My Soul Is a Witness

Other books from Gloria Wade-Gayles

Rooted Against the Wind:
Personal Essays

Pushed Back to Strength:
A Black Woman's Journey Home

Anointed to Fly (poetry)

No Crystal Stair:
Visions of Race and Sex in Black Women's Fiction

My Soul Is a Witness

African-American Women's Spirituality

Edited by Gloria Wade-Gayles

Beacon Press
Boston

Beacon Press
25 Beacon Street
Boston, Massachusetts   02108-2892

Beacon Press books
are published under the auspices of
the Unitarian Universalist Association of Congregations.

99 98 97   8 7 6 5 4 3

Text design by Sara Eisenman
Composition by Wilsted & Taylor

Library of Congress Cataloging-in-Publication Data

My soul is a witness: African-American women's spirituality /
edited by Gloria Wade-Gayles.
p.   cm.
Includes bibliographical references and index.
ISBN 0-8070-0934-2 (cloth)
ISBN 0-8070-0935-0 (paper)
1. Afro-Americans—Religion.   2. Women—Religious life.
3. Spiritual life.   I. Wade-Gayles, Gloria Jean.
BL625.2.M8   1995
277.3'082'08996073—dc20
94-23479
CIP

With love everlasting

for

my sister Faye

Contents

Acknowledgments

How bountiful were my blessings as I worked on this anthology! Let me call them by name:

Deborah Hatfield of Spelman College, a computer whiz and a spiritual sister, was with me from the very beginning. Her assistance was invaluable. Other Spelman women were always close by: Candace Raven, Iris Adkins-Singleton, and Audree Irons assisted me with correspondence, faxing, and the removal of computer viruses; Ann Warner provided solutions to the oil-and-water relationship between my teaching and my writing; Mona Phillips showed me that both are valuable and both should be done well; Beverly Guy-Sheftall sent me frequent FYI memoranda on new books in the field; and Lois Moreland, by example, testified to the calming power of spirituality.

As teachers are always taught by students, so was I taught by Atlanta University students, young scholars I call them, whose passion for our literature and culture was infectious. Reading with insight, they highlighted sections of Black women's texts I would otherwise have missed. I must highlight the names of two of them: Alicia Coleman, whose excellent papers on nineteenth-century Black women's spiritual autobiographies dovetailed with my own research, and Melanie Mims, a very talented young scholar whose thorough research yielded rich harvests for this anthology.

I also owe thanks to other friends and colleagues in academia: John Gates, who gave me a key card to the NYU Library and access to his computer and his laughter; and most especially my young-scholar students and my supportive colleagues at Bennett College, who welcomed me into a truly spiritual family. During the revision and galley stages of the book, their enthusiasm kept my own very high.

Friends outside academia were no less supportive: Geraldine Gilliam, my unselfish friend, "picked me up" when I was weary from writing; Leah McNeil called from Boston at the right time to tell me to "finish the book!";

Charles Finch and Mwalimu Imara introduced me to spiritual riches of Kemetic culture; Julie Hunter, Janice Sikes, and my namesake Gloria at the Atlanta African-American Research Library trusted me with first edition copies of Black women's autobiographies; and Jim Hunt was simply and genuinely my cheering-on friend.

Of course I drew strength and encouragement from the love and support of my family: my son Jonathan; my daughter Monica; my nephew Loren; my cousins Bruce, Kelly, and Ginger; my uncles Jack and Hosea; and Aunt Mae, my spiritual anchor.

It was at Beacon Press that all of these blessings bore fruit. Beacon is the publishing house the Spirit built. Inside is Tisha Hooks, a generous / gentle and talented young woman on her way to being a fine editor. She embraced the book, and me. Inside is Deb Chasman, a senior editor who gave meaning to the saying I hear among writers: "A talented editor is everything." She was my everything-and-then-some editor, a preeminent blessing. The three of us sang together during the birthing of this book, becoming spiritual sisters / friends.

Finally, and most especially, I thank the women whose writings are included herein and those whose writings will be included in other anthologies that witness for the Spirit.

Introduction

Making lists at the end of every day was as necessary to my mother's awaking the next as setting the clock to ring at a designated hour. I can see her now, sitting at the kitchen table, in her right hand a yellow pencil she had sharpened to an almost point with a black-handled paring knife. Open before her on the table is a small spiral notebook, blue, red, or green, depending on which one she pulled from the plastic-wrapped package of three purchased at the five-and-dime, several at a time when they were on sale. She thinks, as if in meditation, and then she writes therein her responsibilities for "a new beginning." She makes a to-do list, a to-buy list, and an important-information list.

When I was a child, I thought my mother's daily list-making a boring routine, a mere habit rooted in her penchant for organization. But when I became a woman and, as the Scripture says, "put away childish things," I realized that the activity was part of a spiritual ritual: first the lists, then the meditation, and before turning off the light, the prayers. It was, therefore, with an unsettling feeling, a dread really, that I accepted the list my mother forced me to take on the night before the morning of her death. I would need it, she said. I remember the small notebook, wired at the top and dark blue in color, and the important information she had written therein with a firm hand: names of doctors and medicines and the numbers of her Blue Cross, life, and burial policies. My mother's spirituality in life and in death started me on a search for my own, giving me a "new beginning." It is that search, I am convinced, that led me humbly to this anthology. I know my responsibilities: I must "do what the Spirit says do" and serve as a conduit for the testimonies included herein.

Many of them found their way to me through seemingly chance connections and casual conversations that appeared to have no connection to this anthology. Meeting a historian at a conference in California. Discussing aging and death with a friend while we counted the number of times we circled the Atlanta airport on a superjet. Accepting roses from the garden of a friend who loves the feel of the soil between her fingers. Hearing Aretha's voice as background in the answering machine message of a former student. Comforting a friend who was experiencing consummate grief following the death of her mother. Being awakened at five in the morning by something that told me to call Bernice Reagon, calling her at seven, hearing her answer the phone almost immediately with "I was thinking about the spirituality anthology," and the next day receiving "Sing Oh Barren," a song from her genius / from the Spirit never before published. The Spirit brought together the contributors who sing at high octaves.

They witness for the Spirit without defining it. I doubt that anyone can because the Spirit, or spirituality, defies definition—a fact that speaks to its power as much as it reflects its mystery. Like the wind, it cannot be seen, and yet, like the wind, it is surely there, and we bear witness to its presence, its power. We cannot hold it in our hands and put it on a scale, but we feel the weight, the force, of its influence in our lives. We cannot hear it, but we hear ourselves speaking and singing and testifying because it moves, inspires, and directs us to do so.

But not always. Sometimes—or often—we attribute to luck, to happenstance, or to our own abilities that which belongs to the workings of the Spirit in our lives. At least nonbelievers do. I was once among them, vociferous and arrogant in my unbelief. In my late twenties, and maybe even as late as my forties—yes, that late—I thought people who believed in the working of something as invisible and undefinable as "the Spirit" were flirting with an illogic that, if they were not careful, could have dangerous consequences. They could become disconnected from the real world which, in my thinking then, meant the world we see and hear and move in as corporeal beings. My mother knew of my unbelief and knew also why, at the time, I chose it above her teaching example of spirituality. It was my way of demonstrating that I had become an intellectual, that coveted identity which gives a Black woman validation in white America, though not, I should add, inclusion in the small circles reserved for those with power and influence. It was my way, I suppose, of demonstrating that I belonged, my way of assimilating, of stepping back from "the folk" when the camera lens searched for a picture of Black people who pray and sing and get happy in their souls; who testify about a "way out of no way" and make that "way" with juju and voodoo and incantations to an unseen power; who speak with clarity and certainty, and in details, about departed loved ones who visit them from the "other side," bringing advice which, when followed, removes stumbling blocks physical strength cannot budge; who read messages in dreams, in sudden changes in the direction of the wind, in the rhythm of a rainstorm, in a bird that suddenly appears and just as suddenly disappears, in a full moon that seems within reach of their touch, in a star that is missing from a constellation, in strange happenings that have no earthly explanation; who know that an unseen power directs them to the bosom of the earth for herbs that cure as man-made medicines cannot and that this same power blesses them with songs that heal the soul as surely as herbs heal the body; who see the work of the divine in a patch of collard greens, a bed of petunias, a child "spat out" by a mother, and in themselves; who sing they can't "feel no ways tired" because always morning comes, and man "can't make morning"; who believe in miracles, including themselves among them, which, like mornings, are the work of the force that governs the universe, which they sometimes call God, other times Jesus, and almost always the Unseen Spirit; who are certain deep down in their souls that this Spirit loves them, protects them, dwells with them, and gives them "blessed assurance" that when their bodies leave this world, their souls will live forever in a world that knows no boundaries of space or time. Which explains why they refuse to be diminished, and are not.

Such thinking, such behavior, such a belief system, I learned in college, is out of consonance with white-male Western thinking which not only teaches dualism of the body and the soul, but also elevation of the body over the soul. In a sense, then, I sought validation at the cost of my own soul.

That was no easy task, given the resonance of the Spirit in my upbringing. Indeed, it is no easy task for any African-American who has witnessed the spirituality of our mothers and grandmothers and women in our community. The testimonies in this anthology, richly textured and diverse, speak to specific ways in which that spirituality expresses itself, resonating individually and collectively with a teaching fundamental to the socialization of most African-American women: Nourish the Spirit within. Invoke it, receive it, and yield to its power. It is, therefore, no accident that our Ancestors' songs

3

were called "spirituals"; that others describe us as "spiritual" people, "spirited" people, or "soulful" people when the context, they assume, is secular rather than spiritual; and that forms of the words Spirit and Soul find their way into discussions about African-American women. Nor is it an accident that "Amazing Grace," though written by a white man seeking penitence for transporting our Ancestors in the hold of a slave ship, is associated primarily with African-Americans. Irony, yes. But the working of the Spirit most especially. We sing this song so movingly, giving it African tonality, because it speaks to the belief that Grace Amazing is the Spirit working in our lives, transforming us and others.

Some readers might ask: But doesn't that song belong to religion rather than to spirituality? And aren't the people who sing it in churches religious rather than spiritual? After all, religion and spirituality are like oil and water: insoluble. Or like tonal and atonal notes: beyond harmony. Arguably, there could, or should, be a line of demarcation between the two. Institutionalized religion requires us to be a congregation following an unchanging order of worship and believing in a dogma, both of which have been linked to oppression throughout the history of human civilization. But spirituality frees us to worship wherever, however, and with whomever we so desire, each time anew and each time in celebration of the divine that is in us and in the entire universe.

These major differences aside, however, codifying experiences, and people, as religious or spiritual—denying them the right to breathe in the same space and doubting their ability to achieve the same goal—is tantamount to playing god, goddess, or the Spirit and, thereby, assuming a power we as finite beings simply do not possess: to see within a person's soul. Codifying (a polite word, I suppose, for judging) blocks our view of the way in which spirituality and religion can be in concert, one immersing us in the other and, together, teaching us the joy of an examined life which, by definition, leads to the highest expression of self. That is the testimony of many contributors in this anthology; they are in religion but not mentally imprisoned or spiritually short-circuited. They witness in church and outside as religious / spiritual women.

From them we learn that "The Old Ship of Zion" our mothers sang and yet sing might not be dramatically different from the spiritual altars at which we sing today. Both promise spiritual salvation, communication with and succor from an unseen power, a sense of connectedness to the universe— everything and everyone within it—and immersion in worship that transcends material concerns, indeed this material world. We also learn that when our mothers sang "My soul is a witness for my Lord," they were reaching toward and for the Spirit no less than we. And when we hear them sing— really hear them sing—we chafe less at the male-naming word of that for which they were and still are witnessing and find renewal, indeed inspiration, in the *how* of their worship. With their *soul*, they tell us. The presence of such women as the subject of, voice in, and inspiration for many of the testimonials in this anthology precluded codification. Hence the absence of broken chords in the songs, pauses in the prayers, and rough seams in the spiritual garments worn or being prepared for our wearing. Everything herein falls on a continuum that moves toward the highest self.

Many of the contributors in this anthology express that self by disconnecting from traditional notions of God as man / He with whom we can communicate only with the assistance of a mediator who, traditionally, has been man / he. Some pray to a Mother / Father God; others, to the Goddess and goddesses. In either case, they are beneficiaries of our Ancestors' struggle to ensure that we would be liberated from all manner of oppression, most especially that which held the Spirit within us bound rather than free.

Perhaps this diverse gathering of women whose witnessing spans centuries lends credibility to the old saying, "There is nothing new under the sun." Today, enlightened and liberated, we make the designs in our spiritual fabric, but the threads we use are gifts from African-American women of the past, untangled by their love. Today we aggressively reject—Thank God! Thank the Spirit!—male-controlled pulpits. So did many of our foremothers and mothers. Without a movement, they went into pulpits declaring the equality of their gender before God and the Spirit. Today we gather as enlightened women to celebrate our spiritual bonding which is also our empowerment, or especially our empowerment. So did they. Today we celebrate the power of affirmations, crystals, herbs, oils, incantations to the Spirit, and the blood flood of being woman. So did they. Today we reclaim and worship the goddess, or goddesses, rejecting the man-image of god. It is quite possible that early in our history, our foremothers, on these shores, did so as well. I believe they did. Unfortunately, many of the truths about who they were as spiritual women did not find their way into written records. But there is a sense in these writings that we have always been on one ship, even when we gave it different names, and that we were always headed for one destination. Perhaps that is what we learn in works written especially for this anthology and in those written centuries ago when we were free to claim our spirituality, but not our humanity.

Some explanation is needed here, however, of what our spirituality meant to those who acknowledged it, even asked us to "perform" it. In the words of a Negro spiritual, "their eyes were blind / they could not see." They did not understand that in worship they called "primitive," we were respecting and connecting to / with the unseen power that governs the universe. Nor did they understand that we imaged ourselves as a people imbued with spiritual power, a belief we retained from African culture. They did not know we appropriated the religion they gave us, invested it with the Spirit, and transformed it into a force that kept our humanity intact. We hear this transformation in the writings of Old Elizabeth, Jarena Lee, Rebecca Jackson, and others; in testimonials of "visitations of the Spirit"; in spirituals that kept our people sane during bondage; and in the analyses of women scholars who write about our spiritual ancestors with both insight and passion. The remarkable spirituality of slave women is the dominant chord in the spiritual singing in this anthology. Contemporary testimonials only improvise that chord, leaving it and returning to it with new chords that harmonize with and amplify the old.

Focusing on Black women's spirituality raises the question: If we cannot define spirituality, how can we, then, write about a spirituality that is distinctive to African-American women? Having acknowledged that we cannot see it, how can we suddenly ascribe to it such material qualities as race and gender? We cannot. *My Soul Is a Witness* does not. But we can, and should, celebrate the way our connection to the Spirit bears the lineaments of our race, gender, and culture. The Spirit speaks in the voice of, sings the songs of, dresses in the symbols of, wears the face of, and moves in the rhythm of the people who receive it. Doing so for African-American women, it produces spiritual songs, spiritual chants, spiritual rituals, spiritual movements, spiritual symbols, spiritual needs, and spiritual energies that are distinctly Black and woman.

This fact underscores the need for *My Soul Is a Witness* and for other books that will bring African-Americans together to witness for the Spirit. And there must be other books. The volume of writings submitted to this, the first, prophesy that there will be. Manuscripts came from all across the nation, from Canada, and even from the Netherlands, so many in number that if all had been included here—and I wish they could have been—*My Soul Is a Witness* would be several volumes, rather than one. Contributors responded to a call which said simply, "Reach inside, deep, and write what the Spirit says write." Many added personal notes: "At last!" "I've been wanting to tell our story." "This I owe my mother." "This isn't about the Goddess, but it's spiritual." And "We need this anthology!" It was not by accident that their responses echoed testimonies of African-American women who reached inside, deep, when there was no call for an anthology, or that I found myself using many of those testimonies as epigraphs in *My Soul Is a Witness*. Testifying for the Spirit knows no boundaries of time. Clearly, in these spiritually destitute times, we are reaching toward spiritual health and empowerment as did our mothers before us.

My reference to our "mothers" (identifiable as a group by race, gender, culture, and history) does not suggest a monolith. They were not. Are not. Nor are the women and men whose testimonials are gifts to this anthology. They do not sing one song; pray one prayer; worship the same God; chant the same mantra; call on the same orisha; heal and meditate and celebrate our spirituality in the same way. They worship in temples, in churches, in candle-lighted rooms, in gardens, in the light of a full moon, in the quiet of their inner selves, or in the music of memory. They are Christians (of different denominations), Muslims, Buddhists, agnostics, goddess-worshippers, and, believing in no God, even atheists. They are priestesses, monks, preachers, psychics, spiritualists, and healers. They are poets, novelists, historians, physicians, psychologists, sociologists, social workers, administrators, theologians, teachers, editors, and dancers. They are African-Americans of different hues and different ages. They have in common their belief that only when we are spiritually connected can we realize our highest selves, become one with all of humanity (as the Spirit says we must), and transform the world in which we live. They do not define spirituality. Instead, they witness for the Spirit. Lighting candles with them, praying prayers with them, chanting mantras with them, and singing witnessing songs with them at high octaves, we may be started on a search for our own spirituality, our own new beginnings.

PART I

Boarding "The Old Ship of Zion": Witnessing for Our Mothers' Faith

'Tis the old ship of Zion
'Tis the old ship of Zion
'Tis the old ship of Zion
Git on board, git on board.

It was good for my dear mother.
It was good for my dear mother.
It was good for my dear mother.
Git on board, git on board.
—*NEGRO SPIRITUAL*

In my mother's house, there is still God.
—*LORRAINE HANSBERRY*, A Raisin in the Sun

Nobody in the whole wide world to look to but God.
—*OLD ELIZABETH*, bondswoman and minister,
born in Maryland, 1766

That instant, it appeared to me as if a garment which had entirely enveloped
my whole person, even to my fingers' ends, split at the crown of my head,
and was stripped away from me, passing like a shadow from my sight—
when the glory of God seemed to cover me in its stead.
—*JARENA LEE*, 1836

And while I was thus engaged, it seemed as if I heard my God rustling in the
tops of the mulberry trees. Oh, how precious was this day to my soul!
—*ZILPHA ELAW*, 1836

While I was praying to be filled with the Holy Spirit, extraordinary fears overtook me. I saw myself having to jump over a deep chasm of leaping fiery flame to meet Jesus, who was standing to meet me on the other side. If I missed, I would "lose my soul." Incalculable fear! I decided it was worth the risk. I jumped. Instantly, I experienced Joy and Peace.
—*LOIS B. MORELAND,* 1994

"Just a Closer Walk with Thee." That's my favorite song. I started serving the Lord at an early age and I just keep on loving and serving Him.
—*BERNICE TRESCOTT,* 90 years old, 1994

I was converted at fifteen years old in Kember County, Mississippi, and I've stayed with the Lord all my life. I'm still singing, "Jesus Keep Me Near the Cross," and I read the Scripture all the time and I recite the 23rd Psalm. That keeps me strong.
I thank you for putting me in this book about the Spirit.
—*LETHA HARRISON,* 105 years old, 1994

Our Grandmothers

Maya Angelou

She lay, skin down on the moist dirt,
the canebrake rustling
with the whispers of leaves, and
loud longing of hounds and
the ransack of hunters crackling the near branches.

She muttered, lifting her head a nod toward freedom,
I shall not, I shall not be moved.

She gathered her babies,
their tears slick as oil on black faces,
their young eyes canvassing mornings of madness.
Momma, is Master going to sell you
from us tomorrow?

Yes.
Unless you keep walking more
and talking less.
Yes.
Unless the keeper of our lives
releases me from all commandments.
Yes.
And your lives,
never mine to live,
will be executed upon the killing floor of innocents.
Unless you match my heart and words,
saying with me,

I shall not be moved.

In Virginia tobacco fields,
leaning into the curve
on Steinway
pianos, along Arkansas roads,
in the red hills of Georgia,
into the palms of her chained hands, she
cried against calamity,
You have tried to destroy me
and though I perish daily,

I shall not be moved.

Her universe, often
summarized into one black body
falling finally from the tree to her feet,
made her cry each time in a new voice.
All my past hastens to defeat,
and strangers claim the glory of my love,
Iniquity has bound me to his bed,

yet, I must not be moved.

She heard the names,
swirling ribbons in the wind of history:
nigger, nigger bitch, heifer,
mammy, property, creature, ape, baboon,
whore, hot tail, thing, it.
She said, But my description cannot
fit your tongue, for
I have a certain way of being in this world,

and I shall not, I shall not be moved.

No angel stretched protecting wings
above the heads of her children,
fluttering and urging the winds of reason
into the confusion of their lives.
They sprouted like young weeds,
but she could not shield their growth
from the grinding blades of ignorance, nor
shape them into symbolic topiaries.
She sent them away,
underground, overland, in coaches and
shoeless.
When you learn, teach.
When you get, give.
As for me,

I shall not be moved.

She stood in midocean, seeking dry land.
She searched God's face.
Assured,
she placed her fire of service
on the altar, and though
clothed in the finery of faith,
when she appeared at the temple door,
no sign welcomed
Black Grandmother. Enter here.

Into the crashing sound,
into wickedness, she cried,
No one, no, nor no one million
ones dare deny me God. I go forth
alone, and stand as ten thousand.
The Divine upon my right
impels me to pull forever
at the latch on Freedom's gate.

The Holy Spirit upon my left leads my
feet without ceasing into the camp of the
righteous and into the tents of the free.

These momma faces, lemon-yellow, plum-purple,
honey-brown, have grimaced and twisted
down a pyramid of years.
She is Sheba and Sojourner,
   Harriet and Zora,
   Mary Bethune and Angela,
   Annie to Zenobia.

She stands
before the abortion clinic,
confounded by the lack of choices.
In the Welfare line,
reduced to the pity of handouts.
Ordained in the pulpit, shielded
by the mysteries.
In the operating room,
husbanding life.
In the choir loft,
holding God in her throat.
On lonely street corners,
hawking her body.
In the classroom, loving the
children to understanding.

Centered on the world's stage,
she sings to her loves and beloveds,
to her foes and detractors:

However I am perceived and deceived,
however my ignorance and conceits,
lay aside your fears that I will be undone.

for I shall not be moved.

Southern Women

Carla J. Harris

Southern women's voices—
  flow and bounce,
  stroll and skip,
never harsh, never hard,
always loving and warm.

Southern women's hands—
  touch and stroke,
  hold and soothe,
never heavy, never hard,
always calm and sure.

  Young and old,
  gentle and wise,
  sedate and sassy,
never brazen, never bold,
always soft and strong.

Grandmother and mother,
  sister and daughter,
  niece and cousin,
Southern women all—

    in mind—
    in heart—
    in spirit—
    from them—
    I come.

Surviving the Blight

Katie Geneva Cannon

*And when we (to use Alice Walker's lovely phrase) go in search of our
mothers' gardens, it's not really to learn who trampled on them or
how or even why—we usually know that already. Rather, it's to
learn what our mothers planted there, what they thought as they
sowed, and how they survived the blighting of so many fruits.*
—*SHERLEY ANNE WILLIAMS*

I am most aware of the rich lore I inherited from my mother's garden in
Kannapolis, North Carolina. I recall particularly the stories shared during
devastating thunderstorms. Whenever there are gusty winds and heavy rain
accompanied by lightning and thunder, the Cannon household became
and still becomes a folklore sanctuary. We turn off all the lights, unplug electrical appliances, and leave the supper dishes sitting in the kitchen sink.
When the whole family is seated strategically around the kerosene lantern,
my mother, Corine Lytle Cannon, moves into her role as creative story-
teller.

My mother's style is to reminisce around a stock of historical images,
themes, and cultural expressions which tell the story of the origin of Black
people in America. Much of what she recounts is based on the testimony
shared across generations that her father, Emmanuel Clayton Lytle, born August 21, 1865, was the only free child in his family. My grandfather's parents,
siblings, and all who preceded him were born into slavery. One of our favorite
family legends centers around my maternal great-grandmother, Mary Nance
Lytle, born in 1832. When freedom finally came, Grandma Mary walked hundreds of miles, from plantation to plantation, looking for the children that
had been taken from her and sold as slaves. With only instinct to guide her,
Grandma Mary persisted until she found all of her children and brought and
united her family back together.

As direct descendants of African American slaves, my family understands
such tales as the indispensable source of Black people's historical confidence and spiritual persistence despite all oppression. My mother's keen
memory and her extraordinary artistic sense enable her to pass on eye-

witnessed accounts from freed relatives to succeeding generations. These narratives are the soil where my inheritance from my mother's garden grew.

Exploitation of Slave Workers

Be it in the Piedmont section, in tidewater Virginia, in the rice districts of South Carolina, or in the lower Mississippi Valley, stories abound concerning my ancestors' lot, memories of stripes and torture. Their labor was coerced without wages, extorted by brute force. Slaveholders inflicted on slaves any severity they deemed necessary to make slaves perform required tasks and meted out any sort or degree of punishment for failure to perform them or for otherwise incurring their displeasure.

The rigor of bondage meant that chattel slaves worked always at the discretion of their owners. They could not sell their own labor. My forebearers had no say-so as to where, for whom, or how they would work. Slaveholders appointed the nature of work, the times for labor and rest, and the amount of work slaves were required to perform. The fruit of Black labor could not convert to financial and material gains for Black people and their families. Black people were exploited both for white people's profit and their pleasure.

Hovering over all of my cultural inheritance is the devastating reality that the chattel tenure excluded any sort of social recognition of Black people as thinking, religious, and moral beings. My ancestors were forbidden by stringent laws to acquire education or obtain the means to buy their own freedom. The dominant legal and social attitude was that slaves were to bekept ignorant, living on marginal existence, fed or famished, clothed or left naked, sheltered or unsheltered as served the slaveholder. In North Carolina it was a crime to distribute any pamphlet or book, including the Bible, among slaves. Only under rigidly specified conditions could Black people take part in services of worship. Preaching the gospel, assembling together, or learning to read and write were understood simply as obstacles to maximization of slave identity. Black people were the only people in the United States ever explicitly forbidden by law to read and write.

Cultural Inheritance

Despite the devastations of slavery, with its unremitting exercise of raw planter power and unconstrained coercion, my ancestors had from nightfall to daybreak to foster, sustain, and transmit cultural mechanisms that enabled them to cope with such bondage. In spite of every form of institutional constraint, Afro-American slaves were able to create another "world," a counterculture within the white-defined world, complete with their own folklore, spirituals, and religious practices. These tales, songs, and prayers are the most distinctive cultural windows through which I was taught to see the nature and range of Black people's response to the dehumanizing pressures of slavery and plantation life. Even with cultural self-expression outlawed, my ancestors never surrendered their humanity nor lost sight of a vision of freedom and justice they believed to be their due. There was a critical difference between what whites tried to teach and what slaves actually learned. Against all odds, Afro-American slaves created a culture saturated with their values and shaped by their dreams.

The folktales I have heard all my life were created by slaves throughout the antebellum South as a strategy for coping with oppression and for turning their everyday world upside down. Operating beneath a veil of pseudo-complacency, Black women and men tapped into a profound sense of cultural cohesion, creating an expressive system of coded messages to communicate what they considered good, worthful, and meaningful. Since their survival depended on keeping their true feelings undetected in the presence of whites, Afro-Americans employed the wit, intelligence, and ingenuity of Buh Fox, Buh Rabbit, the Squinch Owl, and others to overwhelm and defeat the powerful foes, Ole Massa and his wife. An ancient Black verse describes this proactive phenomenon of folktales in this way:

Got one mind for white folks to see,
Nother for what I know is me
He don't know, he don't know my mind.   *(Hemenway, p. xxi)*

Many of the slave stories have a defensive verbal dimension so esoteric that white people missed their meaning altogether. Langston Hughes and Arna Bontemps elaborate this point in the following manner:

While masters of slaves went to some length to get rid of tribal languages and some tribal customs, like certain practices of sorcery, they accepted the animal stories as a harmless way to ease time or entertain the master's children. That the folk tales of these Negro slaves were actually projections of personal experiences and hopes and defeats in terms of symbols appears to have gone unnoticed.

(p. viii)

Scores and scores of Blacks projected their everyday experiences and their own sensibilities onto legendary figures like High John de Conqueror, John the Trickster, and Efram as a challenge to the slave system. As C. Eric Lincoln has written: "Every black community in the South has its multitudes of legends illustrating blacks' superior strength, sexual prowess and moral integrity. 'Mr. Charlie' is never a match for the cunning of 'Ol' John.' And 'Miss Ann,' though she is 'as good a ol' white woman' as can be found anywhere, remains in the minds of the black southerner a white woman, and therefore a legitimate target for the machinations of her black servant, 'Annie Mae' " (p. 35).

Folklore flourished in a dialectical relationship with white supremacy, providing the essential medium by which the themes of freedom, resistance, and self-determination were evoked, preserved, and passed by word of mouth from generation to generation. Older slaves used folktales to reveal to their fellow slaves what they knew. As tradition-bearers, they distilled this compendium of folk wisdom into instructional materials to teach younger slaves how to survive. The reappropriation of their own experiences afforded the slaves opportunities to strip away the social absurdity of chattelhood so carefully camouflaged in the dominant culture. In other words, folklore was the mask the slaves wore in order to indict slavery and to question the society in which it flourished. By objectifying their lives in folktales, Afro-American slaves were able to assert the dignity of their own persona and the invincibility of their cause.

Spirituals Like many raconteurs, my mother always includes music in her storytelling sessions. While waiting for the ongoing storm to subside, my mother invites the family to join her in singing Afro-American Spirituals. Beating time with our hands or feet, we sing about Mary weeping, Martha mourning, Peter sinking, and Thomas doubting. This genre of Black sacred music is a vital part of my family's religious tradition.

The music we listen to and sing at home accords with my ancestors, who were musicians who fashioned their songs from biblical lore, traditional African tunes, Protestant hymns, and the crucible of their experiences under slavery. Using their own distinct phrases, improvisational structure, polyrhythms, and call and response patterns, Black women and men expressed their consciousness and identity as a religious people. Some of their songs were slow, drawn out "sorrow-tunes" that reflected the mood of suffering in the midst of unspeakable cruelty.

Nobody knows de trubble I sees,
Nobody knows but Jesus,
Nobody knows de trubble I sees,
Glory hallelu!

Other Spirituals were liturgical shouts and jubilees, songs with reference to a future happy time. These required upbeat tempos accompanied by rhythmic clapping and holy dancing.

Oh, my soul got happy when I come out the wilderness,
Come out the wilderness,
Come out the wilderness,
Oh my soul got happy
When I come out the wilderness,
I'm leanin' on the Lawd—

A number of Spirituals were veiled protest songs used to announce secret meetings, planned escapes, and the route and risk of the freedom trail.

Steal away, steal away,
Steal away to Jesus!
Steal away, steal away home,
I ain't got long to stay here.

In essence, Spirituals were the indispensable device that slaves, forbidden by slaveholders to worship or, in most cases, even to pray, used to transmit a worldview fundamentally different from and opposed to that of slaveholders. For instance, slaveholders spoke of slavery being "God ordained" while slaves sang

Oh Freedom! Oh Freedom!
Oh Freedom, I love thee!
And before I'd be a slave,

23

I'd be buried in my grave,
And go home to my Lord and be free.

The Spirituals express my ancestors' unflinching faith that they, too, were People of God.

As Spiritual singers, slaves were not bothered by the chronological distance between the biblical era and their present. Operating on a sense of sacred time, they extended time backwards so as to experience an immediate intimacy with biblical persons as faith relatives. In other words, the characters, scenes, and events from the Bible came dramatically alive in the midst of their estrangement. The trials and triumphs of Noah riding out the flood, Moses telling Pharaoh to let God's people go, Jacob wrestling all night with an angel, Daniel being delivered from the lion's den, Shadrach, Mesach, and Abednego walking in the midst of flames, Joshua fighting the battle of Jericho, and Jesus praying in the Garden of Gethsemane are some of the Bible stories my foreparents committed to music as they interpreted their experience against a wider narrative of hope and courage.

Prayer When the rainfall's intensity and the winds' velocity drop and the lightning and thunder recede, I know that the end of the storytelling is near. Believing that a direct personal relationship with God exists, my mother always concludes her stories with a long prayer of intercession, praise, and thanksgiving. Kneeling beside the couch, she prays for the needs of both the immediate and extended family. She celebrates God's goodness, majesty, and mercy. She frequently enunciates thanks for the gifts of the earth and for all the blessings received. After a period of silence, my mother then provides time for every family member to bear witness to the immediate power of Jesus as "heart fixer and mind regulator."

This sacred corporate event is the direct and natural antecedent to the oral folklore and the religious music inherited from Afro-American slaves. Hence, I grew up understanding Black folks' prayer tradition to be the authentic living bridge between Black people's stories, Black people's music, and Black people's source of faith.

In the past, my ancestors met in secluded places—woods, gullies, ravines, and thickets (aptly called "hush harbors")—to pray without being detected. Adeline Hodges, born a slave in Alabama, attests to the importance of prayer:

"De slaves warn't 'lowed to go to church, but dey would whisper roun, and all meet in de woods and pray. De only time I 'members my pa was one time when I was a li'l chile, he set me on a log by him an' prayed . . . " (Rawick, p. 35). Sometimes they prayed while huddled behind wet quilts and rags that had been hung up in the form of a church or tabernacle in order to prevent their words from penetrating into the open air. Other times they formed a circle on their knees and spoke their words into and over a vessel of water to drown out the sound. Ellen Butler, born a slave in Louisiana in 1859, witnesses to this dimension of slave religion: "Massa never 'lowed us slaves to go to church but they have big holes in the fields they gits down in and prays. They done that way 'cause the white folks didn't want them to pray. They used to pray for freedom" (Rawick, p. 35).

The tradition of the slaves' "hush harbor" prayer meetings lives on in my parents' home. With the abiding strength of the family legends planted in our own hearts, my mother invites each one of us to pray, quote Scripture, lead a song, or give a testimony. Speaking under the unction and guidance of the Holy Spirit, my father, Esau Cannon, testifies about his personal experience with God. My Grandmother, Rosa Lytle, "lines out" in long-metered style her favorite Psalms and Spirituals. The rest of the family interjects Bible verses between the singing. The last thing we utter before retiring to bed is always Grandma Rosie's prayer:

And, when waste and age
and shock and strife
shall have sapped
these walls of life,
Then take this dust
that's earthly worn
and mold it
into heavenly form.

Such is my inheritance.

Works Cited

Hemenway, Robert E. "Introduction" to Zora Neale Hurston, *Mules and Men*. Blooming-
ton: Indiana University Press, 1978.

Hughes, Langston, and Arna Bontemps, eds. *The Book of Negro Folklore*. New York: Dodd,
Mead & Company, 1958.

Lincoln, C. Eric. *The Black Muslims in America*. Boston: Beacon Press, 1973.

Rawick, George. *From Sundown to Sunup: The Making of the Black Community*. Westport,
Conn.: Greenwood Publishing Company, 1972.

Williams, Sherley Anne. "Foreword" to Zora Neale Hurston, *Their Eyes Were Watching
God*. Champaign-Urbana: University of Illinois Press, 1978.

Hattie on the Block

Dolores Kendrick

Remember me?
   I'm the woman you nailed to a tree
      after the twilight died.

Carrie, you be still, now,
   don't make no noise.
Mama will protect you
   from all the shoutin' an' screamin'
   an' biddin' that's goin' on
      right now. Hold on. Hold onto Mama.
   Won't be long now,
   they done had they lunch,
   an' somethin' will happen to take
   the fear outta your bones
      an' the sweat off of your eyelids
   an' drain them to the sweet winds
   for the birds to eat. Somethin' will happen;

Happens that I be a slave woman,
maybe that makes me property,
not a human bein' like all
you who come to buy me,
see if I'm sturdy, can hold ground,
can withstand the elements, bear fruit
when the seed is in me, like the Lord's land,
sing for my supper when the seasons come,
give death the mortgage on my bones.

Don't come near me! Stay away!
I'm not buyable yet,
I'm a bit unleavened.

Still, Carrie, be still, child. Don't cry,
    don't let them see you cry, honey,
there's a victory in that. Keep the tears
    inward, outta they sight.
Hold onto my apron, tear it, if you want,
    hold hard while we crush the evil
pushin' its way through that crowd of shoppers
yellin' before us an' standin' there
mockin' us with money an' all the changers
    in the temple, but they all look good,
    don't they? Nice coats an' trousers,
    bright shoes, sturdy hats, ever seen
    a finer lookin' peoples than that?

Evil be pretty sometimes, don't it?

Money look good, even if it be for your soul.

Souls cain't be bought.
I won't be of much use to anybody
who buys me without my Carrie here.
I be crippled, needin' crutches: who gonna
pay for them? Or will I have to work
the fields limpin' about with my mind
catchin' butterflies, when I should be
pickin' cotton, 'cause my soul be amputated
when you bought me without my Carrie
for a few dollars cheaper?
No, don't, I beg you, don't touch me!
Stay back. I cain't leave this block
in holo-cust!

That's it, Carrie, hang tight
    My, your forehead be hot,
fever comin' on I 'spect, an' your

28

mother's fever gone cold
makin' it more dangerous when
   it be exposed to the elements
that gather up 'round her now,
   this early, bright mornin'
spoiled an' festerin' in the mouths
   of all these happy buyers who need
the disease of your Mama's wrath
   so they can recover from their own
dyin'.

Dyin' today if I be sold without my Carrie.
I promise you that.

Look on us before you lay
your money down. What we cost? $2,500?

Good price. Buy what you breed.

Masters, Owners, Buyers, Fathers, Sons,
Take vengeance on your dollar!
God help me, I be His maidservant,
I be His witness to this sale of womanflesh
in the twenty-eighth year of my delivery!

Carrie, look! Wipe your eyes, child.
See. They finished the biddin'. Money
be paid. We's together, God heard my
haltin' words through the ears of these
deafened people, you an' me from this strange
pulpit. Look lively, child. We be sold,
but we ain't bought.

The Elders

Mari Evans

With their bad feet
and their gray hair
and Amazing Grace how sweet the sound
cardboard fans
with a colored family seasonal
gift from Baker's Funeral Home
stirring heat and hallelujahs
No hiding place down here, son
I asked Jesus to change your name, child
Help me Jesus
through one more day
And, yesma'am, I dont mind working late
again and nosir, I'm feeling fine
it be a long time before you need a
younger man t'work this job
And swing low sweet chariot Lawd
somewhere there's a crown f'me
Be our heritage
      our strength
The way they moved from can to can't
preparing the way
thowing down the road
Say want you to have more'n I had child
Say be more than I am, go
Go where there aint no limits
See you standing at the top a that mountain
lookin down

With their bad feet
and their gray hair
bony symbols of indomitable will

having triumphed over Goree
endured the Middle Passage
survived cotton and cane
branding iron and bull whip
crossed Deep River into Canaan
strode through dust bowl and depression
Smiled through smoking Watts and
Newark, smoldering Detroit and
locked old arms with young to sing
surely We Shall Overcome

And now
be saying Walk Together Children
we went through the undergrowth
with only cane knives and we
cut it down to size
Fight the fight, wage the wars
and win
It's in y'blood

With their bad feet
and their gray hair
they be our heritage
our strength
Torn tents pitched
at the foot of the mountain
having moved from can to can't
they be our national treasure
they be
    our priceless charge

"Will the Circle Be Unbroken":
African-American Women's
Spirituality in Sacred
Song Traditions

Lisa Pertillar Brevard

"Oh the stars in the elements are falling,
And the moon drips away in the blood."

Former African-American slave Granny tearfully sang these words during an interview conducted in southern Alabama in 1910 by Radcliffe College alumna and N.A.A.C.P. treasurer Mary White Ovington (1865–1951). The lyrics to Granny's sacred folk song reflect an African-American folk belief that, upon reaching one hundred years of age, one will see the stars "drop from de sky" (Blassingame, p. 541). Said the centenarian, "I was at a wonder when I saw it" (p. 541). For Granny, this vision and song not only document her unusually advanced age (like most slaves, her exact date of birth was not officially recorded); they also serve as a capstone to a life in which she witnessed her children sold away from her, and many years later learned that she and other slaves had been freed by President Lincoln's Emancipation Proclamation. Granny's plaintive intonation and spiritual interpretation of this song mark her as a member of a long line of African-American women singers in the rural southern sacred folk-song tradition.

Granny's age and geographical locale also indicate her grounding in southern, rural African-American folk traditions. In "Afro-American Scholars and Afro-American Culture: Notes Toward a Historiography," Richard A. Long identifies three "overlapping phases" of African-American culture: the "Folk Rural," the "Folk Urban," and the "Trans-Urban":

According to Bernice Johnson Reagon in her booklet accompanying the 1980 audio recording, *Voices of the Civil Rights Movement, 1960–1966*, the song "Will the Circle Be Unbroken" "is part of the Southern Baptist tradition. It was used throughout the Civil Rights Movement in its original form and was often sung at points of crisis" (p. 19).

The origins of the Folk Rural phase lie in the beginning of the Black experience on these shores. Its artifacts are the spiritual and the worksong, the sermon and the folktale, the quilt and the hoedown. The Folk Urban phase springs up after the Civil War and is . . . the urbanization of the folk with blues and jazz, the cakewalk and the parade, the concert party and the pageant. The Trans-Urban phase, which is anticipated even in the [eighteen-]nineties, comes into full form in the [nineteen-]twenties . . . facilitated by rapidity of transportation and the expansion of the media, further facilitated by a broadening of the base of literacy and the easier post–World War I access to artifacts of the mainline culture.

(p. 5)

Granny still clearly belongs to, and speaks out of, the Folk Rural phase, even as time and technology "phase it out." Her steadfast moorings in African-American Folk Rural traditions speak to the legacy of slavery-like conditions which persisted in the South for African-American peoples long after the formal practice of slavery had been abolished. During slavery and into the civil rights movement, African-American women were instrumental in bolstering the social and political life of their communities through sacred song.

Former Alabama slave Henry Baker, during an interview conducted by Thomas Campbell in 1938, recalled the central role of African-American women as community leaders of sacred song and worship traditions: "A'nt Ca'line Calloway, A'nt Mandy Phillips en Emeron White en Racheal Mac-Mullens dem wimmen, dey wuz a sight, dey sut'only did know how tuh worship God. Dey wuz de leaders in prayin' tuh de lawd fer our freedom" (Blassingame, p. 661). Many of these "wimmen's" prayers for freedom were made through such African-American spiritual songs as "Rest fer de Weary on de Other Side ub Jurd'n" (p. 656); "Sometimes I Feel Like a Motherless Child"; and "Swing Low, Sweet Chariot."

Baker, born in Alabama in 1854, describes A'nt Roney's use of the spiritual "Let Evah Day Be Sunday," when she learned the whereabouts of her sister, who had been torn from her during slavery: ". . . We wuz all comin' from prayer meetin' one night en she wuz shoutin' 'Thank God we is all free.' In slavery time her suster wuz sep'rated frum huh en she didn't know wha she wuz en aftuh freedom she had don' found her. She come 'long dat night en sung dis song":

Let evah day be Sunday
Let evah day be Sunday
Let evah day be Sunday
By 'em by.

Yuh heah ol' Hell a howlin'
Yuh'll heah ol' Hell a howlin'
Yuh'll heah ol' Hell a howlin'
Let evah day be Sunday
By 'em by   (pp. 660–61)

For the African-American slave, Sunday, according to the Bible, and some-times according to the whims of the White master, was a "day of rest," and also a time for slaves to reflect upon their lives and aspirations, often through music and religious worship.

Spirituals and worship traditions nurtured during slavery survived African-Americans' second "middle passage" during the twentieth century, when many migrated northward and westward between 1915 and 1940 in search of better employment opportunities in factories and increased access to formal education. Spirituals and sacred worship traditions were the cor-nerstones of African-American life during this uncertain period, as they moved from sharecropping in the South (which prescribed a specific socio-economic and geographic "place" for African-Americans) to other regions of the country, where they were sure neither of what their occupations would be nor of what their chances were for realizing their personal, communal, po-litical, social, and economic aspirations. In northern and western cities, African-American spirituals often became relegated to church and domestic spheres, since the pace and noise of factory work, as well as the multicultural, multiracial composition of the workforce, precluded the raising of spirituals, a communal song form. Secular survivals of the spiritual can be found during this "Folk Urban" period, however, in poetry.

African-American Dayton, Ohio, native Paul Laurence Dunbar (1872–1906) captured the spirit, purpose, and historic role of African-American women song leaders of the spiritual in his poem "When Malindy Sings":

G'way an' quit dat noise, Miss Lucy—
  Put dat music book away
What's de use to keep on tryin'?
  Ef you practise t'well you're gray,
You cain't sta't no notes a-flyin'
  Lak de ones dat rants an' rings
F'om de kitchen to de big woods
  While Malindy sings . . .

Oh, hit's sweetah dan de music
  Of an edicated band
An' hit's dearah dan de battle's
  Song o' triumph in de lan'.
It seems holier dan evening'
  When de solemn chu'ch bell rings,
Ez I sit an' ca'mly listen
  While Malindy sings . . .

Let me listen, I can hyeah it,
  Th'oo de bresh of angels' wings,
Sof' an' sweet, "Swing Low, Sweet Chariot,"
  Ez Malindy sings.   (Hughes, p. 39)

Dunbar's poem attests to the survival not only of the spiritual during the Folk Urban phase, but also to the survival of cultural aesthetics in which members of the African-American community (in this case the narrator) comment upon and critique the performance of the spiritual, which is rooted in the oral tradition, and cannot be fully understood or interpreted simply through reducing it to musical notation and the written word.

This was one of the lessons taught by African-American Smithsonian curator, songleader, and civil rights activist Bernice Johnson Reagon in her lecture-demonstration, "God's Gon' Trouble the Water" at Emory University on March 18, 1992. Beginning her presentation with a solo a cappella version of the spiritual "Wade in the Water" (from which the title of her presentation is taken), Reagon explained how the concept of "trouble" is often interpreted in African-American communities as a choice which one must make in order to move into another physical, psychological, and/or spiritual space. Noting her childhood interpretation of this song in rural Georgia, Reagon recalled that she could not understand why one would actively choose to get oneself into trouble. As she matured, however, she began to see that "getting into trouble" could be "good," ultimately—that the struggle toward sociopolitical change, while difficult and often fraught with "trouble," ultimately could produce positive results for individuals and communities. Seeing and hearing how members of church communities in "Worth, Mitchell and Dougherty Counties, Georgia" (Reagon, liner notes, *Spirituals in Concert*) utilized sacred song traditions to claim places for themselves on earth and in heaven, Reagon explained that African-American women's "attitude" expressed during the raising of such songs as "I Got a Right to the Tree of Life" spiritually and psychologically secured their "place" in the afterworld. Such convictions, Reagon said, are cornerstones of African-American survival in the New World, which paved the way for community galvanizing required in the process of sociopolitical change, most obviously realized during the civil rights movement.

Acknowledging the limitations of early studies in African-American oral culture, Reagon explained that historians often entered African-American communities with preconceived notions of what they wanted to find, and, upon locating one or two individuals within the community who would attest to the literal interpretation of Bible-based songs, proceeded to catalog only the literal interpretation of sacred folk songs, unaware that the literal interpretation is often used as a basis for metaphorical interpretations which then are often applied to everyday life experiences. Reagon concluded that so powerful are the metaphorical and connotative interpretations of African-American folk songs, especially spirituals, that taking these meanings and corresponding attitudes away from them "castrates the songs."

Noting that African-American spirituals were a primary means by which singers claimed space for themselves in heaven, Reagon explained how congregations commanded physical space with the sounds of their voices. The translation of this experience into sociopolitical activism, then, is quite similar for African-Americans who tried to claim physical and social "spaces" which, by law, were not designed for African-Americans to occupy, much less utilize. Acknowledging the important role that select White Americans played in helping to secure African-American constitutional rights to "life, liberty and the pursuit of happiness" (Heffner, p. 15), Reagon offered a story about a White Pennsylvania Quaker man who constructed his home to accommodate a crawl space in which runaway slaves could hide. This concrete example of physical space being opened to slaves utilizing the Underground Railroad is comparable to her explanation of the phenomenon of sacred folksong traditions being linked to specific geographic areas:

> If you go to another church, you may know the words or the melody, but you cannot *raise* that particular song [there]. . . . You have to *lay back* and *listen* . . . to what is being communicated through that song at that particular time and place.
>
> (Reagon, "God's Gon' Trouble")

As Harriet Tubman's use of African-American spirituals attests, the links between spirituality, spirituals, and the occupation of physical space are an integral part of African-American history and oral culture. Tubman's interviewer between 1859 and 1965 declared that, as she prepared to take fellow slaves northward, "she was afraid of being betrayed, if anyone knew of her intentions; so she passed through the street singing,—'Good bye, I'm going to leave you, / Good bye, I'll meet you in the kingdom,'—and similar snatches of Methodist songs," and that as she passed by her master, Dr. Thompson, "she sung yet louder, bowing down to him,—'Good bye, I'm going for to leave you.'" The interviewer poetically paraphrased Thompson's reaction thusly: "as her voice came floating back in the evening air it seemed as if—'A wave of trouble never rolled / Across her peaceful breast'" (Blassingame, pp. 458–59).

In *Spirits that Dwell in Deep Woods*, volume 1, *The Prayer and Praise Hymns of the Black Religious Experience*, Wyatt Tee Walker describes the "mesmerizing effect" (Walker, p. 45) of the "prayer chant" "Lord Have Mercy," which regularly was led during his childhood in New Jersey by North Carolina native Louvenia Saunders:

> Lord have mercy,
> Lord have mercy,
> Lord have mercy,
>   On my soul.

Lord I need thee,
Lord I need thee,
Lord I need thee,
  Save me Lord.

Lord please answer,
Lord please answer,
Lord please answer,
  One more time.

  Heal my body,
  Heal my body,
  Heal my body,
Make me whole.

Cleanse my spirit,
Cleanse my spirit,
Cleanse my spirit,
  Make me pure.

Send your power,
Send your power,
Send your power,
  Right now Lord.   *(p. 43)*

This chant is a site of individual and community transformation: it enables participants to engage in a direct conversation with the Holy Spirit, which responds with holistic healing and purifying power. Walker says that while biblical references related to the text of this song are many, "none is more appropriate than the Fifty-first Psalm" (pp. 45–46). Says Walker, "This poignant prayer of penitence is attributed to David. Its traditional reference is to his sin against Uriah the Hittite that was exposed by Nathan the prophet. It is a litany of deep remorse for the king's adulterous affair with Bathsheba. The root of this chant is that same godly sorrow for some offense against the will of God" (p. 46). In raising this song during the twentieth century, Saunders is undoubtedly aware of the song's biblical ties; yet, as is true in many areas of

African-American life and culture, she adapts the meaning of the song, if not its lyrics, to apply to current situations.

When African-American sacred folk songs are used for sociopolitical advancement, as during slavery and the civil rights movement, the transformation of lyrics parallels the conceptual transformation which takes place when lyrics first are interpreted literally, then figuratively. When the disenfranchised group confronts the dominant culture, such transformations must be made plain to the targeted audience so as to set forth the purpose of the confrontation and galvanize the singers. During her Emory presentation, Reagon said that her experience of this transformation as a S.N.C.C. activist resulted in her changing the lyrics of the nineteenth-century spiritual "Over My Head I See Trouble in the Air" to leading the song with "Over My Head I Hear Freedom in the Air." This concrete reinterpretation and alternative lyrical application of the song not only served to galvanize the singers and proclaim their purpose in protesting against the inherent inequalities of the Jim Crow system; it also provided the all-important function of linking the protest to past cultural traditions, solidifying its importance to the survival of African-Americans in what was then the present, paving the way for the future.

Undoubtedly, the importance of hearing (the primary conduit of cultural information in oral/aural cultures) over sight is a primary element of African-American protest singing. As Reagon explained, "Sure, we were trying to change the system [of racial and socioeconomic oppression]. But we were also saying, 'If you don't look at us and where we are . . . then *you will die.*'" Her appeal to the visual sense in this statement is somewhat ironic, in that it took the White Americans' hearing of African-American sacred folk songs to change what long had been, visually, stark inequities in the rights accorded Whites and Blacks, particularly in the Deep South. Many White Americans could not "see" the gross injustices of the slavery-based Jim Crow system even though places for "Coloreds" and "Whites" coexisted, and often were so labeled by the dominant culture.

African-American spirituals utilized during the civil rights movement illustrate the power of racism and resulting segregation in preserving sacred folk-song traditions. Field recordings made in 1963 of such spirituals as "Wade in the Water" and the spiritual-like song "Come Bah Yah" (*Voices of the Civil Rights Movement, 1960–1966*) closely approach nineteenth-century

39

performance styles. This phenomenon is undoubtedly linked to sharecropping, slavery's offspring, which African-Americans endured in the Deep South one hundred years after the Emancipation Proclamation. African-American civil rights activist Fannie Lou Hamer (1917–77) spent her entire life fighting against the Jim Crow system. Hamer was "the youngest of twenty children and had spent most of her life in Sunflower County as a sharecropper and timekeeper on the W. D. Marlowe plantation" (Daniel, p. 202). Despite, or perhaps because of, her firm grounding in African-American folk thought and worship traditions, Hamer used her skills as a songleader to transmit her own suffering, and that of her community, to S.N.C.C. and C.O.F.O. members. Like many African-Americans exclusively "schooled" in sharecropping, Hamer's literacy was sharply curtailed. She was allowed only six seasons of formal schooling, attending classes only during "January, February and March, when you didn't have absolutely nothing to do. But the catch was that two of the months you didn't have nothing to wear, you know, you was only where you could kind of go to school in March, because it wasn't too cold that you would almost freeze" (Wright, p. 4).

For Hamer, denying her connection with her rural southern community necessarily meant an annihilation of self. Conversely, by affirming her communal connection—particularly relationships with other African-American women—Hamer began to see herself, from childhood, as an individual rooted in a community which historically had struggled against and survived the ravages of Jim Crow. A major part of claiming both her own community and spirituality meant positively claiming both her African-American heritage and the responsibilities of Black womanhood, as explained to her by her mother when Fannie Lou was about ten years of age:

> Well, one time, I asked my mother why we wasn't white; and she really had a fit when I said that to her. But the reason I said it you know, I would go to her, we would work all the summer and we would have to tie rags around our feet and sacks . . . to keep our feet warm while we would go out and scrap cotton. Well, then we wouldn't have anything to eat; sometime we wouldn't have anything but water and bread. And I asked her why we wasn't white, because they were the people that wasn't working, they were the people that had food because when we will go to their house to wash they [sic] clothes, I would notice they would have very good food, and they wasn't doing anything.

So I said then to make it you had to be white, and I wanted to be white; and she told me . . . said, be grateful that you are black, because if God wanted you to be white, you would have been white, so you accept yourself as a black child, and when you get grown, if I'm dead and gone, you respect yourself as a black woman, and other people will respect you.   (Wright, pp. 2–3)

By accepting herself as a Black child, and then as a Black woman, Hamer solidified her ties to her African-American rural southern heritage and to other African-American women. As a result of this "grounding," she becomes, through geographically- and community-based African-American sacred folk-song traditions, a fitting spokesperson for and with other members of her community, without threatening its status quo.

By projecting her voice in protest song, Hamer projects her experiences, which mesh with those of other members of the community, young and old, male and female. One of the earliest folk songs that she learned from her mother affirmed Black identity; moreover, since it emanated from her mother, it undoubtedly also validated Black womanhood. Says Hamer of her mother, "At night she would sing, you know, songs that would really sank [sic] down in me, and some of the songs was like, 'I would not be a white man, I'll tell you the reason why, I'm afraid my [L]ord might would call on me and I wouldn't be ready to die' " (Wright, pp. 3–4). For Hamer's mother, who may be considered representative of her community, claiming the culture and the history of rural African-Americans necessarily means *proclaiming* it—verbalizing it through folk songs and stories, which often serve as the only documentation of individual and community struggle. By taking up African-American struggle in sacred folk song, Hamer taps a rich tradition, one of the few instances in African-American settings in which women, in the church tradition, may take center stage in leadership. Yet this sense of "taking center stage" is not absolute for the leader, for in order to lead people in and through song, one must be thoroughly versed not only in the philosophy and history of a song (the philosophy and history of a people) but also those song-performance and song-delivery traditions which emanate from, and are supported by, the community in a given geographical setting.

Bernice Johnson Reagon considers the folk-level claiming and proclaiming of African-American history a spiritual process. Says Reagon,

> I'm not sure if it's that sacred music is important as history as it is that history is
> sacred for African Americans. History is sacred because it is the only chance you
> have of knowing who you are outside of what's being rained down upon you from
> a hostile environment. And when you go to the documents created inside the cul-
> ture, you get another story. You get another history. The history is sacred and the
> highest, most hallowed songs in tones are pulled into service to deliver that
> story.   (Latta, p. 6)

The concept of the sacrality of African-American history parallels the history
of African-American preachers and ministers, the most esteemed members of
African-American folk communities because of their formal training (however little or much) and their inspired messages. Just as Harriet Tubman engaged in community-level political action through the use of spirituals—a
religious and historical text—during slavery, African-American preachers
and ministers straddled the line between the sacred and the political through
the use of biblically linked oral histories, which they also sang, at points.

In accordance with this tradition, Fannie Lou Hamer led a version of a
"hallowed" Christmas spiritual, "Go Tell It on the Mountain," during a Mississippi Freedom Democratic Party (M.F.D.P.) mass meeting held in Greenwood, Mississippi, during the 1960s. The original words of this song (the edited version of which became the official anthem of the M.F.D.P.) follow:

Go tell it on the mountain,
Over the hills and everywhere,
Go tell it on the mountain,
That Jesus Christ is born.

When interpreting and transmitting this Christmas song for the purpose of
creating sociopolitical change, Hamer edits the text, so that she sings,

Go tell it on the mountain,
Over the hills and everywhere,
Go tell it on the mountain,
To let my people go!   *(Voices of the Civil Rights Movement*, side 2, band 6)

By retaining its original melody, the song reminds singers of the joy of the
birth of Christ, which also symbolizes the "rebirth" of all mass meeting participants. Hamer's substitution of socially specific language concretizes the
song's immediate relevance to the singers. A fitting theme for the M.F.D.P.,

and often led by Hamer, it also befits Hamer's robust voice and social, political, and spiritual identity.

Another and a prime example of an oppression-preserved spiritual is "Wade in the Water," led by Hamer during a mass demonstration in Greenwood in 1963. A transcription follows:

Congregation: *Wade in the water,*

Wade in the water, children,

Wade in the water,

God's gonna trouble the water.

Hamer: *Well, you can hinder me here, and you can hinder me there —*

Congregation: *God's gonna trouble the water.*

Hamer: *But the Lord in Heaven's gonna hear my prayer.*

Congregation: *God's gonna trouble the water.*

Hamer: *Come on and —*

Congregation: *Wade in the water,*

Wade in the water, children

Wade in the water (Oh, Lordy)

God's gonna trouble the water.

Wade in the water, (Come on and)

Wade in the water, children,

Wade in the water.

Hamer: *I know that —*

Congregation: *God's gonna trouble the water*

God's gonna trouble the water

Hamer: *You know that —*

Congregation: *God's gonna trouble the water*

God's gonna trouble the water.

(*Voices of the Civil Rights Movement*, side 2, band 7)

Fannie Lou Hamer leads this song utilizing traditional text, settling on terms which apply to the general concerns of the demonstrators, acting as both songleader and soloist (Reagon, *Voices*, p. 15). Here Hamer makes reference to chronic, pervasive oppression endured by African-Americans as a result of slavery and Jim Crow. This song is thematically and musically linked to other spirituals in that it employs the pentatonic scale; antiphony (call-and-response); syncopation (courtesy of handclaps provided by various members of the congregation); thematic reference to daily concerns of the community; a conviction that the singers have a direct connection to God; and repetition of simple words and phrases to heighten the emotional experience (Shaw, pp. 9–10). Hamer's highly personal approach to leading this song stems from her mother's influence, since, like her mother, she explains everyday trials from a personal perspective through song. Despite such personalization, or perhaps because of it, the congregation participates throughout. Hamer acts as a community commentator on the oppression endured by African-Americans in Greenwood. Yet she does not speak entirely *for* them. Rather, she leaves sufficient room for other community members to contribute in raising the song (there occur ad libs of "Oh, Lordy" and "Come on and" by the congregation). This example of "Wade in the Water" contains virtually all of the elements which qualify it as a traditional spiritual.

Nor was Fannie Lou Hamer's political musical expression limited to spirituals. Like many twentieth-century African-Americans, she hopped aboard and helped to conduct the "gospel train," much as Harriet Tubman conducted the Underground Railroad. One of Hamer's most moving performances is the spiritual-derived "This Little Light of Mine," which is often performed as a gospel song in African-American churches:

This little light of mine, I'm gonna let it shine,
This little light of mine, I'm gonna let it shine,
This little light of mine, I'm gonna let it shine,
Let it shine, let it shine, let it shine.

Gospel music, a twentieth-century political music form and style of performance, sprang from African-American spirituals and churches, absorbing and radiating the hope and trauma of the second middle passage from southern plantations to urban ghettos. Its most famous performer is New Orleans, Louisiana, native Mahalia Jackson (1911–72), whose million-selling gospel recording "Move On Up a Little Higher" (1947) had both earthly and heavenly connotations.

Going sightseeing when I get up higher
(and I'm going to) walk and never tire
Then I'm going to march around the altar.
I'm going to try and never falter.

I'm going to move on up a little higher
(Then I'm going to) meet Abraham and Isaac
(Then I'll) move on up a little higher
(And I'm going to) meet the Prophet Daniel

Then I'm going to live (up there with Jesus)
Then I'm going to live on in glory
After 'while . . .   (Reagon, "We'll Understand," pp. 204–6)

Its composer, born in Memphis, Tennessee, Rev. William Herbert Brewster, Sr. (ca. 1897–1987), said about his song:

> The fight for rights here in Memphis was pretty tough on the Black church. The lily white, the black, and the tan were locking horns; and the idea struck me and I wrote that song. We'll have to move in the field of education. Move into the professions and move into politics. Move in anything that any other race has to have to survive. That was a protest idea and inspiration. I was trying to inspire Black people to move up higher. Don't be satisfied with the mediocre. . . . That was my doctrine. Before the freedom fights started, before the Martin Luther King days, I had to lead a lot of protest meetings. In order to get my message over, there were things that were almost dangerous to say, but you could sing it. Mahalia [Jackson] knew what to do with it. She could throw the verse out there.
>
>   (Reagon, "We'll Understand," p. 201)

Jackson also sang a gospel version of the "Battle Hymn of the Republic" during the Kennedy administration's centennial celebration for the Emancipation Proclamation in Washington, D.C., on September 22, 1963. So powerful was her rendition of this song that "partisan rivalries among the politicians [which had been] subdued by the state occasion [were] washed completely away by Mahalia Jackson's performance" (Branch, p. 642). By "gospelizing" this patriotic song, Jackson showed the power of African-American gospel music spirituality in straddling the line between the sacred and the political.

As a leader of African-American sacred song traditions from spirituals to gospels, Fannie Lou Hamer stands at the crossroads of the sacred and the political. Her work demonstrates that the composition and voicing of the sacred as the political in African-American culture did not end with the Emancipation Proclamation of 1863; rather, this process, like those involved in the struggle for justice, was simply transformed as circumstances required. "This Little Light of Mine" was more than a song for Fannie Lou Hamer. It was an ethos and a mode of sacred and political action. Her voice was a beacon of spirituality, strength, and resistance.

Works Cited

Blassingame, John W. *Slave Testimony: Two Centuries of Speeches, Interviews, and Autobiographies*. Baton Rouge: Louisiana State University Press, 1977.

Branch, Taylor. *Parting the Waters: America During the King Years, 1954–63*. New York: Touchstone/Simon & Schuster, 1988.

Daniel, Pete. *Standing at the Crossroads: Southern Life in the Twentieth Century*. New York: Hill & Wang, 1986.

Dunbar, Paul Laurence. "When Malindy Sings." 1895. Pp. 37–39 in *The Poetry of the Negro, 1746–1970*. Ed. Langston Hughes and Arna Bontemps. Garden City, New York: Anchor Press/Doubleday, 1970.

Heffner, Richard D. *A Documentary History of the United States*. New York: Mentor, 1976.

Kathleen Battle/Jessye Norman: Spirituals in Concert. Recording 18, March 1990, Carnegie Hall. Deutsche Grammophon 429, 790-4, 1991.

Latta, Judi Moore. "Sacred Songs as History." Interview with Bernice Johnson Reagon. Recorded August 4, 1992. Washington, D.C.: National Public Radio Archives, Wade in the Water Program.

Long, Richard A. "Afro-American Scholars and Afro-American Culture: Notes Toward a Historiography." Pp. 3–9 in *Black American Culture and Scholarship: Contemporary Issues*. Ed. Bernice Johnson Reagon. Washington, D.C.: Smithsonian, 1985.

Reagon, Bernice Johnson. "God's Gon' Trouble the Water," Lecture-demonstration at Emory University, Atlanta, Georgia. White Hall, March 18, 1992.

Reagon, Bernice Johnson. Annotations (liner notes) for *Kathleen Battle/Jessye Norman: Spirituals in Concert*. Deutsche Grammophon, 429, 790-4, 1991.

Reagon, Bernice Johnson. *Voices of the Civil Rights Movement: Black American Freedom Songs, 1960–1966*. Booklet accompanying audiorecording of the same title. Smithsonian/Folkways Records R023, 1980.

Reagon, Bernice Johnson, ed. *"We'll Understand It Better By and By": Pioneering African American Gospel Composers*. Washington, D.C.: Smithsonian, 1992.

Shaw, Arnold. *Black Popular Music in America*. New York: Schirmer, 1986.

Voices of the Civil Rights Movement: Black American Freedom Songs, 1960–1966. Field recording. Smithsonian Collection/Smithsonian Folkways Records R023, 1980.

Walker, Wyatt Tee. *Spirits that Dwell in Deep Woods, Vol. 1, The Prayer and Praise Hymns of the Black Religious Experience.* 2d ed. New York: Martin Luther King Fellows Press, 1992.

Wright, Robert. Interview with Fannie Lou Hamer. Recorded August 9, 1968, in Ruleville, Mississippi. Washington, D.C.: Moorland-Spingarn Res. Ctr., Howard University.

"In the Morning, When I Rise":
My Hands in Spiritual Soil

Fleda Mask Jackson

The sound of harmonious singing and thunderous handclapping, the rhythm of crescendoed sermons and the muted tones of whispered prayers, all make participation in Sunday morning services a special element of my spiritual life. Yet, while I cherish this sacred affirmation of faith, this time of community, my spirituality is equally nurtured by the solitude I experience in a more intimate setting.

From my earliest memories of a father who planted strawberries and tomatoes (and a lot of other fruits and vegetables) and especially those of a mother with an unrefuted green thumb, I have developed a passion for gardening. It is one, however, that goes beyond a desire for the touch of soil and seed. For with the passage of each season, my backyard paradise has become a spiritual sanctuary. It is where I am most in touch with myself and with God.

I come from generations of gardeners, spanning over a millennium. My foremothers and forefathers tilled and planted freely in Africa for sustenance of the body and soul. In ancient Egypt, my ancestors developed the first formal gardens, organizing plants and flowers along the Nile as they worshipped the sun.

Even in the misery and pain of bondage, I'm certain that, for some, a glimpse of blooming trees and shrubs provided a brief moment of hope for the future. For those fortunate slaves who were permitted a patch of earth where they grew vegetables to supplement a meager diet, the harvest of their own bounty must have provided some sense of autonomy. And for all who attempted and succeeded in escaping, they recognized the plants, flowers, and trees as beacons lighting their paths to freedom.

Mama loved her garden as did her mother. Grandma Laura, the daughter of slaves, was the midwife and herb doctor in her small rural community. She was a skilled healer with the ability to go into the woods and forage for a wide range of plants and herbs used in her potions and elixirs. I don't know whether she prayed or engaged in some special ritual as part of the preparation of her medicine. But I do know that she was a spiritual woman.

While she had the reputation of being deeply religious, Laura Staton was also known to have a fierce temper, one that was controlled only by her religious convictions. Once when a neighbor dug a ditch between their properties and placed the soil on her side, my grandmother threatened to do bodily harm. Pacing throughout the house, she told my sister Maedell, "If I wasn't a Christian, I'd kill him."

Grandma Laura was known to pray and shout anytime, anywhere. In her house, in her yard, in the road, anytime the spirit moved her. On Sunday morning, in the church, she sat in the "Amen corner" on the front row urging the pastor on. And when the sermon or a song really moved her, she would stand and shout, moving in a circle around the walls, and back to her seat.

In her garden there were vegetables and plants, tomatoes, beans, corn, and flowers of all kinds, but no grass. She, like so many African-American gardeners in the rural South, would sweep her yard with a stiff broom made from branches, resulting in it being, as Maedell said, "as neat as a pin."

My mama was a praying woman. I have a perpetual image of her clad in a fancy nightgown, kneeling beside her bed, with tiny coffee brown hands clasped together. She would chant for long periods, asking, I know, for God to watch over us. She continued this prayer in church every Sunday. I don't recall seeing her shout, but I remember her holding tightly a laced handkerchief she used to wipe away the tears that flowed as she listened to the sermon.

Prayer and churchgoing were only two aspects of Mama's spiritual life. She believed that there were individuals who had a gift to see the future, not as competitors to God, but as messengers, as were the prophets in the Bible. And so, several times a year, she took the train to visit a woman in South Carolina to receive a reading.

I accompanied her once to the small town where the reader lived. Her house, situated near the railroad track dividing the black community from the rest of the town, stood out from all the others in the neighborhood. Most of the houses in the area were in obvious states of disrepair and very few were painted. By contrast, this two-story, glistening white frame structure with a large porch seemed to tower over the others. It was not only different from those in its immediate surroundings but for me it was one of the most beautiful I had ever seen. The inside was equally splendid, decorated with fine antiques, china, and crystal. Even as I think of it now, it seemed like a place for weddings and tea parties rather than spiritual readings.

After entering the house, I was instructed to sit at one end of the room while Mama and the reader, with their backs turned to me, stood at the other end to discuss the visit. From time to time they would turn and glance at me. I knew that I was the topic of the conversation, especially after the woman fixed her eyes on me, studying my every movement. It seemed as if she could look right through me. Like all thirteen-year-olds, I was self-conscious and this experience made me even more so. I was relieved when they finally told me to go outside and play with the children from the neighborhood.

I don't know what took place between Mama and the woman after I left, but I believe it was a good reading. There was something about the way Mama watched me afterward (even when she didn't know that I was aware of her gaze) that made me feel the reader had conveyed some positive prediction.

The praying, the readings, the churchgoing—all seemed to come together for Mama in her garden. She had learned from her mother the art of using plants and herbs to treat our ailments. Wearing an asafetida ball around her neck in the winter (an herb said to ward off germs), she would mix all types of concoctions to fight colds and infections. But the focus of Mama's gardening was actually less on medicinal herbs and more on decorative flowers and plants. She simply loved them—all kinds—and she collected them wherever she went.

It is a custom among many of my elderly relatives and friends always to give a token or gift of some kind to visitors as they depart. So I always leave their homes with a plate of food, or candy and fruit, or as in the case of one set of relatives, with blankets and sheets from their considerable collection.

Mama understood and participated in this custom, and I've come to wonder if this is why many of her visits to friends ended with a tour of their gardens. If they planted vegetables, of course, we left with a bag of tomatoes or squash, whatever they had in abundance. But whether they planted vegetables or not, she always looked for the flower and plant garden. Once there, Mama would comment on plants that had attracted her attention. It was understood that the host should offer a cutting or a seedling of that or some other plant. They couldn't refuse her.

The acquisition of these plants was not about collecting volume; instead it was truly symbolic. Countless times I heard Mama, when showing off her garden, tell visitors, "this plant came from my cousin," or "that one from a friend, a neighbor." The plants, you see, were constant representatives of the person, his or her garden, the visit.

Increasingly, I have come to understand and appreciate this practice. Recently an ailing relative insisted I plant a flowering bush in my backyard. This, she said, would mean that when she was gone, I could look out my window and see the bush which would remind me of her. I regret that so few of my friends have gardens where I can pinch off a little of this or that and make them a permanent part of my landscape.

As Mama's gardening apprentice, I helped pull weeds, trim away dead branches, and keep the plants watered. Wearing an oversized orange straw hat to protect her from the sun, she led me from plant to plant, instructing me on how to care for them. But of all the times that she showed me the garden, one in particular stands out.

Once, in the middle of the night, she awakened me. This time it wasn't the chill of the cold washcloth pressed to my cheeks or a tug to the sleeve of my nightgown that awakened me. It was something in her voice. A strong whisper, full of excitement, drew me from my bed and led me to what was then an unknown destination. There had been times before when I had been asleep for hours and in the middle of my "good sleep" when Mama would get me up to take the long train trip to visit relatives who lived farther South. Each time I protested, resisting her putting on my clothes with limp arms and wobbly legs, or her combing my hair by turning my head swiftly from side to side. Despite the protest, we never missed the train on my account, and I always enjoyed the travel and the visit once we reached our destination.

I didn't protest this time. It was midnight and yet the glow from a full moon made it easy to move through the house without touching a button or switch. Like an imprinted animal, I followed Mama through the bedroom, down the hall, through the kitchen to the porch, and out the door to our backyard. By now I was fully awake but in a calm state. I could feel the still, yet balmy air of a summer night and smell lingering fragrances from the prized flowers and shrubs that adorned her garden, our "outside room," and gave even me, a twelve-year-old, a sense of peace and anticipation.

The reflections of the moon blanketed the whole area, making it possible to see the gym sets, toolhouses, and someday-to-be-repaired automobiles in our neighbors' yards. It seemed every inch of our yard was so illuminated that I could almost distinguish individual blades of grass. But what I remember most is how it seemed that a portion of the moon's rays had been reserved to spotlight a corner of Mama's garden. She moved quickly to this area, beckoning me to follow.

I had never seen her move so quickly. She, in her sixties, had discarded the aches and pains which periodically plagued her and now on half-toe she practically ran to the spot. As if we had traded ages, I followed more slowly, hesitantly. I guess because, even though I was in the light of the moon, I was still in the dark.

As a child, and even now, I like brightly colored flowers, reds and pinks, purples and yellows. Therefore, I had not paid particular attention to the area of the yard where Mama was standing. Here were planted shrubs with leaves of interesting shapes and colors (characteristics I have now come to admire and appreciate), but no flowers. Of course, I hadn't noticed the potted plant that had been placed among them.

As a succulent, with thick grayish green leaves, it looked like a cactus. But as the night advanced, I realized that it was much more. This plant would not only change the appearance of a corner in the garden, but, for me, represent the beginning of a spiritual journey.

Throughout our home Mama had pictures of places she had visited or wanted to visit. She prized a book she had purchased during a cross-country train ride. In it were photographs of the Rocky Mountains and other spectacular places lying between our home in Virginia and the state of California. She often talked about this trip and also about places she had not yet seen, imagining what it would be like one day to visit them.

The favorite in her collection of travel books was one on the Seven Wonders of the World, which included the Pyramids.

Mama wanted to see the Pyramids and the other buildings touted as manmade miracles. But on this night she awaited another kind of miracle, a wonder which far exceeded man-made places and tombs. She had gotten me up to witness a rare occurrence. For now in the middle of the night, under the light of the moon, our plant was about to bloom.

She prepared me for this event by telling me that the plant was a Night Blooming Cyrrus, a rare flower that blossoms infrequently and only at night. I have always wondered how she knew this was about to happen. I suppose there must have been some change in the color of the leaves where the flowers burst forth, but that night her knowledge seemed mystical.

As the cluster of petals pushed out, she crouched over to see the plant closely. Like time-lapsed photography, we recorded, in our minds, each frame of movement as the bud became a flower in full bloom. I recall that when this happened, our reverent silence turned to laughter and then back to reverence as Mama and I bowed our heads and each whispered a prayer. I don't recall her exact words, but after the prayer she talked about our having witnessed one of God's miracles. It truly was a spiritual moment.

It is this and other memories that have brought me to this phase of my life where I seek the peace and tranquility I find in my garden.

In the morning when I rise
In the morning when I rise
Give me Jesus

Anytime in my garden is special, but there is something particularly rejuvenating about it in the morning. Even during periods of sorrow, pain, and disappointment, in the morning, in this place, I am reminded that there is always hope. There is always possibility. There is always redemption. And before the silence of the preceding night is broken by noises of an awakening world, I rise. When the first light passes through the gently swaying pine trees lining the majestic hills in my backyard, I pray.

Sometimes before I utter a few simple words, I turn the pages of my tattered Bible (a baptism present at the age of ten) and read from my favorite scripture.

I look unto the hills from which cometh my help
My help cometh from the Lord.

It is at the end of this reading that I stand or kneel by the edge of the tiny creek intersecting my yard and say the simple words, "Lord, give me strength, Lord, show me the way." Where peaceful waters flow, I ask for the stamina and direction to face life's challenges. Mama knelt by her bed to pray, but Mama also prayed in her garden.

My early morning prayer marks the beginning of my daily journey. But it does not mean the end of my time of spiritual solitude in the garden. Even during the hottest days of August, whether I stand and survey the land or prune and weed, I find solace and peace here. The tranquil sound of rushing water from the tiny brook, the sight of the rising hills, and the rainbow of colors from an array of flowers create my own paradise in the midst of an urban area too often plagued by misery and despair.

In my garden I am reminded of the beauty of life, of its endless power of renewal. A seed grows into a plant, a plant produces a flower, in the flower there are seeds, and these seeds produce a new plant. I have come to believe that this cycle is for human beings as well. While I grieve and mourn for deceased friends, for a mother, for a father, for a sister, I know that they are not gone, but have merely entered a different phase of life. I know this, because I hear their voices. Voices that advise me, that forewarn me, that embrace me. They are always with me.

I plant year round. In late spring, petunias, impatiens, and zinnia; in late summer and early fall, mums; by winter, pansies, tulip and daffodil bulbs. But in January, I do a special planting. In the midst of preparing the traditional New Year's dinner, while the blackeyed peas and collard greens slowly simmer, I leave the kitchen to engage in my own ritual.

Every year, on January 1, I plant and bury in my garden. Planting and burying are actually the same physical process but with different objectives. Planting is intended to produce life, to begin anew. Burying, on the other hand, is aimed at the cessation of something, an ending of some kind. As the old year ends, I write down on tiny pieces of paper all the negative emotions, feelings, and fears that blocked or prohibited me from accomplishing the things I desire, and I bury them in an isolated corner in my yard. I then pray to God asking for help in erasing those things which impede my spiritual and physical well-being. I try to forgive but I don't always succeed. I suppose there is a fighting woman in me just like in Grandma Laura.

In another area of the yard, near the water, where it is sunny, I plant "hope," "faith," "love," "friendship," and other things that I desire to grow and blossom during the year. After doing so, I get on my knees and pray and sing, thanking God for my life. Amazingly, in this spot my flowers are particularly beautiful. They are fertilized with special ingredients.

I have delighted in watching my infant son, Kari, see the world of my garden with new eyes. His unsuccessful attempts to catch the wings of a bird, to hold fast to a single blade of grass, and to revive a crushed flower have reminded me of how precious yet fleeting life can be. While I see the world through lenses different from my baby boy's, my faith is nonetheless renewed in this place. It is a faith that I hope both of my children, Kimya and Kari, will develop.

In my garden, I have a sense of connectedness to the Ancestors. I am bonded to all who have witnessed the power and beauty of a supreme being in the blossom of a morning glory, in the fragrance of a honeysuckle or a rose, and from the silky touch of the leaves of the Formosa tree. My grandmother is here. My mother is here. And most important, God is here.

"Mary Don't You Weep": Becoming My Mother's Son

Anthony Walton

*I feel sorry for anybody that could let hate wrap them up. Ain't no such
thing as I can hate anybody and hope to see God's face.*
—*FANNIE LOU HAMER*

*I don't know what my mama want to stay here for
This ole world ain't been no friend to her*
—*SPIRITUAL*

Pharaoh's army got drowned in the Red Sea
—*SPIRITUAL*

My strongest, and fondest, memories from childhood center on listening
to my mother sing. All day and all night, hanging clothes or washing
dishes, cooking meals or putting us to bed, she was carrying a song, a gospel
song or a spiritual, almost never the blues. Amaaaaazing Grace. Trust and
Obey. Standing On The Promises. In The Garden. These and so many others
were the music of my childhood, my mother charming me, my mother comforting me, my mother ignoring me. These songs were the soundtrack of my
mother's faith and, therefore, her life.

It is impossible to separate my mother's deep religious feeling from the rest
of her life. Virtually anything you said to her (or say, to this day) was answered
by some quoted scripture, or a fragment of song. She might smile and say,
"Well, it's like Isaiah 54," or "It's like that song Mahalia used to sing . . ."
and break into a verse and chorus of some treasured spiritual.

I do not mean to suggest that my mother, Dorothy, is some kind of addle-
brained Pollyanna. She was born, out-of-wedlock, to a teenage mother in rural Mississippi, and survived the Jim Crow South of the forties and fifties to
make her way north to Illinois to a satisfying family life and a modicum of career success. She started out in Chicago as a domestic and nanny, and worked
her way up by age fifty to her current position as supervisor of accounting and

data systems for a large suburban school district. Along the way, she was exhibited an iron-fisted toughness that has enabled her to shepherd a husband and three children mostly whole through some very bleak times for black Americans, including members of her extended family. She's like the character of Mary Rambo in Ralph Ellison's *Invisible Man*, taking care of and covering for everybody, with very little thanks. But that's where the bedrock foundation of her faith is crucial, and where I've personally come into several kinds of contact with it.

It seems as though much of my life has been spent in conflict with my mother and her spirituality, though I didn't necessarily know it at the time. When I was a little boy, doing little boy things, there wasn't much at stake, or so it seemed, but as I got older, and the differences became more fundamental, our clashes could be titanic. School, church, dating, "the proper comportment for a young man," we'd go round and round and even when I thought I'd won, I'd lost. I'd find myself hearing, doing what she wanted against *my* will, one of those songs coming back into my head. If I was troubled, I'd remember she'd said, "King David used the music to chase the demons away"; if I was sad, nothing could comfort me quite like "Sometimes I Feel Like a Motherless Child"; if I was happy, nothing could quite express it like Aretha's "Wholly Holy." I had grown up, against all my wishes, my mother's son.

It is as I've grown older, however, that the full magnitude of my mother's faith and the effect that it has had on her, her family, and the entire country, if not world, has come to me. How did my mother and the thousands—if not millions—of black women like her, the field hands and domestics, the cooks and government clerks, who have endured every kind of trial and humiliation from white folks (and other blacks) only to have to come home and provide strength and succor to husbands and children, develop a more nuanced understanding of the Christian faith than virtually anyone this side of Kierkegaard, Gandhi, and Martin Luther King? For that is what those women did, coming to a natural (and literal) understanding of Jesus' message of "intentional suffering" that became both a transformative personal power *and* an integral strand of the fabric of black American culture and community. *I am weak but thou art strong . . . A way out of no way . . . Was blind but now I see . . .*

This genius for the Christian faith was one of the principal factors that allowed black people to survive and thrive in North America, and eventually provided the backbone for the movement that was the most significant move toward true freedom that blacks have as yet accomplished. What was Martin Luther King's great insight and application of nonviolence but a refining of the faith of the mothers? This consonance could be seen and heard in the symbols and songs of the movement as well, *Precious Lord, Take My Hand . . . Go Tell It on the Mountain . . . We Shall Overcome.* The very songs sung by my mother and her mother before her and *her* mother before her, the songs of a people, the songs that became a worldview and a way of life.

Thought of like this, it makes sense, because the words and melody of *We Shall Overcome* make equal sense sung while scrubbing someone else's floor or marching over the Edmund Pettus Bridge (or tearing down the Berlin Wall). And while we stand in awe before the story of Margaret Garner (dramatized in Toni Morrison's *Beloved*) who killed her child rather than allow her to go back into slavery, we stand more firmly in awe and appreciation before those black women who shepherded their loved ones through, whatever. It is then that we remember that Christianity is the religion of losers, or slaves, and we see how it is that the black mother, the most disadvantaged, was able to grasp onto the teachings of that religion and make them real.

So real that the expression of self and belief that these women evolved has become *the* American mode of expressing spiritual belief and personal transformation. Think of the (culturally speaking) Cuban Gloria Estefan or the poor white Wynonna and Naomi Judd: when, in the wake of extreme personal tribulation these artists wanted to make it clear how much they had grown, or been redeemed, they chose to express themselves in African-American cultural forms, in the gospel- and spiritual-like songs "Coming Out of the Dark" and "Love Can Build a Bridge." (Estefan goes so far as to riff repeatedly, "I see the light, I see the light" over a large gospel chorus in her best Aretha Franklin imitation.) That these women's "home" cultures are often, at best, at odds with black America only reinforces the universal nature and impact of African-American experience: any time Americans want to declare spiritual profundity, they reach for the forms and tonalities that were developed and refined by people like my mother, people on the boundaries and margins of society expressing their belief in the possibility of a way out of no way.

And so it goes. I spoke earlier of my conflicts with my mother, and I have yet another, even now, that may be the most significant one of all. I make my way in the world, trying to master worldly ways with varying success, telling myself that I can't be a Christian, that I got to study war, that the problem of black folks is that the time of suffering is over, it's time to *fight*, time to stop fighting each other and go after, metaphorically and literally, white folks.

Then I hear my mother singing, "Ain't gonna study war no more." I say, "Mama, that's why black folks is down, and I'm gonna study war in the evening, I'm gonna study war in the morning, I'm gonna study war in the in-between." But every time I pick up the sword and prepare to do what I think will be some damage, I can't do it. I hear my mother singing, and I wonder, in the time of Bosnia and Belfast, of South Africa and Los Angeles, where has war gotten us? Is this my mother's lesson? Her revenge? Is she saving me from sin? Showing me a better way? *Oh, Mary don't you weep. And tell Martha not to mourn.*

The Power

Dorothy Perry Thompson

for Lottie Roberson Corbitt

I

I saw it
in the swift toe dancing
Grandma did to
"You got a robe,
I got a robe,"

in the way the others
followed their leader
and the light scraping
on the wooden floor
became a thumping frenzy:
"You got shoes,
I got shoes,"

in the way Grandma lifted the light voile
of her skirt just above her knees,
raised the cardboard funeral home fan
high toward heaven
and soared.

I saw it
in the way Mr. Freeman
smiled up from his hymnal
and didn't mind showing
tobacco-stained teeth,

in the way Grandma sat,
her finger tracing words

in the book in her lap,
and her mind tracing centuries
of ancient sound:
young Mattie Daffney
screaming in her cabin
for Abyssinia Ned
graying Mattie crooning,
rocking babies,
still at the head of
Master Brown's slave row;
black, bald Mattie
moaning through
"Sometimes I feel
like a motherless chile."

I saw it
in the way Mr. Freeman
made his cane unnecessary
hobbling up from the pew
for a standing "Amen!"

I cry when a deacon announces
the white frame building
finally will come down.

II

I miss the bell tower,
the worn wooden steps
leading to two front entrances
of Old Samaria. I miss
the trees on Big Meeting Sunday.
They shaded picnic tables
and opened trunks of cars ladened
with lemon pound cakes, home-fried chicken,
sweet potato pies,

big boys sweating in seersucker suits
and growing girls in white cotton dresses.

Now on the 3rd Sunday in July,
we all pile through
the one small door
of the new brick building.
Rev. Crumlin speaks
through a shiny microphone.
He gets through charity
and hope of 2nd Corinthians,
and faith wells up, first
in Grandma's bosom, then
in all the congregation as they join her in
"We've come this far by faith,
leaning on the Lord."

When, finally, we leave the sanctuary,
my legs are shaking
and I tell Grandma
I felt trembling, like old wooden planks
(not concrete) beneath the new red carpet.
She asks if I saw how the sun shone
on the figure of Jesus
in the stained glass window.

We crowd into the small dining room
and wait for paper plates
passed down by the Senior Usher Board.
I want summer gnats, outside,
Mama Rhodie's pie from the trunk of her car,
but settle for the Kentucky Colonel's
little custard cup.

The top of a gray head
catches my eye:
Mr. Freeman being rolled in
for the Meeting feast.
When he nears our table,
he meets Grandma's "Praise the Lord"
with a brown-stained grin,

and I see it,

older than Samaria
and seersucker suits,
older than Matti Daffney
and sweet potato pies:

I clap for the shouters
in Old Samaria Baptist Church.
I celebrate board-shaking feeling
in a moving black ritual,
Grandma and a little old man
whose mighty faith stands them up
to mouth ancient memory.

I celebrate the power
that moves us to speak into chrome
our holy phrases,
to meld with concrete
our sacred songs,
to know that wherever
we're gathered together
the power is there.

I clap for the power.
I clap for the power.
I clap for the power.
Amen. Amen.

The Spirit Keeps the Memory of
the Ancestors Alive

Rosalyn Terborg-Penn

In October 1969, Ma dreamed that she was crying at her mother's grave. Six months later in April 1970, my grandmother, Mabel Van Horn, died. It was then that my mother, Jeanne Terborg, realized that she had prophetic dreams. From time to time she reminds us of what happened shortly after she married and left Indianapolis for Brooklyn in the 1940s. She had dreamed that her brother and his friend were lying on the ground with an automobile tire on top of them. Soon after she learned that they had been in a car accident. The ability frightened her. I later realized her ability as a source of power.

Two months after Mabel's death, in June 1970, Grandpa, her husband Earl, died. A few weeks later, my father's uncle, Gus Bierman, passed away also. It had been a terrible spring. My parents' generation was emotionally and physically drained. My father's mother, Delia Bierman Terborg, grieved not only the loss of her brother, but also because now she was the only remaining family member in her generation.

The evening after the burial, my father, Jacques Terborg, Sr., napped on the living room couch and had a vision of Uncle Gus, moving down the stairway toward him. His fright awakened him and Uncle Gus disappeared. In hearing the story later in the evening, my brother and I asked if Uncle had communicated with my father. We were both intrigued, but not frightened by what we heard. It was then that Daddy shared things from his past that we had not known. We knew he had been born in Suriname in South America. We did not know that he had been born with a veil. Years later Daddy told us about his grandfather's sister, Tanta Tet, who lived with them in Paramaribo. A Sephardic Jew, Tanta became very upset when her young grandnephew reported the dreams he would have because many of them came true. The African-descended people in the household, knowing he had been born with a veil, were not disturbed by Jacques's dreams; he repressed them in order to keep the peace. Years and similar stories later, I accepted my father's ability also as a source of power and wondered if other family members, now passed away, held similar power.

From time to time family members meet to celebrate occasions and talk about the spirits and our various experiences with them. Ma's oldest nephew, Fletcher Robinson, and I have been researching our common ancestry since the mid 1970s, after I began studying for a Ph.D. in history at Howard University. While an undergraduate student at Howard in the 1950s, Fletcher had recovered a biographical sketch of Grandpa's grandfather, James Van Horn, in the 1880 edition of the *History of Fayette County, Indiana*. Fletcher had discovered the Genealogical Reading Room at the Library of Congress and proceeded to research his family. Why a young African American in the 1950s would presume that he would find his Black family's history recorded among the elite families found in the Library of Congress amazes me still, until I reflect—the spirit keeps the memory of the ancestors alive.

It is this spirit that Fletcher believes led me to become a historian so that I could gain the skills needed to help find and preserve the family history. When he put it this way, I had no choice in the matter. So in the early fall of 1978, several months after I received my degree, Fletcher and I traveled to Indianapolis to join his mother, Marian Robinson, and her friend Bob Criss. We were heading for Connersville, Indiana, the Fayette County seat, and the rural community where Grandpa had been born. Bob's father had been an A.M.E. minister assigned to Connersville when Bob was a young boy. As a result, Bob remembered the community and names of some of the African American families who had lived there.

The search was productive. We found plat maps with the Van Horn names listed on them. We found deeds, wills, birth and death records, but we could not find the cemetery my mother remembered traveling to after her grandfather died. Finally, as the day came to an end, we located a burial list that mentioned the graves of two Van Horn women, Eliza (1863) and Nancy (1880). However, no one in the Vital Statistics office knew where this obscure graveyard was located. I probed further, asking questions about the community surrounding the town. Finally, a young clerk told us about the Primitive Baptist Church near the Hanson family farm on Route 1. With no other leads we set out and found the farm. I remember the beauty of it all—the grazing cows, the hills lit by the late afternoon sun, the still well cared for house—

and Aunt Marian uttering that something told her we had found the old Van Horn family house. I now know what that "something" was—the spirit.

A farmhand directed us to the church and cemetery across the road. The church caretaker was leaving the building as we arrived. We asked him if he knew about the Van Horn graves, and he said, "No colored folks buried in this cemetery." I could tell from his expression that he did not want us to enter the cemetery gate. At that moment, a long, white Lincoln Continental pulled into the churchyard and an anxious woman of means ran over to us. "Who are you?" she asked. Without hesitation I answered, "We are the Van Horns." She responded, "I knew one day you would come. I have hoped for that day." Fletcher said it was the spirit of the ancestors who put those words in my mouth. The woman was Mrs. Greenbery Hanson. Her husband's ancestors had purchased the Van Horn property at auction in the 1890s. During the bicentennial year, she had researched the history of the several farms their family owned in Connersville. She was most fascinated to learn that the beautiful house in which her immediate family lived had been built by and was the property of a former slave. Hoping to learn more about James Van Horn and his family, Hanson looked to the day when his descendants would come to find their history. She invited us to join her at the house when we finished our search of the cemetery.

In the meantime, the caretaker observed the scene. After Mrs. Hanson left, he became more cooperative, inviting us to enter the cemetery gate. The four of us divided the cemetery and searched until we found the Van Horn gravestones. They were located at a far end of the cemetery, near the church. Nearby stood tall markers with no names. The caretaker said these, with the remains, had been washed below from a hill above the cemetery many years before. The church minister at the time had decided to place them in the potter's field section of the cemetery, which was adjacent to the area where we found the Van Horn stones. Fletcher asked the caretaker if there were any cemetery records, and he agreed to photocopy a map of family plots he had at home. We parted ways at the cemetery and crossed the road to the old house. There we learned that Mr. Hanson had been told that the graves and markers that had washed downhill to the cemetery during the 1930s were those of African Americans who had been buried on the hill before the church and the cemetery had been built. The next day the caretaker brought the cemetery map to us. One corner of the map was filled with names of family members we had found in the county records—Van Horn, Ferguson, and Roberts. The markers for these graves had disappeared; only shallow, grassy indentations remained in the cemetery. The spirit had revealed this history of our ancestors to us.

Several years passed, and from time to time I would arrange to stop in Connersville on the way home from a trip to Indianapolis or Cincinnati. Fletcher's and my ongoing search for the family history seemed compelled by an unknown force. Once his Cuban housekeeper in Washington, D.C., revealed that protective spirits, which made themselves felt, were present in Fletcher's library. One spirit in particular she described as a man who had been a slave. Fletcher knew immediately that it was the spirit of James Van Horn and showed the housekeeper James's dining room table, now housed in Fletcher's dining room. It was in the library, however, where Fletcher maintained photographs of family members no longer living. Over the years, some of those same photos we had shared, making extra copies for one another.

Three of these photos are restored portraits of James and of Nancy Van Horn, plus a picture of another woman, whom Fletcher said Grandpa identified only as his aunt. At the turn of the century, Grandpa said, his father had restored the old photos, first taken in the 1860s. Fletcher restored them once again in 1970, following Grandpa's passing, and gave me a set. I framed and placed them prominently in my living room.

Perhaps the spirit of at least one of these three ancestors resides with me, the woman whom Grandpa called his aunt. Fletcher and I assumed that this woman, like Grandpa's father, was one of James and Nancy Van Horn's children. We presumed that she was Eliza, who was about twenty when she died in 1863. However, further research discredited our assumptions.

On one of my trips to Frankfort, the Kentucky state capital, I found the family papers of James Van Horn's former owners. There were wills, deeds, family biographical sketches, but also a court case over the ownership of a slave woman called "Yellow Becky," whose given name was Rebecca. In the mid-1980s I had copied the handwritten transcript, thinking that the case was a good example of how slave women had been exploited. Not connecting Rebecca to my ancestors, I set the case aside. However, by 1990 something about

"Yellow Becky" drew me back to her. I seemed compelled to reopen the case and to return to Frankfort to find additional information.

Before the trip, I reexamined some of the old photographs and asked a colleague, who specializes in restorative art, to look at the photo of my nameless aunt. In his opinion, she could not be James's and Nancy's daughter Eliza because she looked too old. The photo put her more in the age range of James. Perhaps she was his sister. Well, this cast the photo in another light. My mind began to play tricks, as the spirit led me to speculate. After reviewing all the extant photos of Van Horn women for six generations, beginning with James and Nancy Van Horn's generation, I found at least one "yellow" female in each generation, except for the one where I had no women's photos:

"Rebecca" - 1800s

Harriet - 1840s

no photo - 1880s

Jeanne - 1910s

Lynne - 1940s

Carmen - 1960s

Arguing my new case, family members seemed convinced that the woman in the photo was James Van Horn's sister, and that several generations of Van Horn women thereafter favored her in looks, but how could we prove that she was Rebecca? Everyone encouraged me to continue the search, so I returned to Frankfort to find the answers to the elusive questions raised by this Pendleton County, Kentucky, court case.

Rebecca was listed in the will and the court case as "Black Hannah's" first-born child, who had been promised to James Van Horn's owner by his grandparents. They had given Hannah as a wedding gift to their daughter and her husband. However, the husband decided to keep Rebecca, a mulatto slave, and she remained with Hannah and her master until he died in the early 1820s. Soon after his death, his wife sold Hannah and then gave Rebecca to another one of her sons, who proceeded to "sell her down the river." This son fraudulently claimed to be his father, Rebecca's owner, and sold her to a notorious slave trade of "fancy women," who was expected to take her by boat down the Ohio River to be sold at Natchez, Mississippi. Instead, the trader decided to keep her as his own concubine, but when she became ill, he brought her back to Pendleton County, Kentucky, for medical care. The year was 1824. It was then that James Van Horn's master petitioned the court for his property stolen by his brother. By 1826 the court awarded Rebecca to her new master, but required him to repay the $500 purchase price to the slave trader within six months, or forfeit the slave.

We learned from James Van Horn's biographical sketch that he had escaped from slavery in Kentucky in 1826 and sought protection among the people in Rush County, Indiana, a Quaker community. Nothing, however, was said about a sister, only that James Van Horn purchased his own freedom from his master a few years later.

What then happened to Rebecca? The court case ended in 1828 with the sheriff being ordered six months later to seize the property of James Van Horn's owner because he could not pay the $500, nor produce Rebecca. In reviewing the sheriff's reports for several years thereafter, the records noted all the property seized—the house, his wife's silverware, horses, wagons, furniture and land, but no slaves. The master, who by the 1830s was penniless, left Kentucky for Indiana.

It was as though Rebecca, like James, had disappeared. There is no indication that she had died. There was no local Pendleton County newspaper at the time, but the Lexington and Louisville newspapers reveal no ads for James and Rebecca. I can only speculate that Rebecca joined James in his flight for freedom.

My family is satisfied and I am, too. The spirits no longer haunt me about claiming Rebecca. From time to time, Ma, Daddy, and I have prophetic dreams. They are often frightening. Daddy, now in his eighties, seems to have accepted them without fear. I am learning to deal with my new-found spiritual power and, with age, will embrace the spirit which keeps the memory of the ancestors alive.

The "Finny-Fanny" Rain: Three Women's Spiritual Bonding on Sapelo Island

Gloria Wade-Gayles with Ellen Finch

As planned, we met up at the Atlanta Airport forty-five minutes before the last flight to Savannah, Georgia, each of us rushing in from a task we had rushed to complete. Onlookers no doubt thought we had not seen each other for a long time, so spirited was our greeting. We hugged tightly with our arms and our eyes and leaned close together in chairs that faced the wide avenue of Delta's Concourse B. Had the chairs not been stationary, we would have pushed them closer and sat in a circle.

Nothing we said was particularly funny, but we laughed frequently and not quietly, probably calling attention to ourselves: three middle-aged Black women acting as excited as schoolgirls going away from home for the first time. We had reason. We were stepping off the treadmill that children, jobs, and other demands keep moving at a breathless pace, making it all but impossible for us to take time out for ourselves and even less for bonding with women friends.

Nothing in our appearance gave curious onlookers a clue as to who we were and why on a week night—Thursday, to be exact—we were waiting for the last flight to Savannah. Ellen, whose full day had not given her time to change, was wearing a dress that would have made her at home at a P.T.A. meeting. Ginger was wearing blue jeans and a sweatshirt. I was wearing a black and green jogging suit. In complexion, we give meaning to a saying among African-Americans that we are so "mixed" as a people that no two of us "favor" (which means resemble), even when we belong to the same family. Ginger is light creme (could "pass" in some circles), Ellen is beige, and I am caramel. These differences in color were reflected in the texture of our hair. Ginger was wearing her silky hair, accented with tiny bits of gray, in a close cropped style around her round face. Ellen had plaited her soft hair into one long braid that was pinned artfully at the top of her head with a decorative barrette. I was wearing my political Afro. In the seventies, it was an Angela

Davis bouffant, but it was now short and, manicured with scissors, neat and round. Even in birthdates my friends and I are different. We ranged in age from early forties to mid-forties to early fifties.

Ginger, Ellen, and I do not fit the typical definition of "friends." Prior to this trip, we had chatted on the phone (but not on a regular basis), but we had never gone shopping together, attended a sorority meeting together, worshipped in church together, or dined together. Our genuine and deep bonding was spiritual, which is why we had chosen to spend our first extended time together on this trip to Sapelo, a place known for its beauty, mystery, and spirituality.

The three of us together chose the date for the trip, but Ginger alone took care of all the arrangements. She booked us (with discount fares and seats together) on the only flight out of Atlanta that would get us to Savannah in time to rent a car and drive the hour and a half to Darien, Georgia, before the last ferry to Sapelo pulled away from the dock at 11:45 P.M. Ginger is the youngest of the group, but only in calendar years. To Ellen and me, she is "an old soul." She is much shorter than I, but when I stand next to Ginger, I look up at her. There is so much about her to admire: her sense of humor, her wit, her intelligence, her love for people, and her ability to wear many hats well. Ginger, the mother of two children and the wife of an anesthesiologist, grew up in Cape May, New Jersey, and graduated from Spelman College, where I now teach. She is herself a physician, a public health administrator, and a Kellogg Fellow. A woman of many talents and inexhaustible energy, she travels extensively around the globe, conducting research on traditional healing and ancient cultures immersed in spirituality. She had traveled to Sapelo some time ago as a researcher, but this time she was traveling as a woman with women friends. Ginger never articulated her need for the trip. It was so like her not to focus on herself, but Ellen and I knew that Ginger was learning to say "Yes" to the voice that told her to write.

There is a saying among African-Americans that "some of us don't need one *single solitary thing* to make us beautiful because we got it natural." That describes Ellen. She is a tall and striking woman and, when she wears African dress, a regal woman. She and I are the same height, but I look up at her as I do at Ginger. And for reason. Ellen is a "good soul." Patient, tolerant, understanding—never one to complain—she exudes calm, gentleness, and strength. She is the contemplative one among us. Her penetrating eyes say that she is always thinking, observing, processing, and feeling. All three of us are affectionate women who find ease in saying, "I love you," but Ellen is affectionate in a way that, years ago, I would have called maternal, but now know to be spiritual.

But "maternal" is an appropriate adjective for Ellen. She has seven children, and she birthed all of them naturally. Like Ginger, she is a woman of many talents. A native of Philadelphia and a graduate of Mount Holyoke College, Ellen is fluent in French and conversant in Wolof, one of the native languages of Senegal. She is a dancer, a writer, a thinker, and a serious student of spiritual rituals, of astrology (she knows all the constellations), and of African culture, especially Kemetic culture. For Ellen and her husband, a physician and a Kemetic scholar, these interests provide the ordering principles of family cohesiveness. We know this from the sacraments of rituals visible in their home, from the African naming ceremonies which introduced the "Village" to their children, and from the African names, two of them Kemetic, which their children were given in those ceremonies. Already immersed in spirituality, Ellen would meditate at Sapelo on her new journey. She was returning to school to study midwifery.

I am the oldest of the three, the only southerner, and the only teacher, in the traditional, narrow sense of the word, that is. I grew up in Memphis, Tennessee, graduated from LeMoyne College, and have spent all of my professional life teaching at historically Black colleges. Like my friends, I, too, am a mother and, like them, I needed the trip to Sapelo, but perhaps more than they. I was recovering from a brutal rape attempt that had occurred four months earlier. Though I was spared the actual rape, I often felt the knife to my throat and the rope around my wrists. Nightmares can be as real as life. At Sapelo, I would begin to heal. Ginger and Ellen, I was certain, were making the trip mainly for my recovery. They never said so, but true friends rarely need to spell out what they are giving, or receiving, from bonding. We spoke about none of these things while we sat, close together, waiting for the plane to be called.

The night was free of rain and blessed with a clear sky. A relief for me. Though I fly frequently, I have not conquered my fear of flying, at least not my fear of the whirring sound the plane makes as it ascends to cruising level,

73

especially small planes like the one in which we would fly. I know that planes are ton-heavy, and yet, in those first few minutes, I fear they are large kites and that no one holds the string.

The flight was smooth and short. In an hour we landed in Savannah and, given Ginger's skill as an administrator and a charisma that makes people anxious to meet her requests, within no more than ten minutes we had a rented car and were pulling away from the airport headed for Brunswick. We listened to tapes of Gullah music and Gullah storytelling that Ginger, the able planner, had brought for our enjoyment, our enlightenment. A little better than an hour later, we reached Brunswick, parked the rented car, and boarded the last ferry to Sapelo, as did women carrying groceries and children and men wearing the clothes in which they work in the city. With pride, we watched a Black man man the ferry. With fascination, we watched white seagulls dive for fish in the white-tipped swirls of water that trailed the ferry. We stood on the deck breathing in air that, though ripe with the smell of fish, was clean and damp. The city disappeared quickly, and we were enveloped in a comforting darkness.

Forty-five minutes later, the ferry reached Sapelo. The sky overhead was clearer than in Atlanta and brighter with stars, but somehow still hinted of rain. A light mist hung in the air, seeming not to reach the soil of Sapelo. When we commented to a woman that it looked like rain, she quickly answered, "Oh, that's just a finny-finny rain." That did not mean rain, she added, in the way we thought of rain. A "finny-finny" rain is different from a sprinkle, light drizzle, or morning mist, all of which we had experienced in the city. A "finny-finny" rain has a unique silence, a unique way of touching your face, of making the air pregnant with mystery and discovery. It welcomed us to Sapelo.

Mr. Bailey, the husband of our hostess, was waiting for us at the end of the ferry's ramp. He is a tall, polite, and somewhat shy man with smiling eyes. We followed him to his car, Ellen and I asking questions all the way about Sapelo, which had once been a slave plantation where our Ancestors harvested rice and cotton and was now a small community of forty-five families, all of whom traced their ancestry to those slaves, knowing many of them by name and in some cases by physical description. Mr. Bailey told us that the number of young people leaving the island for jobs in the city increases each year. They leave because there are no jobs on Sapelo and the state-run ferry trips are too infrequent to accommodate work in the city and residence on the island. The 11:45 P.M. ferry we had taken to the island is available only once a month. Ginger said it could all be fixed so easily, if those who could fix it would. "Just make more trips," she said. Of course she was right.

By 1:15 in the morning, Mr. Bailey turned out of the small parking lot near the ferry and began driving down a road that, though bumpy, was amazingly straight. In ten minutes, or less, he made a right turn off the road into a complex of trailers. In the center was the Baileys' trailer-home; to its right was a trailer-store where residents and visitors could purchase cold sodas, island tee-shirts, and other souvenirs; to its left was the guest trailer, our home on Sapelo. We turned the knob. The door opened. We entered, each of us carrying our one bag, except for Ginger, who had brought a computer for my use and a bag of goodies for the three of us. We felt at home immediately. The living room was furnished with a comfortable sofa and two chairs; the kitchen, with a table and every utensil needed for cooking and eating. Down a narrow hall from the living room were one large bathroom and three bedrooms. Always generous, Ginger took the smallest bedroom, the first one on the left. Ellen, equally generous, took the second one, leaving me the largest room, located at the end of the hall. It had two beds, a full closet, and a table for the computer. By three in the morning, we retired to our individual rooms, falling asleep to the sound of the ocean a short distance away. We slept with our purses in the living room. We slept with the door unlocked.

Ginger and Ellen rose for the dawn walk we had promised to make together, but they did not bother to wake me. They knew I had not slept well; they had heard my screams in the middle of the night. The incident revisited me, even on Sapelo. I remember Ellen walking into the room and holding my hands and Ginger covering me with the blanket I had thrown off during the nightmare. I do not remember how long they stayed or what they said to me. I remember only that I fell asleep again, certain that I was safe because they were there.

By the time they returned from their walk, I was wide awake. I had taken my shower and was eager to begin our full day of activities. They said nothing about the nightmare. They talked instead about dawn rising on Sapelo.

Ellen was poetic in her description. "The old trees along the road, centuries old," she said, "made the whole morning incredible. I couldn't take my eyes off their thick, twisting branches." An astute student of nature in its many forms, she was fascinated by the way each tree supported a multitude of life systems. "There are vines that are indistinguishable from the trees," she said. "And the Spanish moss!" She was ecstatic about the moss, but she added: "You know, it really isn't moss."

Ginger was in love with the palmettos, "the young, bushy ones full of leaves." And of course the ocean. Ginger loves large bodies of water. The ocean. And low-growing vegetation that, with her skilled eyes, she sees as healing herbs. I am convinced that her Ancestors were the ones who prepared the poultices and potions and applied them lovingly to bruised slaves.

Neither Ginger nor Ellen said, "Gloria, you missed it!" And when, expressing my disappointment, I said, "I wish I had been with you," Ginger reassured me, "It's still there. Waiting for you." Ellen said, "You needed your rest." I felt they were giving more to me than I to them and considered myself blessed.

The finny-finny rain greeted us when we left the trailer. "It's in a capricious mood," Ellen said. And it was. It seemed to be coming and going, disappearing and returning, teasing and confusing us. We did not yet understand its gentle rhythms. Sapelo resembled the land from which our Ancestors were taken as slaves. As in Africa, so, too, on Sapelo, the weather is warm. The ocean is vast. The soil is rich. The spirits are alive. I wondered if Africa also has a finny-finny rain.

By 10:30, we were worshipping at one of the two small churches on the island. It sat a bit back from the road, shaded by a wide canopy of trees. Later we would hear about the miracle that built the church. The story goes that the congregation wanted a new church, needed one badly, but they had no money for the lumber. They prayed and prayed hard. Then, the story goes, a fierce storm demolished a church located on another island, and the lumber from that church floated across the ocean to Sapelo. The congregation praised God as they built their new church.

Sapelo and other rural areas, for obvious reasons, use itinerant preachers who go to different churches on different Sundays. This was an "off" Sunday for the church in which we were worshipping; the service was, therefore, the responsibility of the trusted Deacons. After morning prayer and one song, the Head-Deacon-in-Charge pointed to Ellen: "You will teach Sunday School," he instructed her. Ginger and I were delighted and encouraged the Deacon to continue with his persuasion. Ellen quickly explained that she was a visitor, that she had come simply to observe, that she. . . . He did not listen. He said again that she *would* teach the lesson. Ginger and I nearly pushed our reluctant friend from the pew and to the front of the church. She had to obey him, us, and most of all the Spirit.

And so Ellen taught, "in the only way I know how," she told us later. "With personal testimonies and input from the class."

"This is good. This is real good," the Deacon remarked midway through the lesson. "Everybody is talking this morning. Everybody is talking."

Ellen became bolder, drawing on her Catholic faith to make a point in a lesson being "taught" in a rural Baptist church on the island of the Ancestors. By the time the lesson ended forty-five minutes later, everyone in the church had taught in his or her own way. Everyone seemed caught up, as Ellen said later, "in the spiritual web of the three curious women from Atlanta." The feeling was as refreshing as the finny-finny rain that waited for us outside once more.

We returned to our trailer renewed and invigorated by what we had experienced in only a few short hours on Sapelo. Ginger set up the computer she had brought for me. She knew I would be taking notes on the trip, "for your book, Gloria." True friends know your needs before you articulate them. It was that way with Ginger and with Ellen. I turned on the computer, went to the directory as Ginger suggested, and saw "Gloria." I pulled up the "document" and read, "Hi, Gloria. Welcome to Sapelo and to the Spirit. Write. Love, Ginger."

While we talked, I recorded our thoughts on a document that I named, "Three Women's Spiritual Bonding on Sapelo." Our conversation turned naturally to the spirituality of African-American women and to our own search for spirituality.

"I feel connected to the cosmos," Ginger said. "I'm one little miracle, but I'm still a miracle."

"I try to fit into nature without disturbing it," Ellen said. "We are a part of nature. God speaks to us through nature."

I confessed that I had begun to search for the Spirit only after my mother's death. I tried to explain how many experiences I have had since then that I cannot explain. How does my spirituality express itself, or how do I know I have it? By the connection I feel to other people, even people I have not met. "It's as if I sometimes feel that all of us were born at the same time."

"And in the same place," Ginger added.

In the same womb, my friends agreed.

And so we wove our bonds. We talked about the spirit, the Spirit, spirituality, unable to explain that which we cannot see or hear, but feel. We danced with words, all of which came from the presence we had journeyed to the island of finny-finny rain to experience. The Spirit which had guided our individual pathways thus far now joined us and began to move us forward along a new pathway. Together.

We felt that Spirit in a special way during a tour of the island in midafternoon. Mr. Bailey, in a car that threatened to stall but never did, drove down dirt roads bounded on both sides by the magnificent trees we had grown to love. The trees told stories before Mr. Bailey put them into words, especially when we drove onto the grounds of the old plantation and saw quarters in which our Ancestors had once lived as slaves. It is one thing to read about the horrors of slavery. It is quite another to stand on the very earth where the horrors took place. The power of our imagination and our spiritual connection to our Ancestors transported us back in time, and we felt that we were witnessing the suffering of our people in bondage. We became the women in the stories the trees told with Mr. Bailey's voice, our husbands and fathers were the men, and our children were the children stolen, raped, maimed, or sold down the river and, therefore, lost to us forever.

We walked among the huts, marveling at the ingenuity of our Ancestors. They had built their own living quarters from "tabby," a durable concrete-like substance of shells, sand, and water. After more than three hundred years, the huts still stand. We moved in silence from one hut to the next. Ginger remarked that the one in the center was probably used for punishment. We looked inside each hut to the dirt floor on which they slept. In the stillness, we thought we could hear voices—"first a whisper, then a wail, then a shouting song," Ellen said. Each of us believes that the dead never truly leave. That there is no separation between those living and those dead.

Between those who are spirit and those who are flesh. At Sapelo, in the slave quarters, that belief became experience. I understand why African-Americans who visit the concrete fortresses in Africa in which slaves were retained before being packed into the hold of a ship say, to a one, that they heard voices and felt people whom they could not see moving around them. I am convinced that in places where human beings have experienced egregious suffering, the Spirit touches and speaks in a way that it does not in places where they have known joy.

We remained longer at the quarters than at any other place during our stay, leaving reluctantly, without touching, and yet holding onto one another. Tightly. We left knowing that we had been inspired, by the Spirit, to pass on truths of the African holocaust that have not yet penetrated the conscience of this nation.

Not only the holocaust that our African Ancestors suffered, but also the holocaust that destroyed the indigenous people of this island. Deep in the forest on the west side of the island, a mysterious circle with twenty-foot-high walls made of shells is all that remains of their culture. We walked through the shell ring as we had walked through the slave quarters. In reverent silence. In awe of the ingenuity of the people who made the shell walls during one of the many rituals that immersed their culture in spirituality. Native Americans, too, believe that the dead are never dead, that their spirits forever walk the earth. Their history and their lives, indeed their culture, were intertwined with that of African slaves, like the trees wound with vines on Sapelo.

Later that day, we learned more about African history on Sapelo from Mrs. Bailey, a woman with presence and energy. With memory. A griot. In language impressive for its precision and color, she told us the story of how the lumber from the old church floated to Sapelo. How the people grew herbs and plants that cured many ailments. How they passed on the names of their Ancestors to their children. And about the day she died and was resurrected. Her uncles had skillfully carved her casket from fallen trees in preparation for her burial. She was four at the the time. For eight hours she had not breathed. Though there was no question that she was dead, and had been for eight hours, an older woman in the community, for some mysterious reason, decided to try to bring her back to life. She did so by placing garlic under the child's nose. This was, of course, the working of the Spirit.

79

The people, then, Mrs. Bailey explained, believed that all of us can communicate with God. When preparing children to get religion, the elders would remove the children from the community to strengthen them spiritually. When the children were ready, in the elders' opinion, they were told to go out at night and find a place where they thought they could talk with God. That place would always be theirs. Communing with nature meant for them meditating with God. Even now, Mrs. Bailey explained, people on the island go to their special places of communion. There, they are still with God, with the Spirit.

Mrs. Bailey's phenomenal memory is the reason why she was featured in a story in *Essence* on surviving Africanisms on Sapelo and why she is in great demand by researchers who want to write books about our people. Mrs. Bailey grants interviews, but she tells researchers only that which is available in encyclopedias—rainfall, vegetation, dates. The culture, the rituals, the stories—she protects all of that. Researchers, she explained, will write books replete with information, but lacking in the soul of the island. Her house is a museum of documents and artifacts, an art gallery of old photographs, a temple in which she and her family worship the spirit of the Ancestors. Only Mrs. Bailey can write an authentic book on Sapelo. She must. She will. Perhaps that is why the garlic awoke her years ago.

Mrs. Bailey will keep the history alive in a book; Nancy, a woman whom we met in church, keeps the language alive in her telling of fairy tales in Gullah. She agreed after church (she was the secretary) to share her talent with us because Ellen had taught so well. After darkness had fallen, we left the trailer for an evening of storytelling at her home. Once outside, we realized we did not need the flashlights each of us had checked for working batteries before we left the trailer. The sky was clear, clean, radiant in its beauty. There is no pollution on Sapelo; nothing, therefore, dims the brightness of the heavens. We understood why visitors to the island are not allowed to bring cars. Either they walk everywhere or "catch a ride" with one of the few residents who own cars, none of them late models. Like their descendents from Africa, the residents believe that water, air, and earth are gifts from God and gods and goddesses, not to be defiled, not to be taken for granted, but to be used in good ways and to be worshipped in the various ways that speak to their spirituality as a people. They love the stars which are more plentiful on Sapelo than in the city. And brighter. And so perfectly clustered into zodiac signs named by ancient Egyptians, chief among them women.

I couldn't help thinking about my African-American literature class and the students' analysis of Harriet Jacobs's *Incidents in the Life of a Slave Girl*, a classic among slave narratives. I could hear Melissa Johnson, a very bright student from New York, telling the class that all African-Americans should be able to find the North Star and in regular rituals pray to it in thanksgiving. I remember that Melissa was fighting back tears. Ellen, Ginger, and I studied the stars, they with greater skill than I, especially Ellen.

"How did they remain sane?" I said.

We knew the answer. They believed in the inevitability of freedom, in the eventual triumph of good over evil, in the power of the Spirit. When people suffer, they find solace in the Spirit. Must. In order to remain sane.

"That is why the slaves talked about no shackles being on their souls," I said.

Ginger said, "You can kill the body, but not the soul," referring to a spiritual. It was not by accident, we agreed, that slaves testified about "visitation of the Spirit" and wrote about those visitations in their narratives.

On our walk to Nancy's home, I asked Ellen to tell me again about her experience with the bird. Months ago it had entered her house, mysteriously, since there were no open doors or open windows.

"It was strange," Ellen said. "Suddenly there was a bird in the house. I mean, suddenly it was there. It flew over my shoulder and perched on the mantel next to the picture of the Black Madonna."

Strange because Ellen is afraid of birds. Strange because the season for birds had not begun. Strange because it was the thirteenth day of the month. Strange because before the incident, Kuumba, a psychic in Atlanta, had told Ellen that the Goddess was trying to communicate with her. Strange because after perching on the mantel, the bird disappeared, exiting where there were no windows or open doors. As we talked about Ellen's experience, we knew we were supposed to be on Sapelo.

"Kuumba saw this trip," Ginger said. Weeks before the flight to Savannah, the car ride to the ferry, and the ride in Mr. Bailey's car to our home on Sapelo—before there were plans for a trip of any kind—we had been chosen for this experience. Kuumba had seen Ellen's sojourn on Sapelo.

The walk was a short one down a path which, though made of dirt, was without dust. We knocked on the door, a man answered, we identified ourselves, and seconds later, Nancy greeted us, her voice pitched high and her smile broad and welcoming. Like the Deacon at the church, she was in charge. "Which one of you will play the piano?"

I can't play a tune, though I have wanted all my life to play a piano. Actually, I took lessons when I was a young girl and was doing okay until one day when something unexpected occurred. I remember it as if it happened yesterday. Because my family could not afford a piano, I used the one at church. That day, I entered the church as usual and skipped, as usual, down the center aisle that led to the choir loft that led to the piano. Suddenly before me was an open casket with a body in full view. No one had told me about a wake scheduled for that afternoon. I ran screaming from the church, traumatized by my first look at a dead body. I stopped the piano lessons. I was *not* the person to obey Nancy's orders.

Nancy turned to Ellen and said, "You will play." Kuumba had seen this as well. "You're musical," she had told Ellen weeks ago, repeating it above Ellen's assertion that she was not.

"You will play," Nancy said again. Ellen obeyed, as she had when the Deacon told her to teach. She opened the hymnal the woman had provided and placed her fingers on the right keys. We were there for storytelling, but Nancy had other plans. Church began. Song after song, the four of us sang, clapping our hands spiritedly as if, together, we had worshipped this way many times. We were emotionally full or, as Blacks in the old church say, "filled with the Holy Spirit." We knew each song from a memory we did not know we remembered. "On Jordan's Stormy Banks," "Wade in the Water," "Come Ye Disconsolate," "Onward Christian Soldiers," "Kumbaya," "How Great Thou Art," "Ride on King Jesus," "'Tis de Ole Ship of Zion," and others.

Only after we had worshipped in song for an hour did Nancy begin to tell stories in Gullah. The music of her telling of "Little Red Riding Hood" was every bit as spiritual as our singing of old songs.

When the storytelling ended, I said to Nancy, "You are so very spiritual." Nancy testified. She was in church. Worshipping. Feeling as if she were floating in air. The only thing that stopped her from floating higher was the tug of her son pulling on her dress.

She testified again. When she was a young girl, she loved to climb trees. But no longer. Now she worships trees. "I see them different," she said. "I see in them the handiwork of God."

We walked back to the trailer in deeper reverence, talking among ourselves, one voice indistinguishable from the other. We set our clocks to ring well enough before dawn so that we could witness its arrival on the horizon of the Atlantic Ocean. Again we slept with the door unlocked. We slept soundly. Even I. My healing had begun. Before dawn, we were pulling away from the trailer in Mr. Bailey's car. Ginger knew the road to the ocean only because Ginger and the ocean talk to each other. The ocean directed her. I am sure of that.

Free of umbrellas, empty bottles of tanning lotions, spent beer cans—all debris that beachcombers leave behind—the shore was breathtaking in its beauty. There are no beachcombers on Sapelo, Mrs. Bailey had informed us earlier. The beach belongs only to the people of the island who respect the ocean and its white sandy breast, and to the few visitors who are allowed to stay, but not too long and only under the circumstances that the residents establish. We were alone on the beach. Except for tiny holes made by sand crabs and three short/slim lines which were the footprints of sea gulls, the beach was flawlessly smooth. The water rushed to our feet and then receded, spraying a fine mist that stroked our faces like the finny-finny rain we had come to love. I thought of the Africans of Ibo Landing who walked into the ocean, their chains pulling them under, rather than yield to slavery. The ocean's vastness and the unending, clear sky above humbled us. If there were tears, I did not feel them, for how could I distinguish between the ocean's mist and the finny-finny rain?

The ocean was the first view the Ancestors had of the new world they would never leave. Symbolically, it was the last place we visited before leaving the island. As Mr. Bailey, his kind eyes even kinder, pulled away from the trailer, we were grateful for all we had experienced. I had begun to heal. Ellen was prepared to become a midwife. And Ginger, who had told me to write, had given in to the voice that said to her, "Write." We didn't try to describe the clarity we felt about so many things, but it was evident in our eyes.

We had grown stronger spiritually. We knew we were three small miracles in the universe, three women trying to fit into Nature, three women feeling connected to all people because all of us are born in the same womb. Each of us, to herself, made a promise to grow stronger still in the months and years ahead by seeking spirituality and expressing spirituality in relationships with others.

When I think about our three days and two nights on Sapelo, I realize how infrequently we physically touched one another. We hugged when we met up at the airport, but we did not hug on Sapelo. We touched spiritually and continuously. After our time together on the island, we would change nothing in the way we expressed our bonding. We would not begin to chat on the phone. We would not begin to plan shopping sprees together, worship in church together, or dine out together. We would simply be there for one another in spiritual ways. For me that meant Ginger would continue to leave her Ginger-message on my answering machine: "Love you." Ellen would continue to call, at just the right time, to bless my writer's space with her encouragement. I don't know that I give as much to them as they do to me, but I would continue to give them my love.

Love. That is what we experienced on Sapelo. I am realizing that now as I leave the island, this time in my remembering. Given the history of suffering that the people on Sapelo keep alive in songs, stories, and rituals, they are remarkably a people of love. No rancorous spirit. No rage. Love. They inspired us.

Ginger, Ellen, and I will grow stronger as women friends in the months and years ahead and stronger as women of the Spirit. Like the children of Sapelo, we will find places where we can speak to our God. I am as certain of that as I am that our trip to Sapelo was no accident. It was a gift from the Spirit, as were the talking trees, the vines intertwining with them, the vegetation yielding healing herbs, the slave quarters speaking to us about a history we cannot and must not forget, and the shell ring reminding us that no group has a monopoly on human suffering. Our friendship had been baptized in the spiritual waters of Sapelo which sometimes, often, stroked our faces in a finny-finny rain.

A City Called Heaven

Rachel Harding

the snake in her back
hollering
like a vine struck loose

    voice climbing stair
    scrapes
    each level to
        smoothness

shaken
  on a wing like hunger

inside
her thin arms
her wrists   a percussive trembling

the gourd
rattler
tuning up

    twelve gates
    are a single breath
    trailing ribbons

    the small chime of bells:
    instruction   a map
    fire pellucid in her bones

face
like a salty internal rain
song called out for air—
who is that yonder coming?

turning her weight
in spasms
her hat off   her heat-straightened hair undone

row of saints
to steady the ladder
eyes shut
ring shout
every rung goes a little higher
          higher

Life-Making: The Spirituality
of Ella Jo Baker

Rosemarie and Vincent Harding

To me, faith means treating the truth as true. Jesus believed in the infinite possibilities of an individual soul. His faith was a triumphant realization of the eternal development of the best in man——an optimistic vision of the human aptitude for endless expansion and perfectibility. . . . Religion must be life made true; and life is action, growth, development—— begun now and ending never. And a life made true cannot confine itself——it must reach out and twine around every pulsing interest within reach of its uplifting tendrils.

——A N N A J. C O O P E R, Voice from the South

When we first met Ella Baker in Atlanta in 1961 she was already something of a legendary figure in the Southern Freedom Movement. Having given decades of service in struggles for social justice and human transformation, this fifty-seven-year-old veteran freedom fighter was at the time serving as a highly valued, unpaid, full-time advisor to the Student Non-violent Coordinating Committee (S.N.C.C.), the courageous young shock troops of the Movement. But part of her attractiveness lay in the fact that Ella Baker could not be cast into any neat and hard categories; so now, eight years after her death, she might well initially resist the idea that she belongs in a collection celebrating Black women's spirituality.

Nevertheless, there was something about "Miss Baker" (as nearly all of her student charges, and many others, called her) that suggested the way of a true pastor, a spiritual guide, one who helps us to discover and develop our best path, our deepest resources, one who meets us at the amazing springs of our own spirits. Though she usually tended to avoid the language and the rituals of traditional religion, it was clear that she was always inviting us to move toward those profound levels of our being, those inner spaces that we eventually recognize as the sources of life-giving, energizing spirit. Without ever using the term, she helped us to explore the sacred spaces in our own lives and in the life of the Movement that we shared. For she kept reminding us of the great life-giving strengths, powers, and possibilities that were within us all,

87

and that were so needed for the good of us all. Hers was a spirituality of self-discovery, one that exposed us to the creativity—and therefore the divinity—at the center of our being.

This doughty, nontraditional shepherd in our lives was always helping us to see that the way of our best development did not require weakening or demeaning others. Indeed, by her own example she made it clear that the fullest opening of our personal strengths, skills, and truths required the sharing of our gifts, demanded that we carry on a constant search for and engagement with kindred spirits of every kind.

Ella always assumed that there *were* kindred spirits available, especially if we made clear to ourselves and to others what we were committed to and what we were prepared to risk. So, for instance, while she remained deeply grounded in the African-American experience that had so richly endowed her life, she never saw it as a restricting ground. Rather, she made that Black experience her base for working with and reaching out to all others who wanted to join forces in the urgent humanizing tasks that needed to be accomplished.

In the search for kindred spirits she was an accomplished guide. For she had been working with others for justice and for a compassionate society all of her adult life. By the time we met her she had known decades of service, including a time of organizing domestic workers and developing co-ops in New York City, years of carrying out very risky N.A.A.C.P. organizing across the southern states, and providing crucial skills in the early development of the Southern Christian Leadership Conference. And, of course, she offered essential, catalytic encouragement to the creation of S.N.C.C.

It was especially with the Black and white young people of S.N.C.C. ("Snick") that Ella carried out the essential role of unconventional pastor, wise auntie, and spiritual guide. For instance, we remember vividly that this very articulate, powerfully gifted public speaker never failed to *listen* to the young warriors as they tried to sort out who they were, what they were doing, where they were going, and what the Movement required. She listened to them, took their words and deeds seriously, and worked with them to try to discern the fullest meaning and potentials of all that they were saying, doing, and learning. That had been her role from the very beginning of the student movement, always reminding them that it was *their* movement, but that it was also part of something larger than themselves. So when these young people needed to turn the powerful, largely spontaneous beginnings of the sit-in movement into a more focused and organized thrust toward freedom, justice, and a new social order, it was Ella who encouraged them to see their own best possibilities as agents of profound social change. It was she who urged them to listen to each other, to develop their great leadership capacities, to trust each other with a generosity of spirit and an honest, nurturing commitment that eventually helped to transform many of their lives.

Perhaps we could say that Ella Baker's spirituality was expressed in her profound trust in the young freedom workers. Perhaps we could say that it was demonstrated in her compassionate, demanding toughness with them, as she constantly insisted that they discipline themselves to live up to their own highest possibilities.

Through all of this, one of the most powerful signs of her spirituality was that no one *followed* Ella Baker. Everyone walked with her, and she taught, guided, and learned in the process of walking together. On the way, she was mentor, guide, and model. As a model she made a special contribution to the young women of S.N.C.C. They saw and felt her combination of toughness and compassion, of self-assurance and humility. They saw her capacity to be absolutely fearless in her outspoken advocacy of her beliefs, and at the same time they recognized her ability to listen and try to understand the viewpoints of those with whom she disagreed. They saw her calm, unmistakable signals to insensitive men, demanding that she be respected. They saw her courage, self-discipline, and deep inner strength which refused to be run over, but which also refused to run over others. And at the deepest level of all, beyond gender, race, and class, everyone in the small band of young sisters and brothers knew that Ella Baker loved them and would walk through the valley with them, teaching all the way. What they saw in "Miss Baker," without ever naming it in this way, was the spirituality of compassionate commitment to justice and hope, commitment to human beings of all kinds. It was a spirituality that grew out of a politically aware participation in the life-long struggle for personal and social transformation, a spirituality that arose from her sense of connection to her own deepest spiritual resources.

Of course, although young people were her special passion, this deep-living woman could not confine her spirituality and pastoral care to them.

Her spirit was too rich to be confined, and it engaged many of her adult peers as well. For some, especially some men, her spirit was too strong, too honest, too poised, too outspoken and self-assured. But for other co-workers she was a welcome source of great strength. For instance, Anne Braden and Fannie Lou Hamer, two southerners from very different origins, found in Ella a nourishing spirit. Mrs. Hamer, the Black sharecropper's daughter, was persistently encouraged by Ella Baker to stand and live and speak the great truths of her matchless life. Reciprocally, Ella never failed to wonder and rejoice at the great courage and determination of this woman who did so much and paid such a personal price to re-make her own life, the life of Mississippi, and of the nation. Anne Braden, daughter of southern white aristocrats, committed worker for truth and justice, met Ella and knew that she had found a sister in the struggle and a teacher on the path. For Ella, Anne was one of those dues-paying spirits whom she recognized from profound levels in her own life. And they worked together, both south and north, to embody their shared vision of a just and compassionate society.

For younger and older companions, it was clear that the walking, the embodying, was central. What we discovered was that Ella's spirituality was indeed a spirituality of embodiment, walking the truth in the struggle for new women and men, for a new society. It was in walking with her that we best caught her spirit. Of course, our elder sister/aunt also knew how to make speeches, and she made some very powerful ones. Indeed, even though she would often laughingly deny it, she could even preach inspiring sermons when she had to, lifting the spirits and riveting the determination of men and women in very dangerous and desperate situations all across the South. But it was always the walking together, the thinking together, the laughing together, the amazingly long debates and discussions together—it was in being together with her, and not following her, or being dazzled by her, that we imbibed her great compassionate spirit.

What we saw was a woman who steadfastly refused the limelight, who intentionally stood aside to open the path of personal and political development to others. We watched her insisting that even at the most exciting, triumphant, limelighting moments, someone needed to be working behind the scenes, making sure that the hidden, essential machinery was attended to: the bail arranged, the housing secured, the voters driven back home, the educational materials developed, the mailings sent out, and a thousand other logistical and political details taken in hand. And after every action, no matter how heady and apparently successful, she urged us to engage in self-criticism, in analysis of what we had accomplished, as well as what we had failed to do and be.

Through it all, we recognized that this great-hearted woman also had a magnificent mind, capable of the clearest, wisest analysis, and we realized that she never used these gifts to promote herself, only to teach and develop others, only to forward the cause of racial, economic, and social justice to which she consistently gave herself. So we saw her living modestly, often sacrificially, demonstrating a life of what someone has called "creative insecurity." (At the time she carried a magnificent capacity of laughter, especially at herself; and often we would be almost rocked by the powerful gusts of laughter that would suddenly rise on the waves of her rich contralto voice.) She knew what she was doing, the risks she was taking. So toward the end of her life she kept repeating to us the title of the autobiography that she wanted to write. She said that it should be called, "Making A Life, Instead of Making a Living." The spirituality of life-making—perhaps that was what she most fully embodied.

During her final days, back in Harlem, as she reflected on her own childhood and youth, we learned something about where she had caught *her* spirit. Clearly, much of it had come from her mother, Georgina Ross Baker, a woman who had been a teacher in Halifax County, North Carolina, before she married Blake Baker and moved to Norfolk, Virginia, where Ella was born in 1903. Ella remembered her mother as a strong-willed, outspoken, and self-disciplined woman whose house was always open to any friends and relatives who needed help. (Mrs. Baker seemed especially solicitous about the sick.) Then there was her mother's father, Reverend Mitchell Ross, a Baptist pastor who took young Ella with him in the buggy on many of his pastoral preaching and business trips. He was a real favorite with the young girl. He listened to her. She especially remembered Grandpa Ross letting her sit in one of the big chairs in the pulpit of his churches (he was responsible for four of them) as he preached his deep, restrained, and spirit-filled sermons. These were undoubtedly some of the influences that led her to decide while she was a student at Shaw College in Raleigh in the 1920s that she wanted to be a medical missionary, perhaps in China or Africa.

When the Depression shattered the dream of medical school, Ella Baker went north to Harlem to begin her long career of tending to the dis-ease of her own nation, sharing her spirit, walking her talk, eventually returning south to shepherd some of the great spirits of the next generation, passing on the spirituality of life-making through persons like Diane Nash, Bob Moses, Jane Stembridge, Charles McDew, Casey Heyden, Ruby Doris Smith Robinson, James Forman, Bernice Johnson Reagon, and many others, and some of *their* children. Every time we hear Bernice and those great a cappella artists, Sweet Honey in the Rock, sing, "We Who Believe in Freedom Cannot Rest," we hear the words and catch the life-making spirit of Ella Baker, calling us, challenging us, to make a life, to live, to awaken to the life within us, to live. And we know that though she rests, Ella will not rest while freedom's life is still to be made.

In the turning tides of life she who nurtured us by her capacious spirit now finds her spirit nurtured and awakened by her deepest memories. So the life-making goes on. The sister spirit who worked for new life in Harlem and Mississippi still works, inviting us to new life, to work, urging us to life-making, together, here, everywhere, now.

Gospel

Rita Dove

Swing low so I
can step inside—
a humming ship of voices
bit with all

the wrongs done
done them.
No sound this generous
could fail:

ride joy until
it cracks like an egg,
make sorrow
seethe and whisper.

From a fortress
of animal misery
soars the chill voice
of the tenor, enraptured

with sacrifice.
What do I see,
he complains, notes
brightly rising

towards a sky
blank with promise.
Yet how healthy
the single contralto

settling deeper
into her watery furs!
Carry me home,
she cajoles, bearing

down. Candelabras
brim. But he slips
through God's net and swims
heavenward, warbling.

PART **2**

Testifying:
The Spiritual Anchor in
African-American Culture

I'm gonna do what the Spirit say do.
Oh yes.
I'm gonna do what the Spirit say do.
Oh yes.
If the Spirit say shout
I'm gonna shout, shout, shout!
I'm gonna do what the Spirit say do.
—NEGRO SPIRITUAL

I sets here 'mongst my rags and soot and gits so happy sometimes I jes 'bound
to shout. I shouted de other night in bed. In de kitchen cookin' my little
piece o'flour bread, in de garden workin' out my greens, in de bed—
wherever de grace o' God swells up inside me I git so
overjoyed I bound to praise my God.
—SLAVE NARRATIVE

We would form a circle, each touching those next to us so to physically
express our spiritual closeness. We "testified," speaking on the day's or the
week's experiences. We shared the pain of those experiences and received from
the group affirmations of our existences as suffering beings. As we "lay down
our burdens," we became lighter. As we testified and listened to others
testify, we began to understand ourselves as communal beings, no longer
the "individuals" that the slave system tried to make us. . . . We sang
and moved until we were able to experience totally the spirit within
us. We "got happy". . . . We became, again, a community.
—DONA MARIMBA RICHARDS, Let the Circle Be Unbroken

As a young girl growing up in Mississippi, I witnessed the gathering of
community women that took place in my mother's parlor once a week, or
whenever a sister was in need of prayer. I was fascinated by the shifting
motion in the women's shoulders, the lifting and butterfly opening and
closing of their hands, and the sporadic shaking of their heads. I knew from
these movements and from the songs they sang that they were praying and
testifying; they were celebrating joys and removing sorrows. When I became
an adult and understood the meaning of sisterhood, I realized that the
women became stronger individually and collectively as a result of their
spiritual bonding, and the children were the beneficiaries of their

strength. Working on Sturdy Black Bridges *was my way of
expressing gratitude to the women of my youth.*
— *BETTYE PARKER-SMITH*

*I laugh at myself sometimes when God takes the reins I had intended to take
and turns everything I think is right and real upside down. . . . With God
there is no fixed state. God takes us on a wonderful faith-journey of
living—painfully, honestly, responsibly, and spontaneously.*
— *CARDINAL LINDIWE NYERERE,*
Shrine of the Black Madonna Church

*My soul is a witness for my Lord,
My soul is a witness for my Lord,
My soul is a witness for my Lord,
My soul is a witness for my Lord.*

*God sent His angels de lions for to keep,
An' Daniel laid down an' went to sleep.
Now Daniel was a witness for my Lord.
Now Daniel was a witness for my Lord.*

*O, who'll be a witness for my Lord?
O, who'll be a witness for my Lord?
My soul is a witness for my Lord,
My soul is a witness for my Lord.*
— *NEGRO SPIRITUAL*

how i got ovah II/ It Is Deep II

Carolyn M. Rodgers

for Evangelist Richard D. Henton

just when i thought i had gotten away
my mother
called me on the phone
and did not ask,
but commanded me
to come to church with her.

and because i knew so much
and had "escaped"
i thought it a harmless enough act.

i was not prepared for the Holy Ghost.
i was not prepared to be covered by the
blood of Jesus

i was not ready to be dipped in
                              the water. . . .

i could not drink the water turned wine.

and so i went back another day
trying to understand the mysteries
of mystical life the "intellectual"
purity of mystical light.
and that Sunday evening while i was
sitting there and the holy gospel choir
was singing
        "oh oh oh oh somebody touched me"

somebody touched me.
                    and when i turned around to
see what it was whoever touched me wanted
my mother leaned over and whispered in my ear
        "musta been the hand of the Lord"

From *Gifts of Power*

Rebecca Jackson

*Her dreams are filled with symbols and her own activity. She can fly
through the air like a bird (though higher than birds, and, interestingly,
white women), walk through walls, visit other realms, and converse with
angels. She can touch a hot stove while awake and not be burned, or totter
with eyes closed on the very lip of a steep cellar stair and not fall. She
preaches the word of God as it is revealed to her and discovers she has
the power to pray sick people well and sinful people holy. All glory
for these wonders she gives to God alone and repeatedly describes
herself as "a little child" or "a worm of the dust."*
—*A L I C E   W A L K E R, In Search of Our Mothers' Gardens*

In the year 1850, March 15, a pamphlet was put into my hand, which gave
an account of the spirits visiting the inhabitants of the West with strange
knockings and of the communications to the people, through the alphabet, by
which they have been able to make known to the people that God has sent
them to help the inhabitants of the world. While giving attention to these
things, I had a clear view of God's dealing with me, from July in the year 1830
to the year 1850, that I was greatly astonished at His mercy to a worm of the
dust like me. . . . Through the aid of departed spirits, I have been able to tell
many things before they took place. . . . For all these years I have been under
the tuition of invisible Spirits, who communicate to me from day to day the
will of God concerning me and concerning various events that have taken
place in the earth. But this communication to me has been in words as clear
and distinct as though a person was conversing with me. By this means I have
been able to tell people's thoughts, and to tell them words they have spoken
many miles distant from me. And also to tell them things they would do a year
beforehand, when they had no thought of ever doing such things.

From *Beloved*

Toni Morrison

It was time to lay it all down. Before Paul D. came and sat on her porch steps, words whispered in the keeping room had kept her going. Helped her endure the chastising ghost; refurbished the baby faces of Howard and Buglar and kept them whole in the world because in her dreams she saw only their parts in trees; and kept her husband shadowy but *there*—somewhere. Now Halle's face between the butter press and the churn swelled larger and larger, crowding her eyes and making her head hurt. She wished for Baby Suggs' fingers molding her nape, reshaping it, saying, "Lay em down, Sethe. Sword and shield. Down. Down. Both of em down. Down by the riverside. Sword and shield. Don't study war no more. Lay all that mess down. Sword and shield." And under the pressing fingers and the quiet instructive voice, she would. Her heavy knives of defense against misery, regret, gall, and hurt, she placed one by one on a bank where clear water rushed on below.

Nine years without the fingers or the voice of Baby Suggs was too much. And words whispered in the keeping room were too little. The butter-smeared face of a man God made none sweeter than demanded more: an arch built or a robe sewn. Some fixing ceremony. Sethe decided to go to the Clearing, back where Baby Suggs had danced in sunlight.

Before 124 and everybody in it had closed down, veiled over and shut away; before it had become the plaything of spirits and the home of the chafed, 124 had been a cheerful, buzzing house where Baby Suggs, holy, loved, cautioned, fed, chastised and soothed. Where not one but two pots simmered on the stove; where the lamp burned all night long. Strangers rested there while children tried on their shoes. Messages were left there, for whoever needed them was sure to stop in one day soon. Talk was low and to the point—for Baby Suggs, holy, didn't approve of extra. "Everything depends on knowing how much," she said, and "Good is knowing when to stop."

It was in front of *that* 124 that Sethe climbed off a wagon, her newborn tied to her chest, and felt for the first time the wide arms of her mother-in-law, who had made it to Cincinnati. Who decided that, because slave life had "busted her legs, back, head, eyes, hands, kidneys, womb and tongue," she had nothing left to make a living with but her heart—which she put to work at once. Accepting no title of honor before her name, but allowing a small caress after it, she became an unchurched preacher, one who visited pulpits and opened her great heart to those who could use it. In winter and fall she carried it to AMEs and Baptists, Holinesses and Sanctifieds, the Church of the Redeemer and the Redeemed. Uncalled, unrobed, unanointed, she let her great heart beat in their presence. When warm weather came, Baby Suggs, holy, followed by every black man, woman, and child who could make it through, took her great heart to the Clearing—a wide-open place cut deep in the woods nobody knew for what at the end of a path known only to deer and whoever cleared the land in the first place. In the heat of every Saturday afternoon, she sat in the clearing while the people waited among the trees.

After situating herself on a huge flat-sided rock, Baby Suggs bowed her head and prayed silently. The company watched her from the trees. They knew she was ready when she put her stick down. Then she shouted, "Let the children come!" and they ran from the trees toward her.

"Let your mothers hear you laugh," she told them, and the woods rang. The adults looked on and could not help smiling.

Then "Let the grown men come," she shouted. They stepped out one by one from among the ringing trees.

"Let your wives and your children see you dance," she told them, and groundlife shuddered under their feet.

Finally she called the women to her. "Cry," she told them. "For the living and the dead. Just cry." And without covering their eyes the women let loose.

It started that way: laughing children, dancing men, crying women and then it got mixed up. Women stopped crying and danced; men sat down and cried; children danced, women laughed, children cried until, exhausted and riven, all and each lay about the Clearing damp and gasping for breath. In the silence that followed, Baby Suggs, holy, offered up to them her great big heart.

She did not tell them to clean up their lives or to go and sin no more. She did not tell them they were the blessed of the earth, its inheriting meek, or its glorybound pure.

She told them that the only grace they could have was the grace they could imagine. That if they could not see it, they would not have it.

"Here," she said, "in this here place, we flesh; flesh that weeps, laughs; flesh that dances on bare feet in grass. Love it. Love it hard. Yonder they do not love your flesh. They despise it. They don't love your eyes; they'd just as soon pick em out. No more do they love the skin on your back. Yonder they flay it. And O my people they do not love your hands. Those they only use, tie, bind, chop off, and leave empty. Love your hands! Love them. Raise them up and kiss them. Touch others with them, pat them together, stroke them on your face 'cause they don't love that either. *You* got to love it, *you*! And no, they ain't in love with your mouth. Yonder, out there, they will see it broken and break it again. What you say out of it they will not heed. What you scream from it they do not hear. What you put into it to nourish your body they will snatch away and give you leavins instead. No, they don't love your mouth. *You* got to love it. This is flesh I'm talking about here. Flesh that needs to be loved. Feet that need to rest and to dance; backs that need support; shoulders that need arms, strong arms I'm telling you. And O my people, out yonder, hear me, they do not love your neck unnoosed and straight. So love your neck; put a hand on it, grace it, stroke it and hold it up. And all your inside parts that they'd just as soon slop for hogs, you got to love them. The dark, dark liver—love it, love it, and the beat and beating heart, love that too. More than eyes or feet. More than lungs that have yet to draw free air. More than your life-holding womb and your life-giving private parts, hear me now, love your heart. For this is the prize." Saying no more, she stood up then and danced with her twisted hip the rest of what her heart had to say while the others opened their mouths and gave her the music. Long notes held until the four-part harmony was perfect enough for their deeply loved flesh.

Revelation by Grace

Belvie Rooks

Being bound by the limitations of time, space and causation, we cannot express all of the powers that we possess in reality. The higher we rise above these limiting conditions, the more we can manifest the divine qualities of omniscience and omnipotence.
—SWAMI ABEHEDANANDA

S omething" kept telling me run. Actually it was more on the order of a quiet, insistent urging. But how did I know to respond? What if I hadn't run? What if I had chosen instead simply to ignore that nagging, insistent voice? Would I have even lived long enough to be sorry? Even if I had not been killed, would I have been maimed and crippled for life? What would my life have been like as a disabled or crippled person? These were, and continue to be nagging questions, without answers.

What I could not have understood at the time was that the incident at the creosote plant would have a profound impact on my life, mostly because I would live to have a life.

After all these years the memory of me as a terrified, wide-eyed, ten-year-old girl is still a vivid one: trembling uncontrollably, staring at the spot, now buried under a ton of wooden debris, where a few seconds earlier I had stood. In fact, a half-second earlier. My favorite horse, brown with white-patterned legs, that a few seconds earlier had been begging for just one last pat on the nose, lay partially buried, struggling and whinnying on the outer edges of the debris unable to stand. My heart was beating wildly. Had I not honored an uncontrollable and, at the time, seemingly irrational urge to run, I too could have been lying there. The spot where I had been standing was now completely covered over. Fortunately the horse had been standing behind the fence and had moved quickly enough to not be buried completely.

Always upon reflection, there was nothing rational about my last-minute decision to obey the urging, that persistent voice that kept saying, "run!" Why, after all, would any ten-year-old, on a sunny afternoon, playing with a horse that she loved, suddenly turn and run as if her life depended on it?

Afterwards, I stood rooted to the spot, unable to move, or really grasp what had occurred. Frightened and alone, watching the horse struggle to get up, I tried to understand why I had suddenly responded, and what it was that I had responded to. Having made the decision, there was barely time to take more than five or six, ten-year-old strides before the world in the back of me collapsed.

That afternoon, I had been walking through a creosote plant, a place where railroad ties are treated prior to being laid as railroad track. The railroad ties are soaked in a thick black substance to prevent decay and afterwards are stacked to dry. Each railroad tie weighed about twenty pounds. After being treated, the thick ten by ten logs were often stacked as high as one story to dry. At the time, I only weighed about sixty pounds, the weight of three logs. I had stood transfixed, staring in disbelief at the hundreds of logs now covering the spot where a few moments earlier I had stood.

Could it be that an aspect of embracing spirit is the ability to access a space that allows our life-preserving voices to speak clearly, and with unchallenged authority? Could it be that we are embraced by spirit when we experience those magical moments of connectedness: a sacred gift, that as children we sometimes access without effort?

There was a wonderful feeling of disconnectedness and flight, as if I were both sinking and rising at the same time. I tried to move but couldn't. I tried to speak but no sounds came. I needed to tell my roommate, seated a few feet away studying, that I was dying and that she shouldn't cry or be sad because it was a wonderful experience. With that thought I could feel myself relaxing into the experience. Suddenly, my perspective seemed off, and I found myself at the top of the room, floating just below the ceiling, looking down at my now lifeless body. But who was "I"? Was "I" the lifeless, unconscious body still lying on the bed with the book resting gently across my chest, or was "I" looking down on all of this? Whichever. "I" was confused but happy. Ada sat hunched over her desk still concentrating on the notes for our upcoming anthropology exam. A few minutes earlier "I" had been stretched out on the bed doing the same thing. If "I" were the person still stretched out on the bed, then who or what was the invisible, yet conscious entity now looking down on all of this?

This new experience of duality was confusing. The new "I" now seemed to be the conscious self or the subject, while my old, unconscious body seemed relegated to the status of mere object; simply another aspect of the environment. I was totally conscious and totally frustrated. I kept trying to speak to Ada, but there was no indication that she could hear me. I understood that in a few minutes she would look over and discover my lifeless body. I knew that she would be frightened, hysterical, sad. I thought about all of my friends, my classmates, and my relatives. I could see the entire scenario. The funeral. My burial. The tears. The sadness. The sense of loss that everybody would feel. I desperately needed to get Ada's attention, to let her know that I was all right, that in fact I was still there; that I could not only see her, but that I was able, to my surprise, to understand what she was thinking and feeling. I wanted her to know that even though I was no longer in my body, I was still in the room and totally conscious of everything that was happening.

It was a perfect fall afternoon in San Francisco, warm and sunny. I felt drawn to the window by the happy inviting sounds of children playing on the sidewalk below. As soon as I had the thought, I was at the window. Did this mean that I could just decide where I wanted to go by thinking it? Before going out the window to join in the fun, I hesitated; something held me back.

My next memory is of being back in my body, staring up at the ceiling where, a few minutes earlier, I had been happily gliding about. The question was how to explain all of this to Ada, who was still sitting in the same position studying. I took a deep breath; that part of me that was once again "my body" could breathe again. I remembered thinking that this was not going to be easy, but it would be interesting. "Ada, did you hear me trying to talk to you a few minutes ago?" Without even bothering to look up or turn around, she responded, "No, you haven't said anything, you've been laying there asleep the whole time." Another deep breath. "No, I wasn't really asleep, something happened. I think that I died or something, at any rate, I was floating around on top of the ceiling and I was trying to get your attention . . ." My voice trailed off at the look on her face. Ada was nothing if not rational. When I explained what had happened, she rationally explained that it was probably just a bad dream or a nightmare. I didn't bother to explain that I hadn't felt scared; that it had, in fact, been wonderful. I turned over and picked up the book that I had been studying in preparation for our upcoming Physical Anthropology exam and continued reading about the origin and evolution of the species.

Somewhere, though, a window had been opened—ever so slightly. Perhaps the body and the soul were distinct entities—after all. Maybe Shana, my East Indian friend who had grown up in the West Indies, was right when she said that we were essentially souls that selected particular bodies during different lifetimes. In that context she often laughingly said that "we are not our bodies." That part of the conversation had always been confusing, but so was the experience that I had just had. What if I had given in to the desire to float out of the window? Would I have been able to? Would I have been able to come back? Were the choices mine? If the physical body and the human body evolved over time, then what of the soul's evolutionary journey? Who was "I," really? Was Ada perhaps right? Could it all have been just a bad dream?

The really focused questioning would come later—much later; as if in response to the insights, the teachers, the revelations always seemed to appear magically, as if by grace.

Spirit Never Fails

Paula L. Woods

As I sit amidst the rubble of a city that has experienced the worst earthquake in its history, I am blessed. Not just for the obvious reason, my survival and that of my family and friends, but because the Los Angeles earthquake has been the culmination of my own personal movement back to a spiritual connection that has eluded me for most of my forty years on this earth.

I was always a deeply spiritual child. Not religious—despite my family pedigree of being the granddaughter of an African Methodist Episcopalian minister on my mother's side and the great-granddaughter of another A.M.E. minister on my father's—but spiritual, because as I watched the sun peek over the tops of the houses in my Compton neighborhood, I knew the presence of God as surely as if he were a playmate greeting me each morning. My prayers at night, after I had done the "now-I-lay-me-down-to-sleeps" required by my mother, were often rambling conversations with God long after I was tucked in and the lights were off. God was my playmate, a constant companion who foreshadowed many life events to me as surely as a friend whispering in my ear. In fact, it was the whispering in my ear and my childish innocence in sharing the secrets I had been told that began what I realize now was my separation from the knowledge of my spiritual core, a separation that took most of my life to heal.

My grandfather, Lawrence Woods, was my best friend. He was a tall, imposing man, not because of his size but because of the quiet assurance with which he conducted his business and led his life. His spirit was so centered, so sure, that I thought he owned the Sears store we visited regularly in Compton. Maybe as a child I just didn't understand that when you gave people money you were able to take things out of stores, but I remember being three and watching white store clerks who I'm sure acted against their every racist instinct (which were as strong in California as elsewhere, sunshine notwith-

standing) serve us so courteously that I returned to the house he shared with
Mama Vivian in Watts with a new name for him—Papa Sears.

In his late sixties, after the death of his wife Maud, Papa married Vivian, a
woman approximately my father's age who was very sweet to me but who my
father always believed had married Papa for money. That she wore my grandmother's jewelry was probably only one of her transgressions for my highly
moral father. I was five when Vivian left Papa after seven years of marriage
with the jewelry and a considerable amount of cash to return to Arkansas. My
father pleaded with Papa not to go after her. I was at Papa's house when they
argued, but Papa insisted he was going to Arkansas to bring her back. As we
left the house, my childish concern was that my Papa wasn't ever going to
come back. We stood in the yard of his house in Watts as he bent over me
and, hugging me, said, "Sweet Pea, I'll always be with you." My father took
me home before returning to take my grandfather to Union Station for the
train ride to Arkansas.

Papa came back in a wooden box. He died of a stroke sometime after he
arrived in Arkansas and saw Mama Vivian. I remember so well the day he
died. My mother and I were home when the big black rotary phone rang. I
answered it and Daddy's voice was so strange as he asked for my mother, I
handed the phone over right away. I watched Mama's eyes fill with tears as
she screamed through fingers covering her mouth and ran from the house,
crying, over to a neighbor's. I didn't find out until I followed her that Papa
was dead. I didn't even know what the word meant.

Although my parents meant well, they didn't help me by not explaining
what death was all about and by not allowing me to participate in the laying
of Papa to rest. They told me Papa was in heaven, a place I knew from church
was where God and his son Jesus lived, but Papa had told me before he left
that he would always be with *me*, not in Heaven. So while my parents grieved,
I talked to God and asked him to let me speak to Papa; I wanted to know
about this Heaven place. Every day and night I asked, even when I was left
with friends the day of Papa's funeral.

It was after the funeral that Papa answered me. I had been having nightmares about death for about a week when, one day, my mother outside hanging wash on the line, Papa came to me. He was there, as present to me as he

had ever been. I could see him and feel his big, rough, soft hands holding mine. I asked him about Heaven. What was it like, why did he have to go and leave me? He told me Heaven was all bright light and cobblestoned streets and he was very happy there. He told me people never leave each other, wasn't he with me now? Yes, I countered, but he wasn't *here*. I remember he laughed and said I was right, his body did go into the ground, but *he* would always be with me.

I was so excited that Papa had come to see me, but when I told my mother, she almost hit me, so great was her anger and (I know now) fear. She told my father about it later and they chalked it up to my overactive imagination. Because he didn't come back, I eventually did, too.

A couple of months after Papa's death, my father bought a new station wagon. A 1959 Ford, it was what white people called flesh-colored, but not cocoa-brown like Mama or even creamy pale like Daddy, but Crayola crayon flesh-colored, with a white top and little gold metal balls at the top of the front fenders that I cupped in my hand as I swung around the front-end of the car. My father, who had gotten very quiet since Papa died, decided we were going to take the car on a ride to Perris, California, about ninety miles southeast of Los Angeles, to visit a family friend and do some hunting. My mother and two of my father's friends, Brownie and Garcia, went with us on the trip.

It was late when we got to Mrs. Soares's house in Perris and I had fallen asleep in my mother's lap in the back seat of the car. As they woke me up, I touched the car and said, "Good-bye, car." My mother, who carried me into the house, asked me why I had said good-bye to the car. I told her it was because I wasn't going to see it again. She laughed and said, "Don't be silly; of course you will."

Technically, she was right, but when I did see the station wagon again, the roof had been flattened down to the door panels in an accident. It seemed my father's friends decided to go for a ride in the middle of the night and borrowed my father's keys. I think it was Uncle Brownie who was driving. The accident had injured both him and Uncle Gar badly and almost demolished the car.

That morning, as my parents sat at Mrs. Soares's house in shock talking with the sheriff, I said, "I told you, Mama, we wouldn't see the car any more." Daddy sat and stared at me, but Mama looked at me intensely and told me *never* to do that again. And because their response to my revelation was so fearful, I also began to fear the thing inside me that told me what was going to happen. I became afraid and disconnected from the little voice in my life.

Perhaps these events were only childish imagination, premonitions, coincidence, but they became fewer and fewer as I grew up because when they happened, I froze up and the voice fled me, leaving me confused and fearful. And because I thought it was so unacceptable, so strange, one by one, I lost my spiritual moorings.

My grandfather's death was one of the first wrenchings. Papa and I talked about God a lot which was only right because he was a prominent member of our church, Grant A.M.E. I was a regular attendee of The Cradle, an upstairs nursery with a big plate glass window where we could look into the sanctuary as we colored or listened to stories about Jesus, Joseph, and Mary. I would see Papa many times after church and go to his house and play. Even after Papa died, I still went to church and even began to read stories to the smaller children in The Cradle. I was about eight, though, before I began to notice that my father had stopped attending church except for those rare occasions my mother just insisted. I asked him why.

"I don't go to churches where the people pray on the inside and then stand on the church steps after service and talk about each other. God's not there." My father had been the subject of a significant amount of pressure from the minister of Grant at the time to take my grandfather's place in terms of participation and support of the church and I had heard Daddy say many times how he refused to be pressured into supporting a church. But he was saying something more to me that particular Sunday as I was dressing for church with my mother.

"Church and God are two different things, girl. God is not just in churches; God's everywhere and in everything. Sometimes churches are the hardest places to find Him."

I went to church that Sunday and several more, but my father's words awakened a new perspective in me, a critical eye that began to notice the women standing in clusters talking about another's dress or hat, or the kids who sometimes sat listening to the Word but who more often sneaked out and smoked cigarettes and did much worse behind the church in the alley off 105th Street. I came to understand what my father meant. I soon after announced I wasn't going to church anymore and, amidst the outcry from my mother and my grandmother's prediction that I would become a "h-e-a-t-h-e-n," another avenue for spiritual connection was loosened in my life. Although a wonderful minister, Rev. John Adams, enticed me back to Grant briefly during my junior high school and high school years, I officially "joined" church and participated in activities more to please my mother or hang out with friends than from any deep spiritual connectedness to the place.

My mother's funeral in 1973 was the last time I entered Grant A.M.E. My mother died from a rare form of hepatitis which the doctors could neither determine how she contracted (she neither drank, smoked, nor used drugs) nor stop after it caused her liver to disintegrate in ten days after she had, from all appearances, recovered from the disease after suffering a six-month illness. My mother and I were very close, friends as much as mother and daughter, and her death was a gut-wrenching shock to me at nineteen. Other deaths had crossed my path by then, a grandfather, aunts, but these deaths were distant, somehow alien to me, perhaps because of my family's continued inability to make death part of their lives or their misguided attempts to shield me from it to the extent it became something to be feared. My mother's death could not be denied or experienced second-hand, but the fear of death was so ingrained in me by then that I could hardly bear to see her in the casket (I had never been allowed to see other relatives who had passed). Sitting in the limousine in front of Grant that Friday, I was so torn, so grief-stricken, they almost closed the casket before I jumped out of the car, broke free of the matrons in white who surrounded the car, and walked quickly up the aisle to see my mother's body and say good-bye. Looking down on her, I knew she wasn't there and I thought she was lost to me forever. In fact, from the moment of her death, I felt her withdraw from me and seeing her still, drawn body lying in the casket, I instantaneously forgot the sound of her voice. The stilling of her voice for me was an annihilation worse than her death and a cutting off of another spiritual connection. In his eulogy, Grant's new minister (a man too new to the community to know my mother well) made an unfortunate analogy between life and a horse race, saying that my mother was now in the winner's circle. His words sealed for all time the doors of that church to me.

I didn't enter a church at all for years after my mother's death and rarely had a moment of spiritual connectedness outside of one. If anything, I was profoundly *dis*connected spiritually. For months and years afterward, I had nightmares about my mother, that the doctors had made a mistake, that she had had the liver transplant they had said was too experimental and for which she was too old to be a good candidate, that she tried to talk to me, that I had tried to talk to her but I had no voice or my teeth would shatter in my mouth when I'd try to speak to her. The dreams left me dry-heaving in bed and red-eyed day after day. The anniversary of her death invariably found me ill, not just with headaches or depression, but real illnesses, from flu to conjunctivitis to bladder infections. Each year, she moved further and further away from me. And through it all, I could never conjure her voice, I could never hear her talking to me or remember what she had given me.

Years later, other traumas in my life and a failing relationship forced me to seek therapy, where I began to heal the emotional scars in my life. The opening of those doors and examination of my feelings made me aware that the spiritual side of my life had been atrophying for a long time. The spiritual meanderings I had engaged in up until that time, Eastern religions mostly, took on a deeper significance. But it wasn't until I became involved romantically with Felix, my best male friend, that I began to sense the connection I had been missing.

One time when I was visiting Felix in Chicago, during our long-distance love affair, we went to Rev. Johnnie Colemon's Christ Universal Temple. I had maybe been with him to that church once before, pre-romance, but this time something about the service's allocation of time to pray, to "go within to God," gave me a feeling of connection I had not experienced since my days watching the God-light come up over the neighborhood houses onto the tops of my rubber-capped red Keds.

I pursued Unitarian-type churches when I returned to Los Angeles and finally found a home in the teachings of Ernest Holmes and the Church of Religious Science. It was there that a name was given to the still small voice of my childhood, it was there that my connection to Mother/Father/God was encouraged. And when I found Howard Thurman, the great African American spiritual guide, I knew I had found another spiritual anchor.

My awareness of connections to Spirit began to return, after an almost twenty-year absence. I say awareness, because I know now that what kept me putting one foot in front of the other through the dark days surrounding my mother's death was Spirit. That what allowed me to change majors in the chaotic year after her death, moving from a master's in English literature to one in hospital administration, was Spirit throwing open a door that U.C.L.A. officials all but laughed at me for trying to approach. Or the fellowships, the business success, the vice presidency in a Fortune 1,000 company at thirty-two, finding the love of my life virtually under my nose, were Spirit working in and through me.

We most often turn to God when things are roughest and, in those times, too, Spirit has seen me through and to better things. In 1988, after surviving three corporate restructurings at my job with my paycheck and title intact, I was faced with a new boss whose behavior was what could be called erratic at best. A hard-driving marketing type, he was charged with building volume in our operating division's units and was doing so through an elaborate scheme of marketing programs and tactics that were closely held, although hardly unique, secrets. Working on a derivative strategy with a department-wide consultant, I innocently sent them a copy of an altered schematic for my marketing programs in violation of a memo from my boss not to reveal materials to outsiders. The ensuing hue and cry from my shark-like fellow vice presidents and a few choice subordinates fueled my boss's fire to find me incompetent and weed me out of the department. Daily I watched the scurrying back and forth from co-workers to "tell" about my uncooperativeness, unwillingness to laugh at innocent jokes involving women's body parts or comments to female staff, all additional reasons why I just wasn't a team player and had to go. Although I expected a certain amount of envy as one of only two women and the only African American vice president in the company, the viciousness of the attacks rocked me to the core and forced me to revisit any source of spiritual calm I could find, including long telephone calls to Chicago to Felix, by then my husband, talks with spiritually minded friends and relatives, and even that old standby, the Bible. These were some of the Bible phrases I copied onto index cards and carried in my pocket, like flash cards, reciting them throughout the day like mantras:

> For God hath not given us a spirit of fear, but of power and of love and of a sound mind. (2 Timothy 1:7)

> If God be for us, who can be against us? (Romans 8:31)

Those phrases allowed me to walk the halls with my head up and continue to do my work, which only intensified with deadlines mysteriously shortened and priorities changed daily by my boss. I read:

> The wicked is snared by the transgression of his lips: but the just shall come out of trouble. (Proverbs 12:13)

> He that diligently seeketh good procureth favor: but he that seeketh mischief it shall come unto him. (Proverbs 11:27)

> For they intended evil against thee: they imagined a mischievous device against thee, which they are not able to perform. (Psalms 21:1)

Those phrases allowed me to know that one of my peers would eventually come to his just desserts, which he did and was fired less than two months after my transgression.

I weathered the storm but knew my boss continued to plot my ouster. Felix and I were making the decision to live in one city, Los Angeles, but I was worried about him quitting his job and coming to L.A. with my turmoil and uncertain income. Again, my spiritual flash cards answered:

> Better is a dry morsel and quietness therewith than a house full of sacrifices with strife. (Proverbs 17:1)

> A man's heart deviseth his way: but the Lord directeth his steps. (Proverbs 16:9)

Was it just good timing that made Felix and me talk three days after he arrived about my situation, deciding I could and should leave such a negative environment just hours before I had an unplanned lunch with a friend, an executive at the company, who made my transition out of the company work to my advantage? Was it luck that presented us with our first consulting client one day after returning from a much-needed vacation after leaving that company? Was it coincidence that made me find my file several months later with little positive facts about African Americans I had planned to write into my day planner for when corporate America got me down? Or that that file became *I, Too, Sing America: The African-American Book of Days?* Was it being in love alone that led me to the love letters while doing research for *I, Too* that led to our second book, *I Hear a Symphony: African Americans Celebrate Love?* Was it just lucky that Felix's turning away from art, his first love, to business would come full circle as he selects art for each of our books?

I don't think so.

Spirit was working in and through my life in ways I could only give thanks for every morning as my eyes opened on a life that was unfolding in ways I could only imagine years before.

Four days ago, a Sunday, Felix and I had had a long day. His mother had passed away two weeks before and he had returned from Chicago to client priorities and art due to our new publisher for *I Hear a Symphony*. Our dog, Sampson, had been acting so strangely that Felix had warned me to expect an earthquake. No longer laughing at the ways Spirit speaks to us, I looked at the dog's questioning eyes and made a mental note of foodstuffs in the house.

But that night, I couldn't sleep. Earthquakes were not on my mind, though; I was regretting again that, over two decades after her death, I could not remember the sound of my mother's voice. I was so disturbed by this loss that I arose at 3:30 A.M. and wrote the introduction to the last chapter of *I Hear a Symphony*, which is on the legacy of love. I reflected there, in part, "Love does not cease because we do. The universe, the loving darkness that protects us and supports us, never ends. For those of us who experience the leavetakings, breakups, deaths, separations, we eventually learn one thing— the love is always left behind . . ."

The introduction to the chapter finished, I turned out the bedside light and began, for the first time in years, to remember my mother. The cocoa smoothness of her skin, how she smelled, the look of the dandruff flakes I'd diligently loosen from her scalp the day before her beauty shop appointment, how her wedding ring looked on her hand, the way the little fat pockets jiggled under her arms when she hugged me. My mother was with me, holding me, and I realized her spirit was with me, was guiding me, had never left me.

And when, minutes later, 4:31 A.M., Pacific Standard Time, found our house shaking violently, I rose, watched Felix spring into a closet doorway, stood holding our dog in another doorway, and listened to my mother's crystal break on the kitchen floor, I knew the things that had stood in place for her in my memory could be let go. I had not lost her. My connection to her spirit and that of my grandfathers, my father, other relatives, and friends, would never fail me again.

Ms. Sarah's Recipes, or,
I Am the Butter

Sandra Yvonne Govan

The summer I returned to Charlotte from my one year stay in New York on a Schomburg Scholar in Residence Fellowship, my mother died. The actual date was August 3, 1991, and as is typical with August in North Carolina, the weather outside was hot, humid, sultry. Inside the intensive care unit at Mercy Hospital, in the artificially controlled climate of Ma's room, it was cold, dry, sterile. The nightshift, unlike the nurses who had shared my vigil in the long afternoons, was staffed by white people I did not know, had not yet even met; they seemed strangers self-absorbed and distant; able to chuckle at private jokes, oblivious to my pain, my father's, or even that of my mother as she made her transition, crossing over the threshold separating her home on this earth from the home she had been summoned to enter.

For three weeks, as Ma had lain in the ICU room fading in and out of a semi-comatose state, I had brushed and combed her hair and thought of how she used to do mine. I'd read to her and sang to her and played a tape of selected favorite gospel songs from Beth Eden's Wooten Ensemble, the church choir I'd grown up with, and tried to talk with her. Between the strains of "I've Been 'Buked" ("I've been 'buked and I've been scorned; I've been talked about sure's you're born") and "Thank You Lord" ("thank you for one more day"), I'd try to ask Ma about her church, my childhood, or my brother's— all, for the most part, pleasant memories. The nurses had always wanted to check her reality by asking "placement" questions. They would insistently rouse her, calling her by her first name, young women, black and white, getting familiar, saying "Sarah. Sarah. Do you know where you are?" Or, they would ask her for the day of the week or her name. She had indeed drifted from Charlotte back to Chicago but whether it was Monday or Thursday or the number of fingers on a raised hand was manifestly immaterial to Ma. I could tell by the expressive look she cast upon them; and I knew how to read these disdaining, dismissive "looks" better than anyone. Yet most of their questions she responded to politely, if inaccurately; however, the issue of their doubting her competence clearly irked her. When she deigned to answer, announcing, "Sarah Govan," the exasperation showed clearly in her sometimes proud, sometimes annoyed, tone. But when she was awake enough to talk to me, Ma never used that tone. Instead, it was a softly quizzical, "Sweetie, Sweetie, are you there?" Or, it was the single snap of my name, in the tone used for instructions: "Yvonne!"

Over the years Ma had kept her own counsel, always imparting to me at opportune moments bits of information she thought it necessary for me to know. And now, in this room and from that bed she earnestly wanted me to know something else vitally important about living and life. At the last meal she had tried to take at my table she'd told me two things I thought total non sequiturs. "Women," she said, "can come between fathers and daughters. Be careful." And, "You know, when that liver shuts down, you just can't function." But now, her words simply coiled themselves around the symbols intimately connected to her workaday life as a high school cafeteria manager and thus emerged something like, "Now, Yvonne, you've got to watch the roast carefully. Now, you're going to need so many pounds of pork for the sauce. I bake mine at 350 degrees. Be sure you get the pies right. I always check my meats twice." Each directive was issued carefully and enunciated with great precision . . . except we had not been discussing food.

In one of her last lucid, clear-headed verbal moments just days before she died, Mommy called to me, "Yvonne!" and then announced, "I'm going home." And in my blind denial, for a moment I honestly thought she meant going back to Chicago. Several times when she had roused herself she had asked that I take her out of the hospital. Being hospitalized was not "her plan" and "nobody got [her] permission." Jeffrey and I were engaged in conspiracy against her. "Yvonne, find my shoes; I'm leaving." Indeed, she had tried to escape more than once before being restrained in the ICU. Decentered and weak, she had nonetheless freed one arm and removed some tubes before the staff caught her. As much as I wanted to gather her up and flee that awful place, I could not; what's more, I knew that had she been herself, she would not have wanted me to carry her home because, in her words, it would have been "too much" on me.

But adopting her hard commonsense logic seared my soul. Maybe that is why I've put off trying to write this essay, avoided facing the subject of my mother's death—or even of her life in the last years—because writing would mean confronting feelings, emotions, thoughts, and reflections safely boxed up and secured in the closet. It is not guilt that I could not take her home; it is not the letting go or grieving process, the acknowledgment of loss or "passing" that I mind. It is the memory of that hospital with its images of my mama's arms restrained and weeping and her wedding ring stolen that I mind. Ever my mother's daughter, through training over the years I have learned to put aside or store away feelings I choose not to contend with; yet as someone who writes, and teaches the nuts and bolts of good basic writing, even during those hospital moments I was well aware of a particular duality within. Although it sounds so clinical and almost made me feel a monster, in the last weeks of my mother's life, I actually took notes almost frantically at that hospital, trying to record every word she uttered in order to remember, as if some part of me could indeed acknowledge that she would not be coming home with us again. (And I knew she was no longer calling home Chicago when she told me that her father was coming for her.) Later, as if appalled by my own detached separation, I put the scattered back of envelope scraps away in the proverbial safe place. I had not started to look for them until now, when the moment arrived to stop thinking about it and actually start to write about the connection, perhaps spiritual, my mom and I still maintain.

Let me say now that for reasons only vaguely manifest at the moment, "Mom," "Mama," "Ma," and childhood's "Mommy" became synonymous terms for me at the hospital and even afterward, at the homegoing service. "Mom" as in "my mom," was a possessive; somebody I talked about with my friends. As in, "My mom doesn't make me do laundry or scrub floors; she would rather do it herself." "Mama" was the nurturing warm woman whom I both talked about and to as a kid from four to twelve. She was the authority figure who always had the best last word—"my mama said . . ." was the constant citation my teachers, or the neighbors, heard as I explained my stance or my protest of some small or unjust act. Adults did not always have the last word in Chicago and you could stand up for your rights. It was just how you handled yourself, your tone and how you approached people that made the difference. "Yes m'am. I smacked Stanley. Because I knew he wasn't going to get no whippin' when he got home and he was throwin' rocks at me and he almost broke my glasses. My mama said, 'If somebody hits you, it's okay to defend yourself.' " You did not let anyone "run over you." Mama was also the person who bought my last dolls, even when I was too old, and who sanctioned the miles long, off the block bike trips through white territory to Walker Branch Public Library. Mama introduced me to Agatha Christie's *Murder on the Orient Express* and *They Came to Baghdad* and to World War II spy novels— *Two Eggs on My Plate*. She was also the person who carried me to assorted clinics and two different hospitals "to see about" my legs (one seemed longer) or my spine (I could not stand straight); or she found friends to carry me there when her job prevented her from going. It was at one of these hospitals I discovered my full name. They'd been paging a "Sandra Govan" and when I heard it, I had turned to her and said wonderingly, "Mama, somebody's got a name like mine." And she replied testily, because she was missing work, "Fool, that's you." To that point I had only known "Sweetie" or "Yvonne." She'd just given me a new identity to claim.

"Ma" was the emotionally reserved, stingy with her kisses ("I'll take a plug; you're too old for sugar"), chock-full-of-advice, take-no-mess, got-the-right-answer, call-them-as-you-see-them, speak-your-piece, straightforward person she became from my teen years until the moment she entered Mercy Hospital. And until my own dying day, I will believe that my mother heard me best through the haze of pain or medication whenever I called her "Mommy." When he arrived at Ma's bedside from Iowa, my older brother could say "Ma, it's me," and call her back to some semblance of consciousness. But as her baby girl, I used "Mommy" to reach further back to the time she carried me when I could not walk and combed my hair and petted me as I was now doing for her.

I suppose I only hazard the notion of a "spiritual" bond between us still because my mama was not a Bible thumper; she was not a hymn singer (nor could she really carry a tune); nor was she a closet evangelist, always trying to convert somebody. She went to her new church (Episcopal) below the hill regularly and went to Bible school lessons with two different church groups, but she could still get us all told. And poor Dad sometimes caught hell because he was who he was and not what she wanted him to be; nor could he readily change. A festering sore point that lingered over time in their forty-eight-year marriage despite the romantic love that started it all. (He had been

a soldier on maneuvers in Louisiana; she had been a teacher when they met.)
My mama was not "into" signs or omens or ethereal mystic arts either. Hers
was a simple, quiet, affirming yet nonimposing faith. She never said she'd
meet me on the other side nor spoke of ghosts nor announced that she'd been
visited by her long dead father or any other long-departed relative. I suppose
that is why the fact of our strong seemingly spiritual bond, where her felt
presence in my daily life is tangible and she appears in my dreams and her
voice is all but audible, still surprises me. Ultimately, I suppose my perceptions of her spirituality have nothing to do with the real question; and the fact
of my surprise at the strength of our contact may well be the measure of
what's keeping us together. Clearly, Ma still wants to teach me, still has instructions and advice that she thinks will help me better organize my life. And
since no one, not even St. Peter, has ever stopped Sarah Govan from speaking
her piece, my mama continues her talks with me.

Looking at what's here I see I've started this piece toward the end of Ma's life,
rather than at the beginning which is what Jeffrey, my friend, suggested. The
logic of that sounded good but what is the beginning? Is it an infancy I don't
recall? That beginning in my life when we could not even leave the hospital
together as mother and daughter because I was born with dislocated hips and
had to stay behind. Surely the beginning is not the tortuous period between
my thirteenth and twenty-second birthdays when Ma, world of irony spinning, could barely communicate? (Miraculously, of course, when I turned
twenty-two, she regained her ability to talk to me.) Is it the moment when I
won the graduate fellowship to Emory to study for my Ph.D. and she actually
told me, for the first time that I could remember, that she was proud of me?
Was it my announcement I was buying my first house without waiting for a
tenure decision at UNC-Charlotte and without, if necessary, her help because I knew what I was doing now and they would tenure me. Certainly, that
narrow, sterile, chilled hospital room was not where we as a temperamental
mother/daughter unit began to come to terms with each other and respect
each other; that had happened long ago. But there were still things I did not
do to suit my mother, still things she wanted to give me (she believed in giving
to her children while she lived and could see that we appreciated it) and to
teach me or just to tell me that awful summer. That is why she fought so hard

in her remaining hours here to give me one last recipe among the hundreds she'd collected, why she felt it so important to call my attention to salads and roasts and cakes and baking temperatures. I hear my mama now when I'm in the classroom and I'm forced to tell some recalcitrant student her adages about the duck's back or leading the horse to water. Indeed, my students often receive Ma's teaching secondhand, and I am sometimes more merciful to them about late papers because she "had a time" with me on the subject of constant tardiness. I hear her, on occasion, when Jeffrey and I are out just driving and he starts speeding up despite the speed limit or the car meandering ahead of us. My voice will raise the caustic question, "Why are you driving like a bat out of hell?" And when he turns to me, surprised, I can honestly proclaim my innocence: "Baby, that wasn't me, that was my mama." And then we can both smile because he'd met her, that summer, and they had established a rapport. Her first question to him had concerned "the piece of junk" he'd parked in my garage and "the piece of junk" he was driving.

Plain food; plain talk. No T.V., except for football; Chicago news and talk radio to hear what people were thinking and saying. In the last years, I think also talk radio all day and all night was to stay as informed on this world as long as possible and the huge collection of clipped recipes was to keep envisioning culinary experiments that might be possible had she not gotten ill. But the illness, like most things, Ma kept to herself and she managed it herself, unwilling to surrender control to doctors and often substituting her knowledge of foods that could control some body chemistry as effectively as the medications prescribed. I cannot eat bananas again without thinking, "Well, bananas are high in potassium" or "You can get iron from a number of vegetables; you don't need pills."

When do Ma and I talk now? Well, I think, had I kept a dream record I could document, we still communicate mostly on Saturday mornings. I wake up, smiling, having had the most pleasant dreams. Sometimes I'll see Ma amid a field of green. Once she was emerging from a hammock-type bed slung between some trees in a forest. That one I laughed at because Ma did not like camping—despite having been a den mother for the Cub Scouts and a quasi troop leader with the Girl Scouts. Other times I know we have met in a dream but it fades too quickly when I wake, leaving only the residue of a pleasant exchange. You cannot talk to somebody Saturday morning after Saturday, year after year, and just suddenly stop. And the dreams don't have to come while I'm asleep either. I have daydreams where Ma and I talk and exchange and should I go shopping alone and need a good critical and honest opinion about how some outfit really looks on me, Ma is right there. She reminds me to check the fit in the back because my back is so small still and one hip remains higher than the other despite three hip replacements. She has me check the label to see if the fabric can be washed by hand ("they just put that 'dry clean only' tag in there for those dummies who just throw their things in the machine"). She has me check the seams and the stretch of the fabric and how the outfit will look if I'm standing or if I'm seated.

Ma's other favorite time to visit is when I'm in the kitchen trying to recapture a taste or a texture that I remember from her cooking but one I only watched her make. Everybody's potato salad is different so I never try to match that. And I liked Mama Reed's better anyway. But on luscious sweet potato pie, homemade soup, hot corn pone, fresh fried fish, or the greatest scrambled egg, nobody matched my mom. Her potato pies were perfect, full proud pies with scratch crusts and just a hint of butter (and therefore, not too rich) and sufficient sugar to enhance the sweetness in the potato. For my sake she would not experiment with this most favorite dish, leaving out the ginger or other radical departures because I wanted my pies exactly like they were supposed to be. To her credit she did try to teach me the art but she was not infallible and I was a difficult child. If Ma had some major failings with me, one was that I never learned to swim despite lessons; two was that I never learned to sew, despite lessons; three was that I never learned math despite tutors and long summer hours coping with columns of figures; and four was that I never learned to cook in her house. She therefore had to come to me and coach me through the "right propo'tions" of meal to shortening to hot water because too much water and the pone would be thin. As for the pies, I, too, now experiment; on my last try this past Christmas, I don't think I measured it right for the filling sank in some. It passed muster for Daddy, who actually suggested it needed condensed milk! But Mama's pies had never used condensed milk so that was ruled out. I can do the egg; I can fry the fish; I think I've got the best approximation of her corn pone I'm ever likely to have; and she'd sent me the soup recipe several years earlier. But I will get both the taste and the texture of that pie and she will help me.

Without question, my mama was a woman of singular ability and character. Even now, when people who don't know ask about her, my typical response is a variation on the "up there with St. Peter, directing things in that
mansion" rejoinder. I simply can't see her any other way. I see her with a list
in hand ("Yvonne, make a list; I always make a list") and I know she's making
Pete check things off. I'm sure she's on the welcoming committee, standing
at the gates to receive the friends like Bert Harris who have come to join her.
I'm sure she's telling anybody there who will listen about how pleased she
was with her "homegoing" funeral service—"Yvonne did not let them carry
on. Everything was simply beautiful." I can guess what she thinks about my
dad leaving Morgan Park and moving down into the city to a Hyde Park
apartment but that house was her house; I think we're all glad he's now in his
space and doing well. She doesn't have to worry about him locking doors or
shoveling snow. She worries over my brother's decisions and grieves over my
niece's actions. No rest there. She tells me to stay in contact with my brother
and I do, no matter how irritated I get, because I hear her and know that our
family tie is vitally important to her still.

The connection my mama and I maintain is "spiritual," but I believe its
spirituality is expansive and encompasses more than our culture typically in-
vests in this concept. I understand that my mama talks to me, visits me, helps
me, sees about me. Sometimes, I confess, I still seem to need her approval.
(Would she like my new house? Would she think it too large for me to handle
["Yvonne, you don't need any more room!"] or too much space for me to
"junk up"? Or would she be pleased with what I've done in it? I know she'd
like the way I "set up with" the builder to make him get it right. Will she like
this essay?) Seen from a Christian context, I know that Mama is in God's
heaven, assisting St. Peter; I know, too, that our relationship is perhaps a variation on a long ago Sunday school song: "She walks with me and she talks
with me" and my mama still tells me what it is she wants me to know. Yet
her continued felt presence within me, the words we both utter, can also be
seen from an African spiritual context, best rendered in the lyrics from
"Breaths" by Sweet Honey and the Rock: "Those who have died, have never
never left; the dead are not under the earth. Those who have died have never
never left; the dead have a pact with the living . . ."

Let me finish this by stating the obvious. Every family has its traditions.

One of ours was that at mealtimes, gathered around the kitchen table in our appointed places, we all said a blessing. Daddy usually intoned, "In those days came John the Baptist, preaching in the wilderness of Judeah." My brother invariably rushed "Rice [Rise] Peter, slay and eat." I always petitioned, "Lord, teach us to pray." And Mama, well, her scripture, her prayer at every meal I ever ate in her presence was "God is love." And so was my mama.

On July 12th, the day I took my mama to the hospital, I fell in the bathroom while trying to help her get ready to go. I'd helped her with her clothes and shoes but she insisted on putting in her eye drops herself and packing her things in her bag. Although the disorientation had begun, she realized what had happened and, looking down at me, paid me her highest tribute even as she surrendered part of the will that determined her character, "Sweetie," she said, in her softest quizzical voice, "what are you doing down there? You've got to get up. You're in charge now. I don't know what will happen to us if something happens to you. You're the butter."

The Church of Aretha

Margo V. Perkins

We sing while we work. We hum while we cook. We listen to Aretha
when we are down. It is any wonder, then, that most of our music
finds its roots in the church? . . . When we want to express
how much faith we have in spirit, we sing.
—DONA MARIMBA RICHARDS, from *Let the Circle Be Unbroken*

The old songs are in our collective consciousness, perhaps even in our genes.
They are our spiritual chromosomes. They make us who we are as a people.
—GLORIA SCOTT

When i listen to Aretha Franklin sing, i understand why there came to
be, for instance, a church of Coltrane.* Lovers of John Coltrane's
music honor not just his brilliant saxophone playing, but the spiritual power
of his melodies to transform both space and consciousness. Aretha (her first
name, alone, being sufficient to evoke a mood), like Coltrane, is one of those
rare artists whose unique voice conjures the breadth and depth of African
American experience. I think, therefore, that there really ought to be a
church of Aretha, too. In my own struggle as a grad student to stay sane in
the hostile, culturally alienating environment of one of America's preeminent
ivy institutions, Aretha's music has been an ongoing source of spiritual refuge.
Arising out of the Black gospel and blues traditions, her voice is evocative of
my own earliest recollections of church, of the sense of joy and belongingness
shared among a community united in faith. Though for many reasons, i no
longer feel peace in churches, i find myself still drawn to the music, to the
power of song to heal psychic wounds and to reinvigorate the human spirit.
When i journey to the church of Aretha, for instance, i experience again a
sense of peace, wholeness, and of connection to those life-affirming aspects of
my culture and my community.

I love almost all of Aretha's music, but the songs of the late 1960s and the

*One Mind Evolutionary Transitional Church of Christ in San Francisco, California. In *Chasin' the
Trane: The Music of and Mystique of John Coltrane* (Garden City, N.Y.: Doubleday & Company, 1975),
biographer J. C. Thomas writes: "It is a church that is devoted to, was founded for, and celebrates
the music and spirit of John Coltrane, called Ohnedaruth, or Compassion" (228).

1970s—*vintage* Aretha, if you will—are by far my favorite. Songs like "You're All I Need to Get By," "Bridge Over Troubled Water," "Ain't No Way," "Do Right Woman, Do Right Man," "Dr. Feelgood," "Spanish Harlem," "Something He Can Feel," and "Respect" (to give only a tiny sampling) truly have no contemporary rivals in terms of what they convey about the quality of love and mutual caring between Black women and men, and about the dignity, pride, compassion, and resilience of Black people living in America. It could be that this is merely nostalgia on my part (this, after all, was the music my family played and which i grew up hearing in our home), but i suspect there is an even deeper current at work. On more than one occasion, i've been in the company of other Black women and happened to catch Aretha's voice, perhaps on a radio in the background. Rhetorically, i would call out (more to catch folks' attention than for confirmation): "Isn't that Aretha?" Almost before I could finish the question, i'd hear any other sister say, "Girrrl, yeah." And suddenly it would be as if everybody had tapped into the same collective consciousness: that awareness of what it means to belong to a culture that has retained its humor, its soul, and its humanity despite the historic and continued experience of racist, sexist, capitalist oppression and exploitation. Music acts as a link not only to our personal pasts but also to our shared remembrance of an entire social/national landscape. I think about the positive surge of Black nationalism and cultural pride that marked the late '60s and '70s, about my mother's beautiful halo of an afro, and about all the revolutionary brothers and sisters like Angela Davis, Assata Shakur, Ericka Huggins, and George Jackson who must have drawn some of their passion, determination, and energy from Aretha's music. The sound of Aretha's voice is like an expansive album uniting our individual memories into a collective account of all that it means to be Black in America. This, i believe, is the deeper current at work when i hear Aretha sing.

When i put Aretha on my headphones and stroll through campus or when i play her music (loud) on my stereo at home, it is as if all the things that burden my spirit gradually fall away. Aretha just sings them right out of existence. Her songs transform the sterility of this foreign terrain, beating back the spectre of whiteness and replacing chill and despair with warmth and hope. When i listen to Aretha, i know that there is a holy spirit because nothing else could make me feel so alive. As far as secular music goes, vintage Aretha is about the closest i come to "getting happy." Listening to her wail, it's as if i'm not here anymore, but transported to another space and time, where i experience healing, connection, and a sense of peace. Her music has often been the antidote to my sorrow, protecting and strengthening me to keep pressing on.

I believe that the Spirit dwells in many places. I know that it lives in Aretha because my soul has gone there and been renewed. I think that it would not take long to rally support among my sisters for recognition of a church of Aretha. Even if we never thought to call it such, the concept was laid long ago when we proudly crowned her our queen of soul. Make no mistake, when i speak of the church of Aretha, i am not referring to any material structure. The church of Aretha is merely a way of naming what we already know and feel. I suppose my only question now is—*can i get a witness?*

Defying Alzheimer's: Saving Her Spirit in Song

Carolyn C. Denard

During my grandmother's eighty-fifth year, she developed Alzheimer's disease. We didn't know much about Alzheimer's disease then—not even enough to call it "Alzheimer's"; we just called it "senility." And, because most of our older relatives had died early, what we knew even of senility was second-hand or observed from a distance. Stories told about a relative we had never met or small moments of participation in the life of the elderly relatives of friends we visited were all my two sisters and I knew. My father had died three years earlier at 48. And my mother, now only forty-eight herself, was nowhere near the challenges of senility and old age. Grandmother's situation was new to us; and we had no idea of the journey we were about to witness.

Grandmother would forget the days of the week, where she put the mail, where she was going, how to get home, and what she had just said. She confused who was living with who was dead, her house of fifty years as a married woman with the house she grew up in as a child, school with church, sugar with flour, the list of confusions seemed endless. She would get fully dressed at 3:00 A.M. and knock on the door saying she was ready to go to town. She would leave the house—whether in her own in north Mississippi or in mine later in Atlanta, headed for the Delta where she believed her mother and sister would be waiting. She got lost, she forgot to cook her food before eating it, she forgot our names. We were saddened and amazed at the persistence and severity of what was happening to her.

Occasionally, we thought of those words so dreaded in the Black community: THE NURSING HOME. But we didn't think we could do that—"It would break her spirit," I said. We continued to struggle with solutions as we watched her grow worse every day. I had spent much of my young life with her, and since I was not yet raising a family, I volunteered to assume primary care when we realized she could no longer live alone. I brought her to Atlanta, and I read as much as I could about Alzheimer's. We tried everything: inositol, choline, vitamin B and E supplements, naturopathy, long walks, reality orientation. But every day it seemed as if the little connectors that held the spindles of her brain together were gradually unwinding and getting tangled into a new jumbled pattern that was taking her more and more out of the reality of the present and memories of the past that she and I had once known and shared together joyfully. As a woman who did not know my name or where she was or what day it was, she was becoming a shell of her old vibrant self—the woman I knew and laughed with and whom I had sought out for grandmotherly protection. It broke my heart.

After two years with me, we decided in desperation and with conflicting cultural emotions to place Grandmother in a nursing home. Our worst fears were confirmed. Grandmother didn't understand the dormlike atmosphere of the nursing home. She couldn't tell one room from the other, so she often got lost, and the nurses would find her confused and frightened in someone else's room. She didn't understand why other people that she didn't know were staying in the room with her so she was always ready to go when we came to visit, tired of being at "other folks' house." The nurses decided to use medication to restrain her. The medication further disoriented her, and the long hours of restraint caused muscle contractures in her legs. And most regretfully, her spirit seemed bruised by the uncertainty, the wandering, and the restraint. We could not stand to watch what was happening to her. We had to take her out.

We were finally able to find a personal care home with a woman who took care of two other elderly patients, each with individual rooms. After years of denial and hope, of medication and institutions, things stabilized in the atmosphere of the personal care home. We had finally found a place with which we could be comfortable. I began weekly visits, and for a time we were relatively at peace with her situation. The further deterioration of her mind and body, however, began to take its toll. The most noticeable change in her, beyond the contractures which had left her frozen in a sitting position, was her inability to talk clearly. It went from random incoherency to hardly any responses at all. I would ask benign questions or make no-response-needed comments so that we could at least appear to be having a conversation. Occasionally, she would blurt out unconnected sentences: "Light the fires!" "Get the baby in out of the cold." "Daddy's gone to town." But eventually even those sentences—often totally unrelated to what she was being asked—turned into a constant moan. She didn't talk at all. She just moaned, subdued moans mostly with some occasional crescendos—but always a constant and indistinguishable moan. It got more painful with each visit as even her smile of recognition turned into a blank stare that meant no recognition at all. I was devastated. I had always loved her conversations. Although they had been incoherent and repetitive with the onset of Alzheimer's, they had always been lively. Now, in this later stage, there were no conversations at all. We could no longer talk engagingly the way we always had—with her minister's wife jokes and certainty-of-the-right-way-to-live disapproval of people who didn't know how to hang curtains, act in church, or plant flowers. I longed for her to just talk in sentences again, to know me, to have a shared moment with me. But I couldn't figure out what would make her respond in a way that was shared and remembered.

Since I could no longer talk *to* her, I began bringing someone with me on my visits—that way I could at least talk *around* her just so she could hear the conversation. During one summer visit when my sister had come to Atlanta, we sat out in the backyard with Grandmother at the house where she stayed. Brenda and I talked about our times growing up in the church as little girls with our grandparents. Grandmother's moaning had vaguely reminded us of the responses to the old lining hymns we used to sing at devotions in country churches when there was no piano. My sister and I began to recall some of those old songs, and following our own paths of memory, we tried to think of the words. We began with an old standard, "A Charge to Keep I Have . . . ," but neither of us could think of the second line. As we stared off into our individual windows of memory trying to remember the line, I leaned over to Grandmother in a half-hearted gesture to include her in our conversation and asked, "What were those other words, Grandmother?" "A charge to keep I have . . . A charge to keep I have . . . ," I repeated searchingly, not expecting a response. And then a miracle happened: as clear as a bell with no stuttering or moaning and from a woman who had not spoken even her name clearly in a year she answered, "A God to Glorify!"

My sister and I were astounded. I couldn't speak. My mouth was open as I looked at my grandmother. She was right! Those were the words! Brenda and I shared shocking glances. I smiled at Grandmother, and as if just as surprised as I was by her burst of clarity, she smiled, too. We hugged each other tightly. And for one moment, one grace-filled moment, it seemed the awful monster of Alzheimer's that was daily taking her away from me was held at bay. She had not said "Good morning" or even my name or hers clearly in over a year, but here she had spoken those words from an old country song sung so often in the Black church devotions of her past. A flood of hopeful thoughts raced through my mind. "Did the ravages of Alzheimer's leave something intact after all?" "Was there something in the soul immune from its destruction?" "Was the song so deep in her memory as to be invincible, not wiped out by Alzheimer's, and its accompanying odyssey of medication, nursing homes, strange doctors, and new places?" I held Grandmother for a long time. And with tears in my eyes repeated those words over and over, "A Charge to Keep I have, A God to Glorify. A Charge to Keep I Have, A God to Glorify, A God to Glorify."

I couldn't get what had happened out of my mind for several days. It gave me a new burst of energy and sense of possibility. I didn't ask questions. If I had found a way for her to speak to me, for us to have shared moments together, I wanted to do whatever I could to make those moments happen again and again. I went through old hymn books and my own catalog of memory, writing down songs that I thought she would know. When I went back over to visit the next week, I sang as many songs as I could remember. First there was the favorite for both of us: "Love Lifted Me." It was an old song she had taught me during my childhood vacation Bible school mornings at her house. And she joyfully joined me in the chorus—flat and broken in parts but full of her own spirit—"Love lifted me! Love lifted me! When no-uh-thing else could help, loovve lifftedd mee." What joy! I couldn't believe it! Those visits turned into concerts of our old songs. "Jesus Keep Me Near the Cross," "What a Fellowship," "Blessed Assurance." She often just hummed along or sometimes didn't seem to listen to the verses, but when the chorus came she sang out loud and clear. Whether it was the plea of "Near the Cross, Near the Cross, Be My Glory Ever," or the staccato certainty of "Lean-ing in on the

Ever-last-ing Arms," or the resigned confidence of her own favorite, "This is my story, this is my song, praising my savior all the day long," she'd sing to the top of her voice, and we would be in unison together. Ninety percent of the time she seemed in another world, impenetrable. When we sang together, we enjoyed the same spiritual reality. In those moments of singing she seemed strong and clear—and whole.

The songs were ultimately not able to save Grandmother. The physical ravages of Alzheimer's resulting from the muscle contractures eventually led to double amputations. And while Alzheimer's nearly took her body entirely, it did not take her memory of the song. Her spirit had rested in those old melodies. As I recall now, those songs had been her salvation for a long time. She had sung out her troubles when, as a minister's wife, it didn't seem proper to resist in other ways. I had called them her "Lord, you know" songs because she always began them with those three words. She made up the rest of the words to fit her troubles as she took refuge in her kitchen, washing dishes and wiping counter tops in therapeutic circles. She had sung out loudly at church when there was no one to play the piano, and we had to "line" the songs. I still remember her voice flatly ringing out over the rest. She wasn't in the choir. She wasn't really a great public singer; she had a personal relationship with songs. It all came together as I remembered her history of singing—not showboat singing, but lifesaving singing. And here, at nearly ninety, the songs had seemed to save her spirit again.

The power of the song in my grandmother's life in those last few years humbles me still. I have heard a lot since Grandmother died about "ancestral memory," "individual magic," and "Grace." By whatever name it may be called, something wonderful happened that day when my grandmother's spirit, which I thought had been trampled by Alzheimer's, rose up in song. The songs did not prevent the continued deterioration of her physical body, but they gave her a way to articulate and bring forth her deepest inner spirit. Perhaps that is what the moans had been about all along—her recoiling to her deepest spiritual sense of herself. And maybe when she spoke out so clearly in the backyard that day, the spirit was just breaking through to affirm the words that were describing the nature of her present spiritual journey and the bedrock promise she had made to herself and to God a long time ago. When called upon to testify, she broke through the moans, the confusion, and the tangled and unconnected sentences and spoke out clearly her spiritual mission. She had a charge to keep, she had a God to glorify. It was a promise that not even Alzheimer's, the demon of memory, could make her forget.

"Sing Oh Barren One"

Bernice Johnson Reagon

Spring, 1987, I was blessed to get a call from the Reverend Elaine Hyman. She said, "Bernice, I am going to be installed in a ministerial position and I want you to preach my installation sermon in song. The scriptural reference is Isaiah 54: 1–10." Of course, not remembering Isaiah, I said yes. Elaine sent me the King James and New English translations of the appointed scripture.

Being a bit of a scholar, I decided that I had to go to the source. I pulled out my Bible and began to read Isaiah from chapter I, verse 1. After an intense session, I called Elaine, "Why do you have me in Isaiah? God is so pissed with Israel?" 'Where are you in Isaiah?" she asked. "Chapter 1, I started from the beginning of Isaiah." "Oh my sister, yes, no wonder. Isaiah is really three books and it is really a challenging journey." "But why are you in Isaiah?" I demanded to know. "I don't like Isaiah!" As Elaine answered softly, I could feel her struggling to get me to understand what she was doing and why she needed this particular passage. "The scripture I sent you says where I am as I go into this work. You know that I've gone through some serious personal challenges and am feeling my incompleteness very much these days. Do you know the image of the wounded healer? Well, the idea is that even when you are wounded and hurting, sometimes you can offer healing and solace and yes even leadership. In this passage in Isaiah, God speaks to Israel as a failed woman and commands her to sing. And she responds that she is certainly not the one. Look at her, no children, no husband. And the voice says—'Sing.' "

I went back to my reading thinking, well I can write this song for Elaine and about Elaine, but I still don't like Isaiah's God. I took some notes and went on with my life. Elaine called me as the Installation Sunday neared to see how I was doing and wondered why she had not heard from me. A little defensive, I told her that I was inside of the thing and could not talk about it. Or in other words—don't call me about this piece. The truth be known, I was in deep trouble. I kept going back to Isaiah and kept not wanting to be in

Isaiah. Saturday before the Installation Sunday, I took down some more notes and sang some of the poem into my tape recorder by my bed. With the work unfinished and troubled in mind, with the question, "What is Elaine doing in Isaiah and why does she have me in Isaiah?" ringing in my head, I fell asleep.

I woke up with a start, tears all over my face, grabbed my pad and wrote:

Empty and lonely I was
Wordless and useless I felt
Bounded and closed I wondered
Empty and useless I was

Then I heard the voice.

It wasn't Elaine who needed to be in Isaiah, it was me! I sang the lines into the tape recorder and the verses of the poem I had been struggling with unfolded. I worked through the work, singing for about two hours and went to the church: June 8, 1987.

Sweet Honey in the Rock premiered the work as a choral piece January, 1988, at the St. Anne Parish Church in Brooklyn as a Meet the Composer project. I was now very clear on why I had been sent to Isaiah.

There are so many of us who by all appearances and behaviors have flunked all of the tests of success. We don't look successful, we don't dress right, we don't act like we're making it. Anyone looking at us will feel that we have failed: homeless; female, forty-five years, no husband, no children; Black, male, under twenty-five, with no job; homosexual and just tested HIV positive; thirteen years, female-single, and pregnant. It is you and me—we are as the barren woman in Isaiah—cast out as a failure of no use. It is you and me who must now be heard—it is you who must now SING!

Now, if this calls your name you may be as resistant as I was when Elaine pushed me, but Isaiah addresses our resistance to being the leading voice of the time. In Isaiah, the voice—the same force who is asking you now to step out there and sing—jacked you up a few chapters ago for being unworthy. And in this passage God sounds like a dude on the corner copping a plea to a woman he's trying to get back on his team. "Hey baby, I know I was mad with you, I know I turned away from you, I know I left you, but look—I swear I am with you now." "How long?" I swear by the waters of Noah, even if the mountains depart, even if the hills be removed; I swear my love will never leave you . . .

THUS SAITH THE LORD!
THUS SAITH THE LORD!
SING!!!!SING!!!!SING!!!!

Sing Oh Barren One

Empty and lonely I was
Wordless and useless I felt
Bounded and closed I wandered
Empty and useless I was

Then I heard the voice

Sing oh barren one
Sing out and cry aloud
Sing oh barren one
Sing out and cry aloud

Sing oh barren one
Sing out and cry aloud
   Empty and lonely I was
Sing oh barren one
Sing out and cry aloud
   Wordless and useless I felt
Sing oh barren one
Sing out and cry aloud
   Bounded and closed I wandered
Sing oh barren one
Sing out and cry aloud
   Empty and useless I was

Then I heard

Thou that didst not bear
Thou that didst not travest with child
Break forth into singing and cry aloud

For more are the children of the desolate
Than the children of the married wife
For more are the children of the desolate
Than the children of the married wife

Then I heard

Open wide your curtains
Enlarge the place of your tents
Lengthen your cords
Strengthen your stakes in the ground

For you will spread abroad to the right
    You will spread abroad to the right
You will spread abroad to the left
    You will spread abroad to the left
Your children will build nations
I'll people your valleys
Open wide your curtains
Strengthen the stakes in the ground

Yes, I heard the voice

Sing oh barren one
Sing out and cry aloud
Sing oh barren one
Sing out and cry aloud

Don't be afraid
You will not be put to shame
Don't be confounded
You will forget the shame of your youth
Don't be afraid
The lonely reproach of the days of your widowhood
You will remember no more

Then I heard the voice

Your God is your husband
Yahweh is his name
Your God is your husband
The Holy One of Israel
Is your redeemer
Your God is your husband
God of this place
God of the earth
God of the whole wide universe
Your God is your husband

Sing Sing Sing Sing
Sing and cry aloud
Sing Sing Sing Sing
Sing and cry aloud

It is He who has called you Elaine
You standing like a wife forsaken
It is He who has called you Elaine
You feeling so grieved in spirit
It is He who has called you Elaine
Like a young bride left—cast out alone
It is I who have called you Elaine

To Sing Sing Sing Sing
Sing out and cry aloud
Sing Sing Sing Sing
Sing out and cry aloud

Yes yes you will remember
For a small moment I forsook you
Now with compassion I gather you

Oh yes yes, I know you will remember
How in sweeping anger
From you, one moment I actually hid my face
Now with everlasting love
I have compassion on you

I heard the voice saying

This is like the waters of Noah with me
 This is like the waters of Noah
This is like the waters of Noah with me
 This is like the waters of Noah
As I swore that the waters of Noah
 Waters of Noah
Would be no more
 Waters of Noah
I swear my love and compassion on you
 Waters of Noah

Will be forever
 I will be no more angry with you
Will be forever
 I will never rebuke you anymore
Will be forever
 I swear my love and compassion on you

Even if the mountains depart
 Will be forever
Even if the hills shall be removed
 Will be forever
I promise my grace will never depart from you
 Will be forever
I promise my covenant of peace
 Will be forever
Shall never be removed

Thus saith the Lord

Sing Sing Sing
Sing out and cry aloud
Sing Sing Sing Sing
Sing out and cry aloud

My Soul Is a Witness

How I made it over
coming on over
all these years.
You know my soul looks back in wonder:
How did I make it over?
—sung by M A H A L I A J A C K S O N

PART 3

Challenging Traditions: A New Baptism in the Spirit

i found god in myself
& i loved her / I loved her fiercely
—*N T O Z A K E S H A N G E, For Colored Girls Who Have Considered Suicide,*
When the Rainbow Is Enuf

One can easily place a label on one's "religion," that is, one's religious
affiliation. But matters of the spirit flow from the center. It is as fluid
as a moving stream, embracing whatever is touched
to become a part of the "WHOLE."
—*P I N K E G O R D O N - L A N E*

Our passage into queendom comes when we truly recognize
that we are loving Spirit beings.
—*O P R A H W I N F R E Y,*
Spelman College Commencement Address, 1992

All I do these days is write, take long baths, and suck on Popsicles. I rarely
answer the telephone, and I make myself go to church on Sundays so as not
to offend God. (It's better to stay on speaking terms with God, I rationalize;
I just may need a little grace during delivery.) I try to read the Bible, but I
am only exasperated by its profoundly male point of view. Strange, but while
I've always been aware that the Bible was written from a male perspective
and that it presumes its audience to be male also—I've certainly written
and spoken about its male-centered viewpoint—I've never felt so estranged
from its interests as I do now in pregnancy. I find nothing captivating about
rivalries between barren and fertile women (Sarah and Hagar, Rachel and
Leah). I fail to see the justice in sentencing a woman to the inexorable pain
of childbirth on account of eating an apple (the story of Eve). I find no
solace in virginal births (the story of Mary). And I fail to see the connection
between my world and that of women whose sole ambition seems to be to
bear children, preferably male (virtually every woman in the Bible).
Surely these women are the product of the vain imaginations of men.
I need in the Bible a woman I can recognize, one who is as aggrieved
by pregnancy as she is elated, as fascinated by her sexuality as
she is frightened by it, and as dissatisfied with her life as she is
proud of it. I close the Bible, and I search for God in other ways.
I write letters to God. I write letters to friends. I write to myself.
—*R E N I T A W E E M S, I Asked for Intimacy*

146

and i dance my
creation and my grandmothers gathering
from my bones like great wooden birds
spread their wings
while their long/legged/laughter
stretches the night.
and i taste the
seasons of my birth. mangoes. papayas.
drink my woman/coconut/milks
stalk the ancient grandfathers
sipping on proud afternoons
walk like a song round my waist
tremble like a new/born/child troubled
with new breaths
and my singing
becomes the only sound of a
blue/black/magical/woman. walking.
womb ripe. walking. loud with mornings. walking.
making pilgrimage to herself. walking.
—*S O N I A   S A N C H E Z*, "Earth Mother"

Address to the Ohio Women's Rights Convention

Sojourner Truth

"And ain't I a woman?"

Well, children, where there is so much racket there must be somethin' out o'kilter. I think that 'twixt the Negroes of the North and the South and the women at the North, all talkin' 'bout rights, the white men will be in a fix pretty soon. But what's all this here talkin' 'bout?

That man over there say that women needs to be helped into carriages, and lifted over ditches, and to have the best place everywhere. Nobody ever helps me into carriages, or over mud-puddles, or give me any best place! And ain't I a woman? Look at me! Look at my arm! I have ploughed, and planted, and gathered into barns, and no man could head me! And ain't I a woman? I could work as much and eat as much as a man—when I could get it—and bear the lash as well! And ain't I a woman? I have borne thirteen children, and seen 'em mos' all sold off to slavery, and when I cried out with my mother's grief, none but Jesus heard me! And ain't I a woman?

Then they talk about this thing in the head; what's this they call it? ["Intellect," whispered someone near.] That's it, honey. What's that got to do with women's rights or Negro's rights? If my cup won't hold but a pint and yours holds a quart, wouldn't you be mean not to let me have my little half measure full?

Then that little man in black there, he says women can't have as much rights as men, 'cause Christ wasn't a woman! Where did your Christ come from? Where did your Christ come from? From God and a woman! Man had nothin' to do with Him.

If the first woman God ever made was strong enough to turn the world upside down all alone, these women together ought to be able to turn it back, and get it right side up again? And now they is asking to do it, they better let 'em. 'Bliged to you for hearin' me, and now ole Sojourner hasn't got nothin' more to say.   Akron, Ohio, May 29, 1851

149

Jesus Is a Sister

Johnnetta B. Cole

The African American woman, our Black sister: think of her as the only one in America who with her other sisters of color knows the triple oppression of racism, sexism, and poverty. No, most of you sisters in this chapel are not poor; but the majority of Black women are. Perhaps there is some sister here who honestly believes that she has never known the sting of sexism, but I assure you that all of the rest of us have; and if there is anyone among us who dares to believe that her life is untouched by the incessant barbarism of racism, may she live forever in her land of fantasy.

As the great nineteenth-century African American intellectual Anna J. Cooper put it, "The Black woman is confined by a woman question and a race problem." Might we add—and many of our sisters are also confined by a predicament of poverty.

The Race Problem

With our African American brothers, we were torn from vibrant and advanced West African societies, shackled and thrown into the hull of slaveships to be brought into this "new world" as free labor for white men and women driven by boundless greed. With our brothers, know that we worked in those fields—indeed nine out of every ten African American women slaves worked in those fields.

What a horrible myth has been perpetrated on us—that we were only in Massa's kitchen and anxious to be in his bed. Why, like our menfolks, we were whipped and tortured and yes killed. Even when we were pregnant they beat us. A hole was dug in the ground and our sister forced to lay with her

This speech was delivered on January 9, 1992, in Sisters Chapel at Spelman College for the opening convocation of the spring semester.

150

pregnant belly in the hole, so that the earth protected the unborn child, and future slave, while our sister's back received the lash.

With our brothers, sons, fathers, and husbands, we African American women have known the indignities of the back of the bus, working for Ms. Ann, being the last hired and the first fired, having a cross burning in our front yard because we dared to move into a neighborhood, losing a child because and only because he is Black. With our menfolks we know the worst of education, the poorest of health care, the most dilapidated housing. With African American men, we sisters always have at least twice as much of the worst things in life as white folks have—whether it is cancer, unemployment, AIDS, high blood pressure, death by violent means, imprisonment, low-birth-weight babies, drug addiction, or inferior education. Indeed, indeed, indeed: with our menfolks, we African American women know the race problem.

The Woman Question

There are so many ways in which Black women are different from white women. If you have seen one woman, you haven't seen us all. But there are also ways in which we women, red, yellow, brown, black, and white, are bound together by shared experiences and similar oppression.

What of the commonalities among us womenfolks?

We are the members of the human species who everyone assumes were born able to type, now word process, and thus we are destined to be the secretary for the organization.

We are the ones who can work outside the household as hard as any man, but when we come home exhausted, we're to ask, "How was your day, honey?" bring him his slippers, and start our second shift: getting dinner on the table and the kids at their homework, and a load of wash into the machine.

We are the ones who have yet to receive equal pay for equal work.

We are the ones who are still thought of as irrational silly little creatures unable to do math, play a jazz saxophone, or "president" a college.

Although sometimes known by men, it is mainly we women who know the extraordinary fear of rape and the unbelievable pain of its reality.

Every now and then men appear as sex objects, but it's really women who have their bodies objectified and their minds underrated.

Indeed, indeed, indeed, with other women, African American sisters know the woman question.

The Poverty Predicament

With the dispossessed of America and the rest of the world, a poor Black woman knows what it means to ignore her own hunger so that her children can have a spoonful of rice. She knows what it means to hear that her government has spent money to send a man to the moon, when every night she must stare at that same moon in the discomfort of her homelessness.

With other poor folks, poor Black women know what it means to scrape to buy our kids a toy at Christmas, but because it must be a cheap one, it's broken before noon time. With other poor folks, young Black women know what it means to grow fat from cheap starchy foods. With other poor folks, poor Black women know what it is to be without all of the good things in life, while wallowing in the abundance of all that is not good for you. Indeed, indeed, indeed, with other poor folks, many African American women know the predicament of poverty.

Our African American sister knows oppression because of the race problem, the woman question, and the poverty predicament. But we dare not speak of her in exclusive terms here, for in sharing the first jeopardy with Black men, the second with women, and the third with the poor of the world, there is a universality which connects her with others.

I think it is essential that we understand that this is so, not only in terms of oppression, but also in terms of resistance; this is so not only in terms of struggle, but also in terms of victory.

Of course, African American women, like African American men, have had many a cross to bear, but we have also had our Easter Sunday mornings. With our brothers, we sisters know the bitter sting of racism, but we also know the sweet taste of race pride and accomplishment.

Like our brothers, we sisters are the victims of racism but we are, no less than our brothers, the warriors, artists, writers, politicians, organizers, and intellectuals of our people—resisting and struggling in the interest of freedom.

We spoke of ways in which African American women are like womenfolks everywhere, viewed as the other sex, the weaker sex, always second best. But like womenfolks around the globe, we sisters are also coming on, seeking and finding our rightful place.

For many years now, the good Black woman is said to stand behind her man. But many sisters of today are saying "no more" because the trouble with a woman standing behind her man is that she can't see where she is going! And anyway, say today's women, side by side is best.

Earlier I spoke of ways in which poor Black women, like poor folks everywhere, have been made the wretched of the earth. But let us not forget that out of poverty have often come some of the truly great women and men of this and every land. Let us not forget that those of us with material wealth can learn a great deal from the ingenuity of those with so little. For poor folks have had to make do when don't prevails. Poor folks have had to learn to get blood from a turnip.

The African American woman, then, is the symbol and a reality of the bitter sting of oppression *and* the powerful strength of resistance; our sister illustrates the shame of talents denied *and* the amazing creativity that flowers nevertheless; the Black woman has been forced to be the least among us, but she also symbolizes the best that is in each of us.

Let us turn now to develop the idea that the Black woman, as the least among us, is a symbol of Jesus Christ.

Jesus as the sister? Clearly, it was not an outrageous notion to David Driskell to portray the Black Woman as our Lord.

And yet we must ask why on first hearing this concept we find it difficult to comprehend, indeed some find it a disturbing notion. The answer, I think, is that the idea of Jesus as a Black woman challenges two deeply rooted bases of power in "western civilization," including American society: that which is white and that which is male.

But Jesus sided with, identified with, saved, and was at home with the powerless. And thus how easy it should be for us to see Jesus himself as a Black woman.

Let us remember that an enormous effort has been made to distort Christianity so that it stands in the interest of patriarchy and racism. For example, one of the earliest slaveships that arrived on these shores from Africa was called "The Good Ship Jesus." And how often did southern segregationists quote that passage in the Bible on the children of Ham as the hewers of wood and the drawers of water.

For many women, myself included, there is a sense that theology like everything else has been male dominated. As Jacquelyne Grant says, "Historically, these theologies have emerged out of the experiences of only one-half of the human race. . . . [We need] to bring about a more realistic and wholistic picture of the universe by developing a more wholistic theology" (p. 45).

Jacqueline Grant also reminds us that Jesus is the divine co-sufferer who empowers us in situations of oppression. And "for Christian Black women in the past, Jesus was their central frame of reference. They identified with Jesus because they believed that Jesus identified with them" (p. 212). Jesus was so central in Sojourner Truth's life that she made Jesus the starting point of all her sermons.

A preacher asked her if the Bible was the source of her preaching. "No honey, can't preach from the Bible—can't read a letter. When I preaches, I has jes' one text to preach from, an' I always preaches from this one. My text is 'When I found Jesus!' " (Gilbert, p. 83).

Of course sister Sojourner Truth also taught us, in her famous "Ain't I a Woman Speech," that it is incorrect to link the maleness of Jesus and the sin of Eve with the status of women. Listen to her:

And then that little man in black there, he says women can't have as much rights as men, because Christ wasn't a woman! Where did your Christ come from? Where did your Christ come from? From God and a woman! Man had nothing to do with Him. If the first woman God ever made was strong enough to turn a world upside down all alone, these women together ought to be able to turn it back, and get it right side up again! And now they are asking to do it, the men better let them. And a final message: Sisters, I ain't clear what you be after—if women want any rights more than they got, why don't they just take them and not be talking about it? (Schneir, p. 94)

Yes, Sister Sojourner, the significance of Jesus Christ is not his maleness but his humanity. For indeed, Jesus identified with the little people, with the poor, with the downcast, with women. He affirmed the basic humanity in the least among us and he inspires hope that we may all know true freedom—a resurrected liberated life.

As I bring closure on this morning's "sermon," I turn once again to the words of Sojourner Truth:

> I know that it feel a kind of hissin' and ticklin' like to see a colored woman get up and tell you about things, and woman's rights. We have all been thrown down so low that nobody thought we' ever get up again, but we have been long enough trodden now; we will come up again, and now I am here. . . . I wanted to tell you a mite about Woman's Rights, and so I came out and said so. I am sittin' among you to watch; and every once in a while, I will come out and tell you what time of night it is.   (Schneir, pp. 96–98)

My sisters and brothers, I do hope that you have heard my message in the spirit in which I have given it. I simply wanted to say what time of night it is. I truly believe that in sending us Jesus, our God sent one who identified with the most oppressed. And today in America, that means that the suffering servant is our sister. Clearly, Jesus is The Sister. And as we do unto her, the least among us, so we do unto him.

Let the whole chapel say Amen and Awomen too!

Works Cited

Gilbert, Olive. *Sojourner Truth: Narrative and Book of Life* (1850–1875). Chicago: Johnson Publishing, 1970.

Grant, Jacqueline. *White Women's Christ and Black Women's Jesus*. Atlanta: Scholars Press, 1989.

Schneir, Miriam, ed. *Feminism: The Essential Historical Writings*. New York: Random House, 1972.

God Is Inside You and Inside Everybody Else

Alice Walker

From The Color Purple

Dear Nettie,
     I don't write to God no more, I write to you.

What happen to God? ast Shug.

Who that? I say.

She look at me serious.

Big a devil as you is, I say, you not worried bout no God, surely.

She say, Wait a minute. Hold on just a minute here. Just because I don't harass it like some peoples us know don't mean I ain't got religion.

What God do for me? I ast.

She say, Celie! Like she shock. He gave you life, good health, and a good woman that love you to death.

Yeah, I say, and he give me a lynched daddy, a crazy mama, a lowdown dog of a step pa and a sister I probably won't ever see again. Anyhow, I say, the God I been praying and writing to is a man. And act just like all the other mens I know. Trifling, forgitful and lowdown.

She say, Miss Celie, You better hush. God might hear you.

Let 'im hear me, I say. If he ever listened to poor colored women the world would be a different place, I can tell you.

She talk and she talk, trying to budge me way from blasphemy. But I blaspheme much as I want to.

All my life I never care what people thought bout nothing I did. I say. But deep in my heart I care about God. What he going to think. And come to find out, he don't think. Just sit up here glorying in being deef, I reckon. But it ain't easy, trying to do without God. Even if you know he ain't there, trying to do without him is a strain.

I is a sinner, say Shug. Cause I was born. I don't deny it. But once you find out what's out there waiting for us, what else can you be?

Sinners have more good times, I say.

You know why? she ast.

Cause you ain't all the time worrying bout God, I say.

Naw, that ain't it, she say. Us worry bout God a lot. But once us feel loved by God, us do the best us can to please him with what us like.

You telling me God love you, and you ain't never done nothing for him? I mean, not to go church, sing in the choir, feed the preacher and all like that?

But if God love me, Celie, I don't have to do all that. Unless I want to. There's a lot of other things I can do that I speck God likes.

Like what? I ast.

Oh, she say. I can lay back and just admire stuff. Be happy. Have a good time.

Well, this sound like blasphemy sure nuff.

She say, Celie, tell the truth, have you ever found God in church? I never did. I just found a bunch of folks hoping for him to show. Any God I ever felt in church I brought in with me. And I think all the other folks did too. They come to church to *share* God, not find God.

Some folks didn't have him to share, I said. They the ones didn't speak to me while I was there struggling with my big belly and Mr. ——— children.

Right, she say.

Then she say: Tell me what your God look like, Celie.

Aw naw, I say. I'm too shame. Nobody ever ast me this before, so I'm sort of took by surprise. Besides, when I think about it, it don't seem quite right. but it all I got. I decide to stick up for him, just to see what Shug say.

Okay, I say. He big and old and tall and graybearded and white. He wear white robes and go barefooted.

Blue eyes? she ast.

Sort of bluish-gray. Cool. Big though. White lashes, I say.

She laugh.

Why you laugh? I ast. I don't think it so funny. What you expect him to look like, Mr. ———?

That wouldn't be no improvement, she say. Then she tell me this old white man is the same God she used to see when she prayed. If you wait to find God in church, Celie, she say, that's who is bound to show up, cause that's where he live.

How come? I ast.

Cause that's the one that's in the white folks' white bible.

Shug! I say. God wrote the bible, white folks had nothing to do with it.

How come he look just like them, then? she say. Only bigger? And a heap more hair. How come the bible just like everything else they make, all about them doing one thing and another, and all the colored folks doing is gitting cursed?

I never thought bout that.

Nettie say somewhere in the bible it say Jesus' hair was like lamb's wool, I say.

Well, say Shug, if he came to any of these churches we talking bout he'd have to have it conked before anybody paid him any attention. The last thing niggers want to think about they God is that his hair kinky.

That's the truth, I say.

Ain't no way to read the bible and not think God white, she say. Then she sigh. When I found out I thought God was white, and a man, I lost interest. You mad cause he don't seem to listen to your prayers. Humph! Do the mayor listen to anything colored say? Ask Sofia, she say.

But I don't have to ast Sofia. I know white people never listen to colored, period. If they do, they only listen long enough to be able to tell you what to do.

Here's the thing, say Shug. The thing I believe. God is inside you and inside everybody else. You come into the world with God. But only them that search for it inside find it. And sometimes it just manifest itself even if you not looking, or don't know what you looking for. Trouble do it for most folks, I think. Sorrow, lord. Feeling like shit.

It? I ast.

Yeah, It. God ain't a he or a she, but a It.

But what do it look like? I ast.

Don't look like nothing, she say. It ain't a picture show. It ain't something you can look at apart from anything else, including yourself. I believe God is everything, say Shug. Everything that is or ever was or ever will be. And when you can feel that, and be happy to feel that, you've found it.

Shug a beautiful something, let me tell you. She frown a little, look out cross the yard, lean back in her chair, look like a big rose.

She say, My first step from the old white man was trees. Then air. Then

158

birds. Then other people. But one day when I was sitting quiet and feeling like a motherless child, which I was, it come to me: that feeling of being part of everything, not separate at all. I knew that if I cut a tree, my arm would bleed. And I laughed and I cried and I run all around the house. I knew just what it was. In fact, when it happen, you can't miss it. It sort of like you know what, she say, grinning and rubbing high up on my thigh.

Shug! I say.

Oh, she say. God love all them feelings. That's some of the best stuff God did. And when you know God loves 'em you enjoys 'em a lot more. You can just relax, go with everything that's going, and praise God by liking what you like.

God don't think it dirty? I ast.

Naw, she say. God made it. Listen, God love everything you love—and a mess of stuff you don't. But more than anything else, God love admiration.

You saying God vain? I ast.

Naw, she say. Not vain, just wanting to share a good thing. I think it pisses God off if you walk by the color purple in a field somewhere and don't notice it.

What it do when it pissed off? I ast.

Oh, it make something else. People think pleasing God is all God care about. But any fool living in the world can see it always trying to please us back.

Yeah? I say.

Yeah, she say. It always making little surprises and springing them on us when us least expect.

You mean it want to be loved, just like the bible say.

Yes, Celie, she say. Everything want to be loved. Us sing and dance, make faces and give flower bouquets, trying to be loved. You ever notice that trees do everything to git attention we do, except walk?

Well, us talk and talk bout God, but I'm still adrift. Trying to chase that old white man out of my head. I been so busy thinking bout him I never truly notice nothing God make. Not a blade of corn (how it do that?) not the color purple (where it come from?). Not the little wildflowers. Nothing.

Now that my eyes opening, I feels like a fool. Next to any little scrub of a bush in my yard, Mr. _____'s evil sort of shrink. But not altogether. Still, it is like Shug say, You have to git man off your eyeball, before you can see any-thing a'tall.

Man corrupt everything, say Shug. He on your box of grits, in your head, and all over the radio. He try to make you think he everywhere. Soon as you think he everywhere, you think he God. But he ain't. Whenever you try to pray, and man plop himself on the other end of it, tell him to git lost, say Shug. Conjure up flowers, wind, water, a big rock.

But this hard work, let me tell you. He been there so long, he don't want to budge. He threaten lightening, floods and earthquakes. Us fight. I hardly pray at all. Every time I conjure up a rock, I throw it.

Amen

Exploring New Spaces:
A Dialogue with Black Women
on Religion, Culture,
and Spirituality

Margo V. Perkins

As an African American woman socialized into the southern Black Baptist tradition, I have begun to see Christianity as inextricably bound to my identity. Even if I should someday practice another religion, the most that I will ever be allowed to be (at least in the context of African American culture) is a *not-Christian* or, in other words, an *errant* Christian. In any event, Christianity seems the inescapable point of reference marking African American identity. The rituals, music, and ethos associated with the Baptist religious practice of my youth provide a sense of connection not just to my own family but, even more profoundly, to the history of African Americans on this continent. I am deeply moved by the songs (the gospel chords and rhythms), by the joy of fellowship, and the warm embrace of the elders. To have participated in that ethos of celebration, of giving thanks and praise, is to understand that place where, for instance, Aretha reaches to sing "Bridge Over Troubled Water," or Sweet Honey in the Rock, to raise their freedom songs. Aretha's soulful voice (like the voices of so many others reared in the Black gospel tradition) is the album of my childhood memories, capturing in song the love, reverence, resilience, and resistance of my people. If it were only these impressions that I experienced, my relationship to Christianity would not be an ambivalent one.

However, against the strong sense of place that my ties to Christianity have enabled is the simultaneous experience of profound intellectual alienation. I do not give my consent, for example, to the sexism (misogyny?), to the homophobia, to the proselytism, to the intolerance for/erasure of individual difference—all of which have marked my experiences with Christian culture. I further do not consent to the violent imposition (in the name of religion) of one culture's values and ways of knowing onto another, or to the political misuse of religious doctrine to dominate and exploit. I do not know whether the paradox of Christianity, as both a liberatory *and* an oppressive force in the struggle of African American people historically, is one that I can ever reconcile. It is not enough that my understanding of the precepts change if the practice—the way that I witness Christianity to be operating on me and in the culture—remains the same. My inability to reconcile my personal convictions with my Christian heritage has led me to challenge the assumption that participation in organized religion is the only means to spiritual fulfillment.

The more that I share stories and perceptions with others confronting similar dilemmas, the more it seems to me that this assumption is false. I suspect now that there are myriad paths to spiritual fulfillment. Of course, the assertion begs a definition of what it means to be spiritual; the concept evokes different meanings for different people. My own belief is that to be spiritual is to recognize and honor my inherent connection to other beings, to the earth, and to events in the world around me. It is to affirm life and to tap into the power—the life-sustaining energies and forces that direct the motion of the universe. To be spiritual, as revealed in the art of gifted writers, Ntozake Shange, Alice Walker, and Itabari Njeri, and filmmaker Julie Dash (women whose thoughtful and courageous works have enabled me to synthesize and continually reexamine my own beliefs over the years), is to commune with, to nurture, and to celebrate that which is divine around *and* within us. Shange's choreopoem *For Colored Girls Who Have Considered Suicide When the Rainbow Is Enuf*, for instance, proposes that the goddess can be found inside, while Walker's novel *The Color Purple* shows that the natural world *also* evinces the presence of god. Dash reaffirms in *Daughters of the Dust* not only that there exists a continuum between the living and the spirit worlds, but also that oppressed peoples must often syncretize opposing practices and belief systems to survive and make sense of their experiences. Finally, in her autobiographical *Every Good-bye Ain't Gone*, Njeri's portrayal of the pain of her Marxist intellectual father (who nevertheless cried when he heard Mahalia sing) poignantly captures the dilemma of being simultaneously bound to and alienated from one's own cultural heritage.[1]

To talk openly and critically (as distinct from negatively) about Christianity is to risk having to surrender one's membership card in the African American community. Interestingly, I would argue that I have never so much *re-jected* Christianity as I have simply neglected to embrace it. But since religion is treated as an inheritance, the legitimacy of my claim has gone unheard. A couple years ago, I remember rather exasperatedly blurting out at my family's dinner table that "I was not, after all, a Christian." My confession, though initially greeted with incredulity, was soon attributed to an irresponsible expression of youthful rebellion. In the wake of it, in fact, my family's recalcitrance only increased. That I am currently a *not-Christian* (a sort of purgatorial state of existence) leads them to believe that I will eventually recant. In a society that thrives on labels, one cannot just remain in such an ill-defined state. Meanwhile, no opportunities for proselytizing have been lost; saving a heathen daughter is a serious mission. The lack of space that exists for spiritual difference, particularly within the African American *female* community, where images of Black women bearing crosses is by now almost cliché, means that African American women do not often talk to each other critically about the impact of Christianity on our lives. Disclosure may be punished by ostracism or, even worse, by self-righteous proselytizing from those with whom we share our feelings. To be African American, female, and critical of one's own Christian experience, then, is to be a walking oxymoron. It is to have one's difference erased or dismissed on general principle. Lately I have begun to think, though, that the rejection of Christianity, albeit a transgression of considerable magnitude, is less a crime than to not be at least actively searching for another religion to fill its place. *That* is the unpardonable offense. And because there is no acknowledged distinction between religion and spirituality in America, to not be involved in organized religion is to bear an assumed emptiness.

Recently I shared these feelings with a group of African American women in Ithaca, New York, and to my surprise, they were intrigued by the possibility of opening dialogue around their own thoughts and experiences. In an attempt to create a critical and nonproselytical space to do this, I invited this group of five other women (varying by chance in age, occupation, geographical origin, class, and educational background) to my apartment one hot Sunday afternoon (the irony of the day was not lost on anyone present) to talk about our individual experiences.[2] So rare was the opportunity for such a forum that we continued sharing stories for nearly seven hours. To my delight, diverse views and values emerged as we broke silences and attempted to explore new spaces for being. Three critical areas were outlined for discussion, namely: the meaning of spirituality (with some attention on the concept of morality and the significance of ritual), the nature and impact of our socialization into (Black) Christian culture, and the evolution of our own images and concepts surrounding god/the divine.[3] What follows is a brief excerpt (that both begins and ends *in medias res*) from the *much* longer transcript of that exchange. We agreed that it should become merely one chapter in many necessary dialogues to come.

Wanda I've gone through a lot of phases with understanding god and religion and how I'm supposed to behave. And basically, that was what religion meant to me. Christianity, in particular. It meant that you're supposed to behave a certain way. And if you behave really well, really good, then you're going to be rewarded after you die. I'm not looking for that anymore from god. I think there's something inside of me that will reward me now. I think there's a spirituality inside of me. I don't know exactly what that is, but I can't just give all of that to one "White man" so that, I may, you know, have everlasting life. I don't see religion as being a way of me being spiritual. I mean, to me, religion is a way that you're organized or that you're socialized. It's behaviors. Rituals, these things you're supposed to do over and over again. When I understand god—and this is where I am now in my life, and I don't know where I may be ten years from now—I don't think that I need a church to be in contact with that energy or that supreme being that I know motivates me or directs me or has a purpose for me. I don't need to be in that institution to do that.

Margo Do you feel like that institution actually undermines your purpose?

Wanda Yes, you interfere because what you're doing is you're saying that I can't be me. You want me to behave and do things that you want me to do. You're not willing to accept me as being me. So, I can't go into your institution and believe that I need to change myself because I believe that god intended me to be this way. And if there's some changing that needs to be done, then I believe that I will understand that. And I'm not saying that I would do it, but at least I'd be aware that I don't need a group of people to say that you don't belong here because you don't A, B, C, or D. So, then you don't love me? Are you telling me that you're going to accept me the way that I am? Or are you going to accept me *until* you can change me? I don't understand that.

Sandra   God is about accepting you the way that you are.

Wanda   Right, but these churches aren't. They're not going to accept you the way you are because either you're . . .

Sandra   And that's why they're empty ritual.

Wanda   All of the churches are empty ritual? That's what you're saying?

Sandra   Look. Church is people. And love is about connection. I mean, there has to be something beyond that comes from within you. To *be* someone is to be somehow connected with someone else. We don't live on islands and in vacuums.

Wanda   That whole judging people thing is the main reason, I think, that I don't get along with religion. Because I don't think that that's right. You just can't judge other people. And you know, if it's true that I'm going to meet my maker when I die, then let me pay my own dues; you don't have to start punishing me while I'm here. And if I'm going to get punished, then let me get mine. Because, you know, I know what's in my heart and I think that any supreme being knows what's in my heart.

Rosetta   Alice Walker has a quote in *Possessing the Secret of Joy* that says "religion is an elaborate excuse for what man has done to women and to the earth."[4] It just seems like people use religion to justify the status quo and that's the way you should stay—within that status quo. Actually, I draw a distinction between religion and spirituality. To me, religion is an organized set of beliefs, and spirituality represents a more personalized and intimate relationship with my creator. I feel that there is some type of being that is greater than myself, that I am responsible to, and that I draw power from. And it's a very personal relationship. It's like having a best friend. I don't feel like I need to get down on my knees and say, "thank you, thank you." I just pray informally throughout the day, as if I'm speaking with a good friend.

165

Margo Is even the name problematic for you sometimes? Because I think, as soon as I say "god," there's a White man sitting there. Even that whole idea of a being—I'm not even sure now how I feel about that. I've started to think about spirituality as kind of an energy.

Rosetta I think that energy pervades everything, but it's convenient to think of a centralized source just so I can have something to talk to. Even though I have a problem with gender in Christianity, I still have not been able to overcome calling god a "He." It's just force of habit.

Sandra If it's not a "He," what is it?

Joyce It should just be an essence. A being, a power. You know, some creative force. Something that cares and loves.

Rosetta And calling [god] a "she" . . .

Margo Would that be just as problematic for you?

Joyce I think either way.

Rosetta I definitely can't call [god] "it" because that's just totally impersonal.

Sandra The personalizing allows god to be something that one can address or speak to, like I can speak to you. Just to replace "he" with "she," I don't know that going to that is the answer. I've never thought of god as a White man. (*Expressions of surprise.*) I don't think I have. Maybe I should retract that and say "I don't remember thinking in that way," even when we had pictures. I think part of the reason is because, in school . . . our coloring books came in with pictures and we colored them . . . teachers would do bulletin boards and they'd go to the trouble of coloring—you know—finding brown skin tones. My religion was a critique of whiteness. For me, home and church and school had interconnection. We could not go anyplace without being in the Black community. You were born into a Christian world. I'm not necessarily saying that's how it ought to be now, but that's the benefit that I grew up with. And part of that was, again, that everywhere we went was a critique of White power and White oppression and the ways we were treated, so that our god was someone who disapproved of the way White people acted.

Wanda But that's the same god that I feel controlled us, that allowed us to get to where you were. You know what I'm saying? I'm angry because I do think of god as a one thing, a one being. I mean, what if we had many different spiritual energies? Which is what I truly believe African people believed before we came to this place and many other places that were Christian based. Why is that the only option that I have? That there's one god, one Christ, and if you think about spirits too much, or different gods, then you're crazy. Or you know, that's Satan because "everything that moves is not god" (that's what they say). There are no other spirits accepted other than demons. So, I'm saying, oh there are no *good* spirits?

Phoebe I'm getting to the point where I find god within me. I mean, it's scary for me to say that because I'm not supposed to think like that.

Sandra See, that's the way I grew up. From what I know of theology— that's what theology teaches. I'm saying that god is in you, that god is what comes from within you that is good and right and true, that's just and that tells you there's a way that people should and ought to relate to each other; that the essence is love.

Rosetta Do you find anything useful in the Bible for yourself?

Sandra Oh lots. Yeah. That god is love. That I'm made in the image of god. And that image is love.

Wanda See, that's weird to me because I'm a woman and I don't know whose image I'm made in.

Sandra But see, I grew up thinking that god is neither male nor female. That "He" was a way of speaking. Just like we learn in school that "he" is the neutral. I didn't question that right then. I agree now that that's very gendered language, but back then it didn't have that kind of problem for me. When I thought of being made in the image of god, it was not in terms of gender. It was in terms of love and the capacity to be loved.

Phoebe Nobody can really sit down and say this is what we come from, this is how we got here. Nobody really knows. So, some people have gotten together and put some stuff in a book and that's what we accept. I can't really sit down and think of myself coming from a rib and stuff like that. From the very beginning of the Bible, it makes women look like we were wrong.

Sandra Have any of you read the book, *When God Was a Woman?*[5] I read that book and it gave me some of the most recent insights I have into the Bible and where it came from and what it's about. And what made me think about it was what you said about the story of Eve coming from the rib. There were other creation stories around and with the creation coming from the first god [who] was a woman. The woman who wrote this book pointed out kind of profoundly that that's the biggest myth (I guess basically, lie) that you could ever think of. I mean, it just doesn't compute when you think about it. She indicates that the whole thing was that men were just trying to figure out how they could be prior to women because they don't have wombs, and if you sit down to think about it logically, it must seem that the first being must've come from a woman or come out of a woman.

Phoebe Had to! Then it starts to confuse me with the part of Jesus being conceived with no man.

Wanda Oh, that's over my head.

Phoebe And right there, from young, it was like wait a minute. Something's *wrong* there. I had to start questioning that.

Sandra It's in the New Testament that god really turns into a male being.

Phoebe To have sex with her to get that little boy? To get Jesus?

Margo No sex. That would've been unclean.

Wanda The Virgin Mary did not have sex.

Joyce There you go.

Wanda She was married, sleeping with her husband, but he never touched her. I swear, that's what they taught me in church. I experienced Catholicism as a child. The Virgin Mary, first of all, she was White. So, to me, White women were like the ultimate pure existence. Only White women—because the Black women that I knew, I mean, I knew that the Black women in my family enjoyed sex, the sexual part of their existence. That was understood because this one had a boyfriend and that one had a husband and you knew what they were doing. It was about being together, physical hugging, kissing. That was what I understood as life; we hugged and kissed each other. You didn't not want to be next to people that you loved.

Margo   Are there any rituals that are important to you at this point in your life, and how have they figured into the construction of your own spirituality?

Phoebe   Well, for me, I can't get into rituals. I was trying to be a Muslim. They want you to pray five times a day, all these different hours, face towards Mecca, dress a certain way—all of those things are just too restricting. It makes me feel barred or in jail or something and I don't like that feeling. But I *do* do, like, every day is thank the Being, and since I know Him as Allah, I'll say "Allaahu Akbar."[6] And that's just being thankful for me having another day, thankful for being happy, thankful for having my children, just grateful that I'm alive again, that I have another day to move on. For me just to make it through what I've been through, I do have to thank something, some kind of power, some kind of energy. But I can't get anymore into that because I know I'm not a ritual person.

Wanda   I kind of take music and incense. Incense is still real important. I light candles sometimes.

Phoebe   You did say you always like the smell of the church. (*Laughter.*)

Wanda   I used to try to scare Mark and Dez to leave me alone, right? Because they believe in voodoo and stuff—Mark, in particular—I used to light all of these candles around the house. I would put [them] in, like, this circle and then I would burn all this incense and I would just sit in the dark. (*Exclamations and laughter.*) He would come in and say, this lady has lost it totally. And he would just, like, you know, back up. Every time I'd say, oh, he's starting to get on my nerves, I'd go light my candles. And then he would chill out. It's like, just turning out all the lights and having the candles on, I think it may remind me of being in the church. And having incense burning, which is an important part of the Catholic church. You just have to have frankincense and myrrh in your home. It makes me feel like it's kind of cleansing the atmosphere in the house. So, I would say that's probably what I would do, you know, as a ritual.

Rosetta Something that I have been doing, which I sort of got away from, is . . . I have a subscription to *The Upper Room*, a series of little devotional books. For every day of the week, there's a Bible verse. You read the verse and then there's a little story that's relevant to the theme for the day (which might be forgiveness or joy, etcetera). So, I would read that and it would help me get quiet and focused for the day. And I would try to think about whatever that theme was throughout the day. But I've sort of gotten away from that, and I need to go back. And then I also say a prayer at the end of the day. Just gratitude, you know, "thank you for allowing me to get through the day." And I thank god for my family and for their safety.

Margo What do you think about ancestral spirits? Instead of the traditional Christian prayer in the name of the Father, the Son, and the Holy Ghost, I will often say, "in the name of the ancestors." It makes me feel connected and a part of the continuum, that there's something that I have to live up to because I believe that the ancestors made certain things possible for me.

Sandra I believe, like you say, that the ancestors made things possible. Also, I believe that we are all that has gone before us or we would not be possible. Each one of us is unique, but that uniqueness is built on what preceded us. I think you have to recognize, give thanks, and celebrate, but then how you go about doing that, I don't know (and not that there needs to be some ritual around it). I really don't know. I guess I don't know what I believe about [ancestral] presence as separate as opposed to incorporated.

Wanda I believe—I mean, I'm sure—that I have contact with loved ones that are part of a different existence. I don't know what that existence is: I do believe that it's different from this one. I know that I have contact with the spirit world in different ways. I know that I have the ability to foresee events. I haven't really mastered that as much as I'd like to. I think that's because of the way this world is. I mean, I haven't really been taught, I think, to kind of channel in on certain energies. I know that that's something that my family members have—that ability. And it's like an inside joke in the family. But it's not really anything to take lightly because there are certain people in the family who really have special abilities that we just don't pay a whole lot of attention to. I mean, because people will call you crazy.

Joyce It's funny that you say that because the same thing exists in my family and I wonder to what extent in all Black families. I've never talked about that.

Wanda We get on the phone and if somebody has a dream, you don't be playing. Grandma gets on the phone, Mommy gets on the phone. My sister calls me. It's just like, you have to touch base with everyone if one person has this dream. And you know when that's the dream. I mean, if I have a dream—and I'm calling it a dream because I don't know any way to describe it to you (and it happens usually when I am in a sleep state), I feel that my family members that aren't here anymore will contact me and talk to me. And when they talk to me, it's like you have to make sure that everybody knows what they said. And it's different messages that come out of those conversations. Like, if my mother has a conversation with her loved one, she'll call and tell everybody and then we kind of figure out what we should be expecting. Most people outside of the family would think it's absurd; you know: that's stupid, it's superstitious, you don't know what you're talking about. But we truly believe that it's real spirits coming to visit and letting us know what to expect. Or if somebody's having a hard time, you know, you call them if you haven't heard from them, and usually it's like you call right on time.

Joyce The strange thing is that my mother is very religious, yet she also has that aspect. And I've always wondered how she reconciles the two. Both she and my aunt were that way—extremely mystical.

Wanda I think Black people have that trait. I really believe that it's a sense.

Sandra Why are they irreconcilable?

Joyce Because Christianity teaches you not to listen to that other side.

Margo It's the devil talking.

Joyce Exactly. Yet, for them it wasn't a problem. And I didn't even know that it was such an integral part of their lives until I was much older because they kept it very quiet. And so it's really strange to hear someone else discussing it because I thought that this was just, you know, my mother and my aunt.

Wanda Oh no. It's *dangerous* to discuss it. My sister, I feel, is a child that was able to channel in a lot better than anyone else. And anytime we lost a family member, this kid knew that it was going to happen. You know, it's like you can't interfere with what's going to happen, but you're kind of aware of it. If my sister tells me something, I don't even question that it's going to happen; I just kind of get ready for this to happen. I can remember the anniversary of all my aunts' and uncles' deaths because that month before the month that they died, they always visit me. Always. And I don't think it's just that subconsciously I remember that they died this time or that something happened this time. I just truly believe that this is when they choose to visit the family. But that's not something that you're allowed to exercise in formal religious atmospheres. You just can't.

Phoebe I believe I do have a connection with people I've lost or I've loved because I want to keep a connection. I don't want to separate that part. I don't feel like I'm going to see them again, or something like that, because I think my heaven and hell is right here. I'm not really into looking to a life afterwards. I've lost two sisters, a brother, my father, my children's father. You know, a lot of people who are dear to me. So, I try to keep a real connection. Like, if I dream about them, I know it's something going on. Something has happened. I check myself out. Like I know that my children's father (he died in '87)—I've been dreaming about him regularly. And I said to myself: looking for a man again. (*Laughter.*) I know when I start dreaming about them, I miss them. If I start dreaming about my sister, I'm lonely because she was like my best friend. So, that's how I keep my connection with them here. But I do believe what Wanda was saying that everybody has sort of a sixth sense. I mean, I think, everybody in here has felt déjà vu. Has something ever happened to you that you said, this has gone on before? So, I think everybody really has sort of like a map.

Sandra You asked about other frameworks of morality.

Margo What did you want to say?

Sandra   I don't know. That's what I meant—it's mind-boggling. How do you go about putting together a whole framework of morality? I don't think Christianity is *a* framework of morality.

Joyce   Rules don't make a moral basis.

Margo   Yeah, because if you break the rules, whether or not you *suffer* depends on what your moral integrity is.

Joyce   What motivates you to adhere to those rules.

Margo   Woody Allen has this very interesting film, *Crimes and Misdemeanors*,[7] which addresses this issue of moral integrity. I really believe that people do have different frameworks of morality. I think people have a responsibility to be true to what they believe in, whatever that is.

Sandra   But is there a moral standard against which moral frameworks can be measured?

Margo   I've really come to believe no. I mean, I truly believe the fact that we're human means that unless you are pathologically ill, you know the difference between good and evil. I think that's something we can all understand on a very fundamental level. So, then, if you accept that there's something good about human beings (and that already gives you a framework), and [that] whatever convictions you have you ought to live by, then you have a responsibility to act on what you know and understand to be true.

Joyce   But that also comes from the understanding that your first personal value is yourself. It's first directing internally, saying I'm a worthwhile human being and therefore, if I don't want this to occur to me, I shouldn't want it to occur to others.

Margo   Maybe we should close by talking about our children. How have you approached issues around religion and spirituality in the rearing of your own daughters and sons?

Phoebe   I've never said, "You have to go to church" or "Get up, we're going to church." We might have wound up in the church every once in a while or something like that. Their father was Muslim. He gave them Muslim names. And they connect with Islam. Sometimes I think that I'm not raising them right because I don't have them in church, and I don't have them baptized. I didn't go through all of that with them. My sister, she made sure her kids were baptized and took first communion and all that other kind of stuff. But I didn't. So, I haven't given them a real strong religious background.

Wanda Dez is starting to be angry with me. She's been expressing to me her need to go to church. I think the kids in the school talk about going to church, and the things they do with the church and stuff like that. Desiree's father's family were Pentecostal. They made me dislike church so much. I mean, that was like a weapon that they used. And first of all, I was Jezebel; I did everything, as far as they were concerned, you know, to entice this man (a young man at the time) to do everything against what god intended him to do. He's a deacon in the church and has a wife and three kids now, and they are really upstanding citizens in the church. And it's just like, I've got this little bastard child here. So, I'm very turned off from church. Desiree's not baptized. I don't have any plans to get her baptized or to introduce her to church or formalized religion.

Sandra What about her option to make choices, if, you say, she's saying to you she wants [to go to church]. When you say you don't have any plans, does that mean it's your plan to prevent her from going?

Wanda She's going to have to do that when she leaves my house or when she gets older. When she can go on her own and buy her own Bible and do it herself is when she's going to do it. That's not anything I'm endorsing. There's a lot of things she'd like to do that I'm just not going to allow her to do. And religion and church is one of them. I think that I would be oppressing my own child if I did that because I really think that Christianity is a weapon that's been used against Black people. And I'm not going to teach her to believe in a god that I think has been used to put her and me where we are.

Margo Do you tell *her* that? Do you have those kinds of discussions with her?

Wanda Yes.

Joyce   Does she respect [your explanations?]

Wanda   Uh unh. She wants to go to church. But then, I'm the boss and I say no. And she can't understand what I'm saying. Like she's saying, well, god is not White—because Mark tells her god is Black. So that's all right, then. But it's not just the way that god looks. It's more to it than that. I don't think she can really understand that. I don't want her to ever be able to say that the church was a part of her life, like, early on. Because it seems like when you're exposed to certain things in your formative years, that's always a part of you. I don't really want that to be a part of her. I've always tried to stimulate her politically and spiritually. This church thing has come up a few times, so I can't just dismiss it because she's going to look for it someplace. So I need to give her what I think would be most beneficial to her, so she's not like open, you know, to still need that fulfillment. I'm going to give her something, but I'm not going to give her that.

Joyce   I always know that when my parents would say no about something, it would make me want to do it more than what I originally felt. I mean, I don't want to give advice as to how it should be handled . . .

Wanda   That's why I thought if I can give her another way. Like eventually, if she decides to go to church, she can. But for *me* to introduce her into the spirit world or something like that, I'd like to do it the way that I want to do it. I'm selfish with that. I'd rather her be able to get creative with the way that she understands herself and her spirituality. I want to give her those tools because I don't really have the answer myself. She needs to find that out for herself. And if she really wants to go to church or whatever, she can go ahead. I try to arm her as much as I possibly can, and I really encourage her to pay attention to her inner self, pay attention to those voices, those feelings, or whatever you want to call it; they're telling you something. They're there for a reason. Listening to them will protect you when I can't protect you. *You* can protect you when I can't protect you.

Phoebe   And if you start doing that from young, you'll continue to go on with that feeling.

Wanda Yes, I always did that with her. Always. I'm really trying to prepare her in ways that I wasn't prepared as a young person.

The participants are all members of the Ithaca Black Women's Empowerment Group, *which was organized in January 1993 to provide a supportive forum for Black women to share information and to discuss local, national, and global issues relevant to our lives. Membership is without regard to educational, class, or community residence requirements.*

Wanda Anderson grew up in Edenwald Projects in the Bronx, New York. She moved to Ithaca in 1992, where she says she "lives in the shadows of the Ivy League research institution, Cornell University." An activist and community organizer, Anderson is the founder of the Ithaca Black Women's Empowerment Group. She is additionally the mother of one daughter, Desiree ("Dez"), who she says motivates her resistance to the ways Black women are oppressed and victimized in America.

Phoebe Brown moved to Ithaca for a change from the fast pace of life in Harlem, New York, where she grew up. Through her work as a teen coordinator and counselor, Brown says she encourages young Black kids, in particular, to strive for goals beyond those identified for them by the culture. Brown plans to remain in Ithaca long enough to attend college and also to see her teenage son and daughter finish high school.

Rosetta Haynes is originally from Dunkirk, New York. After graduating from Fisk University, she worked for three years as a senior actuarial specialist in Hartford, Connecticut. Haynes is presently a Ph.D. candidate in English at Cornell University, where she is writing a dissertation in nineteenth-century African American women's spiritual autobiography.

Sandra Hill is a native of Rome, Georgia. She holds a B.S. from Berea College and an M.S.W. from the University of Michigan. Hill has been involved in social work most of her career, and is especially interested in issues concerning equity and access to resources, particularly as these issues affect the Black community. Hill does women's advocacy work in Ithaca through Displaced Homemakers.

Margo Perkins grew up in Silver Spring, Maryland, and is a graduate of Spelman College. She is currently a Ph.D. candidate in English at Cornell University, writing a dissertation on the autobiographies of Black Power activists, Angela Davis, Assata Shakur, and Elaine Brown.

Joyce (a pseudonym) is a native of Cleveland, Ohio, and a recent graduate of Cornell University. For many of the same reasons that disclosure was risky for all involved, she prefers to remain anonymous.

Notes

1. Ntozake Shange, *For Colored Girls Who Have Considered Suicide When the Rainbow Is Enuf* (New York: Bantam, 1981); Alice Walker, *The Color Purple* (New York: Pocket Books, 1982); *Daughters of the Dust*, dir. Julie Dash, American Playhouse, 1992; and Itabari Njeri, *Every Good-bye Ain't Gone* (New York: Vintage, 1990).

2. Biographical information on the participants follows the transcript.

3. Because "God" is a *known* entity is something that we interrogate in our discussion, the word is rendered in lowercase throughout the text.

4. Spoken by the character Raye, in *Possessing the Secret of Joy* (New York: Pocket Books, 1992), p. 235.

5. Merlin Stone, *When God Was a Woman* (New York: Harcourt Brace Jovanovich, 1976).

6. Translated: "Allah is the greatest."

7. *Crimes and Misdemeanors*, dir. Woody Allen, Orion Pictures, 1989.

the hall

Lucille Clifton

in this hall
dark women
scrubbed the aisles
between the pews
on their knees.
they could not rise
to worship.
in this hall
dark women
my sisters and mothers

though i speak with the tongues
of men and of angels and
have not charity . . .

in this hall
dark women,
my sisters and mothers,
i stand
and let the church say
let the church say
let the church say
AMEN.

In Praise of Praying Women

Valerie J. Bridgeman Davis

Right now,
    the church is praying.
By that I mean women are praying,
    mourning, weeping, going on in Jesus' name.
Women are carrying the church on their knees.
    These godly, broken, holy females
who look to You to comprehend
    barren wombs and aching breasts,
and headaches brought on by desire
    for intimate, holy, passionate sex.
Surely,
    You must have some womanly, motherly,
sisterly, lover-ly qualities
    we can identify.
Song of Songs where blurs the line
    of lover and beloved.
All power be to godly women: help us, Mother God.

Let the Church Say Amen

Nikki Giovanni

My air conditioner broke down though I don't think that was the cause of my dream. My mother was sitting, testifying about something, I don't know what. The courtroom was the British sort of courtroom with lots of men in big white wigs. She had, I suppose, finished testifying because I saw myself go to her and hug her. I had my right arm around her shoulder and I was saying, "I love you." "But, Nikki," she said, "they cut off my arms." Then she raised her blue, linen jacket above the elbow and I saw that her arms had, indeed, been cut off. I woke up in a cold sweat just this side of crying. I didn't know what that meant. I still don't but it made me think, once again, why I am who I think I am. I'm not sure, by the way, what this had to do with spirituality so perhaps you should stop now if you are looking for either answers or sense.

It's strange . . . the reasons people do things. I was teaching a creative writing course this spring when I received the happy news that I would be honored with two honorary doctorates, of literature and humane letters, from Rockhurst and Widener College, respectively. Bemoaning to my class that I would have to fly west then east, to Kansas City and Philadelphia, and I hate flying, I was nonetheless delighted about the degrees. "But," I concluded, rather casually I thought, "this is the price we pay for letting our mothers know we are o.k." A couple of the young women looked at me with those blank expressions you occasionally get when one generation has no idea in hell what the other is talking about. "Well," I responded to the looks, "it is all about our mothers, isn't it? Don't tell me," I laughed, "you are doing it all for dear old dad!" I was actually cracking up. I thought I had really connected with them. "I do it for myself," one woman said almost . . . well . . . belligerently. Incredulously I looked at her: "What do you mean?" You know how people talk when they talk to the elderly, the very young, and the handicapped? You know, slow and a bit louder? Enunciating very clearly? "I do it for myself." As in, "There! I said it again." "Nobody does anything for themselves," says I as in Don't Make Another Dumb Statement To The Class And Me This Afternoon. But others joined her. Yeah, came this chorus, I write for myself. I live for myself. Everything I do is self-motivated. I threw up my hands "STOP!" I couldn't believe what I was hearing. Who in their right minds does anything for themselves? Where is the challenge or pleasure in that? Doesn't make any sense to me at all. That's as dumb as living for today.

Like everyone, I guess, I've wondered what kind of slave woman I would have been. In my awake dreams I've seen myself leading the people through swamps and forest to the freedom promised by the North Star. I see myself exhorting us onward ignoring the pain in my back from carrying the old woman along and the blood seeping from my feet for lack of adequate shoes. We fight and kill off the patterollers; we are discouraged when the boat is not at the river but we forge on. I am a hero. I see us through. But in my sleep dreams I recall no such scenario. In all my years of dreams remembered I do not ever remember dreaming in my sleep that I was a heroic slave. Perhaps I don't have a dream of it because my sleep self knows that had I been a slave I would have had the same bad choices that real slaves had: how to accommodate myself to a system that does not admit I exist; how to birth and rear children in the hope for a better tomorrow; how to prepare myself for their life and my death with some sense of dignity; how, most important of all, to find a way to love myself, someone else, and the work that I do. You don't have to be smart to know that the ability to take pride in your own work is one of the hallmarks of sanity. Take away the ability to both work and be proud of it and you can drive anyone insane. That's one reason rich people have schedules; not because they need to be someplace or do something in order to eat and put a roof over their heads but because the need to be needed is so central to human beings. It's not that welfare is cruel, because it isn't; it's not that unemployment compensation is cruel, because it isn't either; but it is a reality that when we separate a group of people, whether by race, gender, or physical ability, and say to them "We, Society, would rather not see you and we will pay you to go away from us; to stay out of our sight," then we have taken away all possibility of pride in their lives. Accepting money is a poor compensation for earning it. White people know that, which is why Social Security was made universal; so that poor whites could maintain their human pride while accepting help. Which is what makes the way society is treating young Black people and Black men so vicious. Society has not universalized their plight . . . they simply are told to disappear.

I wish I could be poet laureate of planet Earth. I'd run a contest on how it feels to be permanently unemployed. What it feels like to wake up in the morning and know, not think or suspect, but know that there is no place you are expected to be; no one is looking for you; no one cares whether you survived the night or not. Isn't there a line in the old gospel song that says, "He woke me up this morning and I was clothed in my right mind . . . the Lord is blessing me"? What blessing can it be to be unneeded? And we want to say to the permanent underclass that they should find a reason? We want to say to the young Black men that they should gather themselves up and stay in school? I think not. They know what they cannot articulate: it is not money but the need to be needed that is unfulfilled. Black people have been poor in money since 1619 but we were rich in fulfilling a need . . . for our labor; for our survival; for our dreams of a better day. I wish I were poet laureate. I would run a poetry contest on what it's like to sit in a wheelchair all day and nobody to talk to; nobody to look at you; nothing to do but sit all day which soon becomes the same as all night which becomes your life. That because you are in a wheelchair you have nothing to offer and no one needs you? But how different can that be from sitting in prison? All day and all night year after year until you barely remember why you came or if there was ever a time when you weren't in prison. And someone doesn't like "Cop Killer"? Someone thinks Sister Soljah is . . . what . . . harsh? There is something called "the truth," and as uncomfortable as it makes some people, others of us know the kids are right. Their response is a logical response. You cannot change the images until the reality changes. I know if I were poet laureate I would not happen to be Black; I would be a Black woman who happened to be poet laureate.

There is that old story I heard at least ten years ago about a young man who read a book that mentioned Malcolm X. The young man was so excited by Malcolm that the next day he went to his teacher and asked "Professor, where can I learn more about Malcolm the tenth?" It was probably a joke someone made up much like snakes in the toilets and alligators in the sewers but it still strikes a chord. Nobody wants to take the time to know anything. Mario Van Peebles didn't want to take the time to learn anything about the

Black cowboys; it was more . . . what . . . fun? . . . to play off current images; Spike Lee doesn't want to learn anything. Why should "facts" get in the way of their movies? But if they knew something about our people they would know that just about the only guarantee is that you will not succeed. You can't be Black, in my opinion, and think about winning the battle . . . you have to go for the war. If you assume failure then at least that frees you to make relevant history. What if Van Peebles assumed he would not make a financially successful movie? Then he would have been free to tell the truth about one Black town and let us win for a change, because *Posse* didn't make a cent anyway and was insulting to boot. Same with Spike Lee and *Malcolm X*. But *Menace II Society* and *Boyz 'n the Hood* both had a vision and integrity. That they were financially successful is a plus; not a necessity. The old folks say it all the time: the half ain't never been told. What's the point of any of us being out there if not to get what little bit of truth we can told to us and for us. Who do these people love and respect?

I always sort of assume there is some little old lady reading my book, listening to me read poetry, watching me on television, and I know I have to speak to her. I can go into an all white audience and deliver the same speech that I would to an all Black audience because I know my grandmother and her Bridge-Flower-Book club friends are always there. I don't have to see them to know that. Even in Sunday school we were taught "He didn't bring me this far to leave me alone." God can get busy somewhere else which, I was told, is why He invented mothers. Grandmothers are even better. How do you go out into the world without a firm sense of those women watching you? Why would you want to be out there if not to continue their story? We have obligations. I'm not the artist who would even begin to say what you should write or paint or sculpt or photograph or tackle for or dunk for or any of that. I only know that if you are doing it for yourself you are in deep trouble. We cannot be the reason we exist let alone the reason we excel. All I know is that we have an obligation to claim who we are and to tell our part of the story.

Maybe I've spent too much time on airplanes or in hotel rooms. I always laugh at myself and say that solitaire could never be punishment for me but that's not true. Just because other people are not around doesn't mean that I am alone. I say it all the time though it is nonetheless true: We are somebody's dream. Somebody, some woman, hundreds of years ago dreamed that one day somebody who looked like her would be able to do . . . what? Eat in a restaurant, go to school, vote, not be cold, own herself, be paid for her labor. Who knows what she dreamed, but we do know that she dreamed. Had she not dreamed we would not be here. We have no right to stop now. We have, in fact, every obligation to continue the dreams, to stand before history's docket and testify: I am here. And here I will stand. Let the church say "Amen."

sunday morning ritual

Imani Constance Johnson Burnett

to the "workshop" for karen

on sunday mornings we come together early
disregarding the raiment of the week
those worn garments of lived out realities,
out-lived fantasies, and prayer
we come together early

spirits are merged in movement
bodies and minds sweat and stretch
imagination expresses the unspoken
in the ever natural rhythms
of a colored history
a black presence
and an undeniable future

at once we have been afrika
in the inner city
ocelot, gazelle, ibis, monkey,
giraffe, wildebeest, zebra,
exotic intimidator and intimidated
we have each stood in a space
that could only contain our individuality
we have each reached inside for joy
we have each witnessed the colors of the rainbow
and watched them manifest in nature
right before our very own eyes
as we come together early
on sunday mornings

we defy myths
we come out of kitchens

strained relationships, jobs,
we come on buses, over freeways,
across mountains
we bring babies, and old secrets
we ignore outside pressures
and stop time to move in tune
we create a concert of intimacy
which disallows personal estrangement

we defy myths cast upon us
we defy myths cast upon us
by energizing the physical,
mental, and magical forces
which testify to our belonging

glory glory glory

we design a fertile promise
we create a new day inspired
we are a commitment to effort
to progress, to dreams,
to the very truth of truths
which is sweet sweet
on sunday mornings
early
when we dance.

Sources of Black Female Spirituality: The Ways of "the Old Folks" and Women Writers

Delores S. Williams

After reading African-American women's autobiographies, novels, and essays, nonblack female students have often asked me questions similar to the ones posed by the late Audre Lorde in her book *Zami: A New Spelling of My Name*. To whom do African-American women owe the power behind their voices? What gives black women the strong will to survive the destructive social and political forces threatening their daily lives? Whom do black women owe for what they have become as women?

Many times I have reflected upon these questions within the context of my own life and its formation from childhood to maturity. I have found it useful first to identify the nature of the power that helped me along the way to develop a voice, survive negative social and political forces, and become who I am as a black woman. Spiritual power has been the motivating force, the catalyst for action, the force sustaining energy. The "mediums" (or media) for this spiritual power have been "the old black folks" and what they taught me about surviving this life as a black woman trying to develop a positive, supportive quality of life for myself and my children.

These "old black folks" came from three different historical and cultural contexts and gave three different kinds of complimenting advice that shaped my spiritual formation. There was Old Elizabeth, the slave woman, whose mother told her in the final analysis she wouldn't "have nobody to look to but God." Old Elizabeth told me through her slave narrative. Translated into my history, the advice of Old Elizabeth's mother meant that sometimes, as a black woman, I might have to stand utterly alone without support. Then I would need to reach deep down into my faith and find support and emotional sustenance. This deep down place had to be fueled by something more energizing, sustaining, and transcendent than human power. This empowering force issued from the divine. I experienced this standing-alone-feeling and the deep down powering force when my husband died suddenly seven years ago, and I became the lone parent for our four children. Spiritual power emerged that kept me going as I moved between "a rock and a hard place" to keep me and my children focused on our family goals.

In addition to Old Elizabeth, the "old black folks" at the black church have continuously taught me the power and strength of community: the joy of the social (as well as the religious) gathering of the community in the suppers, basket meetings, Sunday school picnics, and in festivals celebrating the accomplishments of community members. In the segregated South where I came of age, the black church was, as sociologist C. Eric Lincoln has said, "the Lyceum, the gymnasium," the gathering place, the shouting place, the crying place, the testifying place, the civil rights strategizing place, and the sharing place of the community. It was the place where black women passed along spiritual power and sage advice to the community gathered. It was the place where we black children were told over and over again that we were somebody. It was the place where we were trained to be leaders, where we were advised to be somebody who could make a positive difference in the world for our people. The old black folks at the church, mostly women, were the "hope-hangers" teaching us to hold tightly in our memory and imagination to the power of the community gathered for faith and action. This was our hope for a future that would benefit the entire community: women, men, and children.

The last group of "old black folks" contributing to the development of my spiritual power were the female members of my family: my mother, grandmother, and aunts. They introduced me to and rehearsed me in the African-American prayer tradition. None of these women were fanatics or fundamentalists—though they all had great faith in the authority of the Bible. And the Bible definitely had something to do with the prayer tradition they passed along. But the authority of the Bible was also determined by what the community added to the Bible and called "scripture" right along with the Bible as scripture. Two examples can be cited here. Sociologist of religion Cheryl Townsend Gilkes has pointed to an ancient practice among black folks with which many older black people are familiar. She refers to the text in Psalms: "God, you are my father . . ." For generations black folks have amended the text so that it is passed along to the community as "God, you are my father, my mother, my sister, and my brother." This text, made inclusive by the community, has become incorporated into black prayer traditions. In the prayers I heard and was taught as a child, reference was often made to "God, my father, my mother, my sister, and my brother."

The second example among black people of "scripture" right along with the Bible but not in the Bible comes from my own experience. For years in our household, I heard my mother refer to a text I thought came from the Bible. This text advised us "to cast up the highway; roll down the stones; set up a standard for the people."

Once when I was preparing a presentation to give before a church audience, I decided to use this text to develop my speech. I searched for it in the Bible but could not find it. I telephoned my mother and asked where she had gotten it from the Bible. She told me it was not in the Bible, though it was a "take-off" from Jeremiah. Then I said to her, "but you and grandmaw told us that this text came from the Bible." She reminded me that they had not told us it came from the Bible. They told us it was "scripture." The point here is that this "extra-biblical" tradition in my mother's household functioned as sacred text, alongside the Bible, advising us children how to get on in life. This business of "casting up the highway, rolling down the stones, and setting up a standard for the people" was the directive for my involvement in the black civil rights movement and in the women's movement. This homespun black scripture was always at the heart of the prayer tradition taught by these black women in my family. It was their hope (and it is mine) that the people in our family would not hesitate to get out into the world, to "right" some of the many wrongs done to black people, and thereby to set up a standard of action for future generations. This homespun black scripture was the mandate for justice-seeking which the women in my family passed along.

So, in response to the first question posed above—to whom do African-American women owe the power behind their voices—I say we owe this power to our upright spiritual ancestors, to the lessons they taught us through their religious faith and practices, and to the sacred traditions they used to shape wholesome family life that modeled productive, positive action for the future, that inspired us to keep hope alive. Many of the conduits for this power were and are black women.

The power, itself, is spiritual power which has created the spirituality and tenacious will of many black women to survive the destructive social and political forces in America threatening the daily lives of black women and men. This spiritual power and spirituality has helped black women assume active political postures that opposed the forces oppressing black people. The names Harriett Tubman, Sojourner Truth, Ida Wells Barnett, Rosa Parks, Septima Clark, and Fanny Lou Hamer conjure up memories of the way in which black women have, throughout American history, organized, challenged, and conquered oppressive forces threatening the lives and freedom of African-Americans. All of these women have given evidence of the spiritual power motivating their action.

The response to the last question posed above—whom do black women owe for what they have become as women—certainly incorporates the gifts given by "the old black folks" mentioned above. However, on a more personal note, I point to a source that has helped me become who I am as a black woman. That source is other black women speaking to me through their creation of imaginative literature and through their essays. First, there is Zora Neale Hurston's novel *Their Eyes Were Watching God*. From this book I heard one black woman advise another black woman: "Don't love nobody better'n you do yourself; do, you'll be dying before your time is out." This was subtle advice to me about black women and sacrifice: a meaning I did not translate until years later after I had been a wife and mother for many years. I used Hurston's words as a lens to re-view my life and found myself missing from that life. I began to pick myself up from the sacrificial positions to which I had stooped. This rising up, though a difficult and trying ordeal, has strengthened my spiritual power which sustained me as I struggled to gain self-sight, to shape a career, and simultaneously to be a friendly parent to my children.

In addition to Zora Hurston, I owe Alice Walker whose definitions helped me own everything I had been and was to become as a black woman. Her description of a womanist in her book of essays *In Search of Our Mothers' Gardens* gave so many of us black women "who were out there" the pride and strength to say to feminist and black male pressures: "this is who we black women be" and we are proud of it! Walker began her definition the way so many of us begin our adult life: advising, relating to, scolding, loving our children. But Walker emphasized the mother-daughter relation. She lifted up female leadership in black liberation efforts. She affirmed our body shapes, our love of celebration (associated with food, dancing, nature), and our right to sexual preference. Some of her most instructive words advised against sacrificing ourselves as she described a womanist as "loving herself. Regardless." Many of us black wives, mothers, and lovers of men do not take the time to work through and come to an understanding of what it means to love ourselves regardless of all the obstacles in our lives posed to prevent such understanding. There are many more black women writers who have contributed to my coming to terms with my life: Toni Morrison (*The Bluest Eye, Beloved, Sula*), Margaret Walker (*For My People* and *Jubilee*), Hazel V. Carby (*The Reconstructing Womanhood*), and the late Audre Lorde (*Zami: A New Spelling of My Name*). And in all this mix, the many black females making up "the old black folks" cannot be forgotten. For they have, through the years, demonstrated what ethicist Katie Geneva Cannon identifies as black women's "quiet grace" centering their creativity and spiritual power.

Whenever I reflect upon the sources of my spirituality as a black woman, I think of love, struggle, work, self-sight, justice, and celebration taught me by so many black voices: most of them female. For this I continue to be deeply grateful. For this I celebrate the very force of life itself.

On Discovering Self and Empowerment in Black Women's Literature

Mary Helen Washington

I must begin this speech with a warning.* Having been both Catholic and female all of my life, I am given to examinations of conscience and to great quantities of that most female affliction—unnecessary guilt. As Erica Jong so perceptively writes, "Show me a woman without any guilt . . . and I'll show you a man." But I want you to regard the confessional tone of this speech, not so much as moral laxity, but as formalist strategy: a way of connecting to the women in this audience, who I know will understand how to respond to and interpret its underground meanings and as a way of imposing shape and order on my personal history.

If someone had told me in 1962 at my college graduation that it would take me almost fifteen years to feel committed to and comfortable about the work I had chosen to do, I would not have believed it. Nor would I have believed it if someone had told me that I would live for nearly fifteen years on the periphery of my work, doing only what was necessary to get by, at times enjoying the work, but never committed to it—a kind of marriage of necessity, without passion and without fulfillment. When I left Notre Dame College in June 1962, I had in hand a signed, sealed contract which would deliver me to the Cleveland Public Schools as a certified secondary school teacher the following September. For the first two years of my working life, I taught eleventh and twelfth grade English at Glenville High School where, instead of a honeymoon, I found myself overwhelmed by five classes, mountains of papers, a day that began before 8:00 A.M. and did not end until after 8:00 P.M. when lesson plans were done for the next day. My evenings alternated between sleeping and weeping. In my second year of teaching, the administra-

---

*This commencement address was given in 1989 at Regis College, a Catholic women's college in Weston, Massachusetts, outside of Boston.

192

tion added hall duty and detention period to my schedule, eliminating two of the four free periods I had. I felt, urgently, the call to graduate school.

And so I went to graduate school—mainly to escape work. While graduate studies were actually much harder than teaching high school, I had a sense—much like a new divorce—that I had been granted a reprieve from a life's sentence. I had two more years of not having to commit myself to work, two more years of experimentation, of intellectual excitement, of wild graduate school parties. When those two years of freedom ended, I had a Master's degree in English from the University of Detroit and not the slightest idea of what to do with it. With all that freshly acquired knowledge and high eagerness for intellectual pursuits, I found myself in June of 1966 paralyzed, unable even to initiate a job search—for where was I to go? My colleagues—all white, mostly male—were choosing places like Johns Hopkins, the universities of Texas, Arizona, North Carolina, and Michigan. My female colleagues were going with their husbands. It is only with hindsight that I understand why I could not bring myself even to submit an application, why I could not imagine myself in one of these universities. In 1966 I knew, though only subconsciously, that I would have to enter an academic world in which black people and women existed only on the margins—if even there. My reluctance to enter the ranks of what Virginia Woolf called the procession of the sons of educated men—was an unconscious rebellion against my own exclusion from these ranks. Near the end of the summer of 1966—the summer of my paralysis—the president of St. John College in Cleveland got my name from a list of Catholic college graduates, called me in Detroit, and offered me a job as instructor of English at the college, a small, all women's Catholic college in downtown Cleveland. Once again the decision about my life and my work was made for me, and, eagerly and passively—a bride again—I signed on the dotted line, still trying to give shape to what seemed more and more like a shapeless life. (I realize that my marriage metaphor is leading me into adultery and possible excommunication, but I need it for continuity.)

I taught for two years at St. John College with a luxury schedule that had no study halls, no hall duty, no detentions. I spent lunch hours in downtown Cleveland and bought as many clothes as my $7,500 a year salary would allow. I tried to convey to students my love of literature and to challenge students who lived in worlds so protected they seemed symbolically to be walking around in high-necked lace collars and high-top shoes. Half of my students were nuns who were not allowed to have lunch off campus with a lay professor. Bathrooms for lay faculty women were separate from those for religious women. There was a small scandal when the dean (also a nun) discovered I was teaching John Updike's *Rabbit Run* to freshwomen.

I worked at St. John College with pretty much the same attitude that I had as a temporary Christmas worker tossing mail for the post office, obligated, responsible, but not happy. I organized my classes the way I did the mail, getting all the pieces in the right slot; but I was as distant from and uncommitted to my teaching as I was from the postal zones of metropolitan Cleveland. When those two years were up, I knew it was time to leave this protected cocoon and take another vocational and intellectual risk, but this time my reasons for leaving went far deeper than the need to escape the burdens of hall duty. The year was 1968. Martin Luther King had been assassinated in April. There had been at least three major race riots: Watts in 1965, Detroit and Newark in 1967. I was teaching in an all-white institution so oblivious to the ferment taking place that when King was killed I had to insist (in tears) that the college put up a memorial to him. I was teaching the fiction of Joseph Conrad, Ernest Hemingway, William Faulkner, John Updike, and James Joyce. In two years, I had a total of one black student. When I got a call one night from a former professor asking me to return to the University of Detroit to teach in an Upward Bound Program and to enroll in the doctoral program there, I made the first deliberate decision I had ever made about my working life. The prospect of teaching black students, of being part of the movement for black self-determination was irresistible. I realize something else as I am writing this. In 1967 I was in a small prayer group, a disparate group of nuns, priests, lay people—black and white, married and single— all disenchanted with the old Catholic church and trying to find a way to deepen our faith life. We chose the first Beatitude for reflection ("Blessed are the poor in spirit, for theirs is the kingdom of heaven"), and for a year we wrestled with what it meant to be "poor in spirit." For each of us it meant something surprisingly different from what we had expected when we started. For one couple it meant moving from the suburbs into the city. For one of the priests it meant leaving an affluent white parish to work in an inner-city black one. For me it meant becoming a student again and trying to live on $2,400 a year. For the first time I did not try to avoid the reality of work but consciously engaged in directing my own working life.

This is not simply my personal story. Ask any woman my age (fifty-two) and you will hear a similar story about the inability to make career choices, about indecision, passivity, fear of commitment. It is a story quite familiar to most women of my generation and to black people of every generation who discover that the ostensible privilege of being able to make choices about their work is undermined and inhibited by both internal and external forces. Ambition and independent work for women, especially when that work is in-tellectual activity, is obstructed and discouraged in countless ways. In 1881, when Anna Julia Cooper, an ex-slave and one of the first black women to graduate from Oberlin College, tried to prepare herself for college by enroll-ing in a Greek class, she was confronted with a bias that thwarted her entire academic career. Men were given preferential treatment because they were candidates for the ministry, and women were considered interlopers, their ambitions clearly secondary to the needs of male students:

> A boy, however meager his equipment and shallow his pretentions, had only to declare a floating intention to study theology and he could get all the support, en-couragement, and stimulus he needed, be absolved from work and invested be-forehand with all the dignity of his far away office. While a self-supporting girl had to struggle on by teaching in the summer and working after school hours to keep up with her board bills and actually to fight her way against positive discourage-ment to the higher education. (p. 77)

Ninety years later in an address to women educators, Adrienne Rich echoes Anna Cooper's words that the world of the university (as well as the world outside of it) denies women the resources they need to become self-defined, self-determining, self-confident workers:

> The content of education itself validates men even as it invalidates women. Its very message is that men have been the shapers and thinkers of the world and that this is only natural. The bias of higher education is white and male, racist and sexist; and this bias is expressed in both subtle and blatant ways.

In the university classrooms where I had served my graduate apprentice-ship, I had been taught almost entirely by white males (Joyce Carol Oates was the only woman professor I had at the University of Detroit) in institutions administered entirely by men. I was expected to practice in institutions which were white and male. One has to be reminded that in the 1960s, invisibility was not just a metaphor: in 1961 the University of Detroit, whose faculty and student body were about 98 percent white, refused to allow a chapter of the N.A.A.C.P. on campus on the grounds that black students were merely trying to stir up trouble where there was none. The literature I taught reflected the experiences of whites and males and totally denied mine. I could not commit myself to my work because in the world I was expected to negotiate, my face did not exist.

But my talk today is not about failure, nor is it about exclusion, nor about being faceless. Fortunately for me and for all of us here, the struggles for black equality and the equality of women are being waged in our lifetimes, and these two struggles have radically redefined our vision of human experience and quite literally transformed our lives. In 1970 I joined the newly formed Black Studies Department of the University of Detroit, and I informed my thesis advisors that I would continue in the doctoral program only if I were allowed to write my dissertation on black writers. By 1972, aware that African-American literature had its own exclusions, I began collecting the fiction of black women writers for an anthology, *Black-Eyed Susans*, that was published in 1975. Imagine this: I had been in school almost twenty-six years before I was able to read a text written by a black woman. Suddenly the names proliferated: Harriet Jacobs, Maria Stewart, Ida B. Wells, Charlotte Forten, Sherley Anne Williams, Zora Hurston, Paule Marshall, Alice Walker, Frances Harper, Toni Morrison, Octavia Butler, Alice Childress. I cannot recall the exact moment or the specific writer that introduced me to the constellation of black women writers in whose orbit I would live for the ten years (and probably for the rest of my life). I do know that I felt an immediate sense of community and continuity and joy in that discovery, as though I had found my ancestry, my future, and my own voice. And I do know that my commitment to my work began when I joined this circle of sisters.

And what messages did I find in these writings? Let me tell you about two of the most important ones. The voice of black women in their writings—as far back as slavery—is unequivocally and without the least bit of ambivalence or uncertainty a feminist voice, though of course they didn't use that term. Black women of the nineteenth century fought for the abolition of slavery and racism; they demanded the right to vote for women and black people; the right to speak in public, equal pay for equal work, egalitarian relationships between men and women and the right to be ordained. (Oh yes, they lifted that stone too. In 1819 Jarena Lee interrupted a sermon when the preacher seemed to falter, rose, and began to preach extemporaneously and was thereafter accepted as a preacher in the African Methodist Episcopal Church.) They preached a gospel of emancipation in all the circumstances of women's lives. When Sojourner Truth, born a slave in New York in 1790, was eighty years old, she continued to press for women's rights with a voice that was uncompromising and authoritative:

> I have been forty years a slave and forty years free and would be here forty years more to have equal rights for all. . . . I have done a great deal of work, as much as a man, but did not get so much pay. . . . I used to work in the field and bind grain . . . but men doing no more got twice as much pay . . . we do as much, we eat as much, we want as much. . . . When we get our rights we shall not have to come to you for money, for then we shall have money enough in our own pockets. You have been having our rights for so long that you think, like a slave-holder, that you own us. I know that it is hard for one who has held the reins for so long, to give up, it cuts like a knife. It will feel all the better when it closes up again.
>
> (Loewenberg and Bogin, p. 239)

It never ceases to amaze me that a woman who was sold like a piece of furniture, who never learned to read or write, who supported herself as a field hand and a domestic, could speak so eloquently on behalf of women's equality. She was not alone. Black women of the nineteenth century—though their stories have been excluded from history and literature—were abolitionists, schoolteachers, missionaries, public speakers, evangelists, and writers. With little except personal courage and a belief in the righteousness of their cause, they devoted themselves to the work they called "uplifting the race." For me, that long line of feminists, stretching back to the beginning of the nineteenth century, does not begin with Susan B. Anthony and end with Gloria Steinem (although they can certainly claim a place in it). No, for me, that line begins with the most ordinary slave woman (if *any* slave was ever *ordinary*) who taught us with her pain what it means to be equal to men. It extends through Ida B. Wells, whose one-woman crusade against lynching cost her her job, her safety, years of professional work, and almost her life; to Fannie Lou Hamer, beaten in Mississippi for trying to get blacks to register to vote; to Jo Anne Robinson, who ran off thirty thousand leaflets one night in 1955 to initiate the Montgomery bus boycott and usher in the civil rights movement. The stories of these women have become the stories of my freedom. They who made a way out of no way have taught us—who are educated, privileged, and free—the meaning of commitment.

The second message in black women's writings is that we cannot be committed simply to ourselves. The feminist voice in this literature does not call us to rise up the corporate ladder or the literary ladder or the academic ladder. In fact it calls us to resist these questionable myths of levitation.* It calls us to community; in particular it calls us to identify with the poor, the exploited, the powerless.

I want to take you back to my first year of college, to 1958, when I first boarded the number forty-five bus to go to a Cleveland suburb to school, a suburb not at all unlike Wellesley or Weston, set amid rolling hills, lush landscapes, and upscale shopping malls. From 1958 to 1962 I rode that bus every weekday with black women who worked as domestics for white people in those suburbs. In those four years I do not think I ever really saw those women. Their faces were not in the literature I was reading, nor in the history books, nor in my art and music classes. I didn't see their faces until I encountered them in the literature of black women, and there I saw them not as marginal, not even simply as oppressed though they certainly were. In the literature of black women writers, they were central—main characters struggling to articulate their dreams, their anger, their joy, their hopes for their children, even at times their hopelessness. The West Indian mother Silla in Paule Marshall's 1959 novel *Brown Girl, Brownstones* is a domestic worker, and, much like the women I rode to school with, is tired and despondent after a day of hard, poorly paid work. As she talks to her friends around her kitchen ta-

*A term coined by my colleague at the University of Massachusetts, Boston, Linda Dittmar.

ble, she reminds them about the despair that accompanies such poverty. But even as she expresses that hopelessness, Silla's is a voice of resistance and self-conscious political critique:

> . . . you know what it is to work hard and still never make a head-way? That's Bimshire. One crop. People having to work for next to nothing. The white people treating we like slaves still and we taking it. The rum shop and the church join together to keep we pacify and in ignorance. . . . It's a terrible thing to know that you gon be poor all yuh life, no matter how hard you work. You does stop trying after a time. People does see you and so call you lazy. But it ain laziness. It just that you does give up. You does kind of die inside. (p. 70)

I find that same sense of resistance and critique in the voice of the narrator Claudia in Toni Morrison's *The Bluest Eye*. Near the end of the story when the community is united in outrage and shame over the incestuous pregnancy of a poor black girl, Claudia counters the black community's shame by imagining the beauty of the unborn black baby:

> I thought about the baby that everybody wanted dead, and saw it very clearly. It was in a dark, wet place, its head covered with great O's of wool, the black face holding, like nickels, two clean black eyes, the flared nose, kissing-thick lips, and the living, breathing silk of black skin. No synthetic yellow bangs suspended over marble-blue eyes, no pinched nose and bowline mouth. More strongly than my fondness for Pecola. I felt a need for someone to want the black baby to live—just to counteract the universal love of white baby dolls . . . (p. 148)

In this literature we hear the voices of those who are unheard in this culture; we see the faces of those this society has made faceless; it makes visible those who have been rendered invisible. It is a transforming literature because it reconstructs the experiences of black people, of women especially, in complex and powerful ways. Because we are women and because we are black, we have a vital connection with those who are the least powerful in this society. As Lerone Bennett said once, "In a world that oppresses black people, it is an honor and a privilege to be black." To be "poor in spirit" allows us to recognize that privilege and requires us to be in constant opposition to those aspects of our culture that are racist and sexist or homophobic or which seek in any way to dominate and oppress. It means we listen for the silences, we look for who is absent, we try to name the nameless, to see the faces of those made faceless. It is the only way we shall ever be able to hear our own voices, make our own presence felt, name ourselves, and see our own true, beautiful faces.

Works Cited

Cooper, Anna Julia. *A Voice from the South* (1892). New York: Negro Universities Press, 1969.

Loewenberg, Bert James, and Ruth Bogin, eds. *Black Women in Nineteenth-Century American Life*. University Park: Pennsylvania State University Press, 1976.

Marshall, Paule. *Brown Girl, Brownstones*. Old Westbury: Feminist Press, 1981.

Morrison, Toni. *The Bluest Eye*. New York: Pocket Books, 1970.

Sisters

Anna-Marie McCurdy

save us
oh sisters!
mothers, sistahs
warrior queens
sainted soldiers
save us
the slaughter
the execution
the madness
the extinction
the suffering
of our progeny.
daughters of promise
beloved sisters
save us.
save us!

Nature/loved black woman/child

Leona Nicholas Welch

last night the moon and I
shared secrets of soft black beauty rays
on my face . . . the power of ebony
womanhood   under an ebony sky
GOD MADE ME BLACK WOMAN
dawn dripped downy dew
kisses on rich ruby/brown lips
surge of love/strength rage
quietly in my veins
I am woman draped in tones of
brown morning/mist beauty
GOD MADE ME BLACK BEAUTY
the sun dances a brilliant bugaloo
against soft bristled/edge strands
of bushy natural hair
    quiet vanity smiles play in my soul
    and in my eyes
GOD THE WOMAN OF ME!
cool winds whistle flirtations in
my ear and finger/kiss my hair and
the woman in me sings . . .
"SAY IT LOUD" black woman proud
"BLACK PEARL PRECIOUS LITTLE GIRL"
LOOK AT ME WORLD!!!!!
"people get ready" . . .
dew kissed sun danced

wind sung moon courted nature/loved child
"black pearl   precious . . ."
by God   the black woman in me is ALIVE
IS ALIVE   IS ALIVE   IS ALIVE!!!
BLACK PEARL is
       ALIVE!

Faithful Resistance Risking It All: From Expedience to Radical Obedience

Jacquelyn Grant

Esther 4:13–16

More than anyone, Esther exemplifies what it means to move from concern for pure expedience to radical obedience.

The story is very familiar to all of us. Through the strategizing of Mordecai, her cousin and adoptive father, Esther found herself in the position of queen. The book begins with the dethronement of Queen Vashti for stepping out of her place—the prescribed place for women, and especially the king's wife. It goes on to reveal the king's search for a replacement—a new wife. Following Mordecai's instructions, Esther landed the coveted position of queen, wife of a king. When suddenly Haman's plan to destroy the Jews was made known, Mordecai proceeded to instruct Esther, by messenger, of her responsibility as a Jew.

The focus here is not on Mordecai's motives. Perhaps he was just protecting his own individual interests. Or perhaps it could be argued that he was simply an actor in God's providential plan to provide a savior of the Jews for such a time as that. I'd like to focus on Esther's obedience; we'll call it faithful resistance. Esther had two opportunities for obedience. The first was in Mordecai's initial plan to conceal her heritage and for her to "candidate" for the position of queen. It seems that Esther accepted this challenge with little or no resistance.

The second plan was more risky. Esther at this point was being called upon to stand up for the oppressed Jews. This identification as a Jew and the fact that she was a woman made it doubly risky. After fasting and praying, Esther approached the king and saved her people from destruction. In spite of the positive result, it is clear that obedience in the second instance was a struggle: it required wrestling with what was at stake, primarily her life and personal security. Obedience here was not ordinary; it was faithful resistance and radical obedience.

This story affords us the opportunity to reflect upon the relationship between the personal and the political, the public and the private, the individual and the community. It enables us to focus upon the tensions between expedience and obedience, which can plague our decision-making process. In the Esther story, the tensions most concretely manifest themselves in the second decision of Esther's second opportunity for obedience. Esther had to reveal her identity, and that could cost her life.

Decision one (to conceal her identity in order to succeed) was a personal decision, with only personal glorification and advancement as the issue. Perhaps there was minimal tension here—that which may come from the concealment of one's identity—resulting primarily from the fear of being discovered. In the black experience in America, a comparable phenomenon has been known as "passing." For the most part this involved light-skinned black people who passed for the sake of personal gains, enjoying the benefits of white life in America.

Esther's second decision (to reveal her identity) was one that had a direct impact on the whole Jewish community. In the black community, many more could have passed than did, yet they saw their struggle as tied up with the struggle of black people. The movement of a minority of blacks to the status of middle-class should not cause us to forget that the masses of blacks are not there. They are still disproportionately poor, providing a pool of people from which comes a significant part of the increasingly permanent underclass.

It was not until Esther realized her *connectedness* that she was able to come to the point of declaring, "I shall obey the will of the higher authority. I shall approach the king on behalf of my people, and if I perish, I perish."

Only when Esther had succeeded in extricating herself from personal concerns was she free to affirm her real connectedness with her people and her real purpose in life. Mordecai had been right about her inability to escape, as well as about her being put in her position for just such a time and purpose as this.

The connectedness of life at various levels is demonstrated in this story. Here we see the interlinkages of racism and sexism. Esther could escape the harsh realities of anti-Semitism only for a season, as Mordecai said. And even though she was a queen, she was still a woman, and in jeopardy on occasion. She and her predecessor, Vashti, were under absolute male domination.

The connectedness of people is the only hope of the oppressed. Western culture's individualism must yield to the profound African understanding that says, "I am because we are." We are defined by our community, and if our community is negated, so are we. Thus Fannie Lou Hamer could say to the first African-American congressman from Mississippi since Reconstruction, "We marched on the white folks to make them do right. . . . If you don't do right, we're going to march on you, too." She was saying to him that he is because we are, because the community struggled and fought for rights denied us as a people for centuries.

African-American womanist scholars have begun to emphasize this type of interconnectedness. Perceiving the interstructuring of racism, classism, and sexism, they have insisted that the "we-ness" informs the "I-ness," even though the "I-ness" is our concrete starting place for all theological analysis. Our one concrete starting place locates us in the whole of reality. From there we recognize that the struggle for liberation is a global struggle. The oppression of blacks in the United States is not unrelated to the oppression of blacks in South Africa and the oppression of the indigenous peoples of Latin America or Australia.

We are as connected together as the links in a chain, which is broken when only one link is broken. Our resistance must be done in unity, but Esther reminds us that it must also be done in faith. She could not know the outcome of her risk taking, but she knew that she must act. As we say, she did not know what the future held, but she did know who held the future. On this basis her obedient resistance could escalate to a radical level. It is summed up in the defiant and faithful declaration, "If I perish, I perish."

Risking it all in faithful resistance to the oppressive and debilitating structures may mean losing a privileged position. For Esther it could have meant the loss of her place as queen in the royal court, or even being booted out altogether. She could have been sentenced to death. But, as Martin Luther King, Jr., used to say, "If you haven't found anything worth dying for, life isn't worth living."

When Esther understood her connectedness, she understood what had to be done. When we understand how our destiny is tied up with that of black people in South Africa, then we will know what we must do. When we understand that our destiny is tied up with that of a homeless mother and children in southwest Atlanta, we'll know what we must do. When we sense our links with Native Americans on reservations, and poor people in Appalachia, and migrant workers across the southern United States, we'll know what we must do.

This risking it all will also mean that men ministers will stand with women in ministry even when they are threatened with expulsion from the ministerial alliance, and with ostracism from the "brethren."

Risking it all will mean that women will have the audacity to preach when some who presume to know the mind of God declare that they can't. These faithful women will step out of the roles prescribed by a patriarchal society, under which the masses of women are suffering. Their faithful resistance does not mean that they will not lose anything. Indeed, Esther could have lost her all, but in fact she won.

When you resist faithfully, when you risk it all, I can't guarantee that you won't lose anything. All I can say is that I serve one who gave up his very life and went to the cross for all humanity. And I stand in a tradition of black women who have declared that if Jesus goes with them, they'll go anywhere.

Their record inspires. Harriet Tubman said she would go, and she conducted hundreds to freedom by the Underground Railroad. Sojourner Truth spoke out fearlessly against racism and sexism. Jarena Lee preached with power even when the church said she could not. Maria Stewart taught and made public addresses when "colored" or "Negro" women were not supposed to. Mary McLeod Bethune founded a school on one dollar and fifty cents and faith. Fannie Lou Hamer challenged a nation sick with sin, from her place among poor women in the state of Mississippi. All these and many, many more took the risks.

But my faith tells me that if we, like Esther, remain faithful to the struggle, we may lose many things, but there is promise of gain.

We'll lose despair, but we have the promise of hope.

We'll lose hatred, but there is the promise of love.

We'll lose ignorance, but we'll gain human insight.
We'll lose separation, but we have the promise of unity.
We'll lose fear, but we'll have the promise of courage.
We may even lose earthly life, but we have the promise of life eternal.

Faithful resistance does not take away the risks, but it keeps us headed for the promise.

We've come this far by faith
Leaning on the Lord,
Trusting in the Lord's holy Word
The Lord's never failed us yet.

On Going Home

Olaive Burrowes Jones

This morning at the beach looking east across the Atlantic and back to Africa, I write about Egypt, about being changed. About being connected consciously with my hundred-thousand-year-old self. About having stepped into my ancestors' sandals and walked forward in them, about finding home.

I sat here on this beach last year thinking I was me. But now this September sitting here I am a hundred times more me. There was Olive, Olaive who had gained fifty-two years and seen and done whatever, and now there is me—me who is old, ancient, timeless, existent and nonexistent too. I am forever more of me now. There is my essence which is flowing from the source into my veins and cells and energies. I am charged with the presence of the GODS who were me even as I am this me now, this newly charged, awakened me. Alive and unafraid.

So in what ways am I different? Perspective is one way I've changed. I was like the blind woman describing the side of an elephant by feeling a little bit of his dermis under her fingers. I couldn't get a fair gestalt. I don't say I have one even now—but suddenly after fifty-two years of life and having spent just a few days in Egypt I am aware that my perspective has expanded from being cramped into 500 years of American history—as though I suddenly sprang to life here in the new world—to at least 100,000 years of ongoing continuous life and accomplishment, all of which is alive and active in my genetic repertoire. This is a real and palpable difference I feel with every breath I take. I feel it in my spine, in my shoulders, in my full height. I feel the presence of that history at my back protecting me, guiding me. There is a phalanx of Gods and Goddesses, of scribes and musicians and physicians and astronomers and queens and kings and artisans and warriors and priests and priestesses and lionesses and phoenixes and pharaohs. All of these are clearly behind me. I feel their presence. Their power, their essence flows into me unchecked.

Growing up Olaive Burrowes, Dr. Burrowes' older daughter in Youngs-town, I was proud. I was smart and played the piano and my family was important. When I was eight, one day I came home from school to look in the mirror to see if I could understand what they were talking about in school. I saw me there as usual. But for the first time I noticed the skin as significant. I saw the brown skin I had seen every day before, but now I was aware that brown skin was relevant. Relevant to what they'd said in school. It meant I was Negro, colored not white. Well, that was OK. Daddy had the same skin, and Mommy did too and so did Muzzy and Big Dad and Aunt Peg and Aunt Lilly and Uncle Jack. All different shades from quite white to my own red brown. And they were fine so what was the problem? It didn't feel like anything was wrong being this brown-skinned person. But one friend at school was a white girl, and for some reason this distinction between a white skin and a brown skin was relevant. Maybe it was even a problem for somebody?

That moment in the mirror I said to myself, OK—so that's what it will be this time. This brown skin, being a Negro will be relevant in this life. I remember projecting out into some imagined future recognizing that that color part would not change—would be permanently with me this time around. (It seems I've never questioned that my soul has many lifetimes.)

For a while throughout the 1950s being a Negro was OK because I was Olaive Burrowes, and I was smart and my father was a doctor and I was different and could play the piano. I was different. It was OK because I was not like the rest. I was "acceptable" and they elected me president of everything. But I was still colored and had to straighten my hair and if it rained all that straightening and curling and fixing was undone. And my boyfriend couldn't be white. Not that I was in love with a white boy. But even if I had been, he just simply couldn't be white. The boy couldn't get to it and neither could I.

As an undergraduate at Oberlin College, I majored in English literature because I loved learning, learning about music, art, literature, about everything. There was and really still is nothing about which I am not curious. The classics, mythology, Italian Renaissance painters, Albrecht Durer, Brueghel, the rococo French, the German romantics, the great English storytellers—all of it I loved and took great delight in relishing and experiencing and knowing as my own.

The years passed and we came to 1962 and sit-ins in Houston, Texas. Malcolm X saying black is not only beautiful but that I was beautiful and I was fine just as I was. And I could wear an Afro and be really black whatever that meant—I was just fine. And then there was Texas Southern University and black professors teaching me history which was the first time ever my story, our story, came from a black source, and teaching me literature and reading James Baldwin and Richard Wright and Ralph Ellison and Langston Hughes and about the Harlem Renaissance. And there was being beatnik in New York and all that Jack Kerouac stuff.

The yoke of being Negro was broken. But graduating into black woman-hood, I still felt confined to a precarious niche described, proscribed not by me.

I played the piano. I was very good. When I auditioned for the piano department at the New England Conservatory of Music, the chairman, Russell Sherman, asked me, after I'd finished playing Mozart and Beethoven, "What do you think of James Baldwin?" The irrelevance of his question for me at that instant struck me dumb. You see, I still didn't realize that being black meant the music I loved could not belong to me. That was what they took from me at the N.E.C.—Russell Sherman and Gunther Schuler (would-be thief of jazz) and all the keepers of the gate of Western culture. They said, "But you are black, you do not belong here, you cannot come here and live. This place, these ideas do not belong to you—you are black."

And so I discovered my irrelevance as a black woman pianist in the closed society of European classical music. My black brothers took it away from me too. My S.N.C.C. brothers and my Black Panther brothers and sisters said that if I loved those things and felt a part of those things I could not be black—I was not black enough. So they could define how to be black and what was required to be black enough. And they would define what was OK to like and love and look like and say and do if one would be BLACK.

Of course music is actually not political. And I could love John Coltrane and Miles Davis and Coleman Hawkins and Dizzie Gillespie and McCoy Tyner, but even there I couldn't be me really. Because the black men own this domain. And while it's OK to play jazz and talk about it and support the music, and support the musicians—the men decide among themselves what's what and who's who. So, Olaive, it's OK to watch and maybe even jump in now and then, but you can't really be a "player"—you're not a man!

And so for 52 years I maneuvered adroitly in this proscribed world loving what I loved but feeling inauthentic as a black, as a person who didn't have anything which I could really claim.

So how did being in Egypt change any of that—all of that? It changed who I am. Who I thought I was. Who I always have been. The brittle edges, the hard edges, the soft edges, the subtle edges, the colorless edges all broke away. Melt down. No edges—no nappy edges, no straight edges, no edges at all. I'm in all of the spaces. All the spaces of being WOMAN, being the first woman or even being man, being the first man too, all of them, all the spaces are filled for 100,000 years by parts of me that have lived and loved and written and played music and healed myself and others and have worshipped and suffered and destroyed and glorified in the thousand lifetimes in between then and now. And I'm connected with it all. I feel it all as I stand 1000 feet tall.

I crawl deep into the pyramid at Giza feeling the vibration of the chamber just as Mother's beating heart feels inside the womb. It takes me back into my SELF—my archetypal self. That complete SELF which *was* before limitations of earthly, bodily life set up the boundaries real and imagined. I feel the rush of birthing myself once again. As I crawl through the cramped, airless passageway that leads to the opening up ahead, the king's chamber, I reactivate my birth process, but this time I am conscious, and I am also not sad this time as I was when I entered this life in 1940. Because now I am going from my tiny limited self consciously into my expanded archetypal SELF. And it is REAL. I am locomoting my way through this birth canal feeling the pull of my ancestors. I am vibrating to their signals to come in and be recognized, be annointed, to be honored and held in their presence. I am *re*-membering myself. I am expanding into my essence. I am re-be-coming. That orphaned waif, the prodigal daughter, the loneliest woman has returned to her home and is utterly welcomed and loved and honored and reestablished in totality.

My joy is palpable, is rich, uncontained. I want only to be there acknowledging them, meeting them again—shouting and dancing my joy. Even as this jubilant celebration goes on internally and I want to be ever so still externally to experience it—the pesky Arab flies are biting for baksheesh, cluttering my field.

Reflecting now on the wealth of my reclaimed inheritance—my stature grows tall, my back is strong and protected, my feet are firmly planted in this my earth. Perhaps most important, I have reclaimed my history, my archetypes—my kings and queens and gods and goddesses, my priests and priestesses, my wise men and powerful women warriors, my myths, and principles and legends. I am reconnected with my origins. That which had been stolen and then denied is reclaimed.

They said your ancestors are slaves and before that were primitive savages. You are barely a few generations removed from the apes. You are reasonably intelligent however and may learn of *our*/not your Greek cultural ancestry and adjust yourself according to *our*/not your cultural heritage. If you will do that we will allow you to be among us, and if you can act like us we will tolerate your impoverished presence near us—not among us.

At first I didn't know it was theirs and not mine too. I thought correctly that it belonged to all of us. But then somewhere about eight, there came that day I crashed into 1948 consciousness, the day I looked in the mirror and saw the self I was to be in this life and realized something was grossly wrong here. Suddenly I was on the outside, beyond the closed gate. The gate to the archetypes was closed and they told me I didn't have any of my own. That never ever felt right. And so I lived amputated, mutilated, dismembered from my whole SELF for forty-four years. Struggling to become, to overcome the shame of being nobody. Orphaned, bastard of primitive savages not far removed from apes. Oh sure, I had family, more than 200 years of accountable family, and love, and education and community and standing and place. But all—all of that wonderful gift which has made my life good and tolerable—was as nothing compared to the riches stolen and denied. They had stolen the ground, the clay, the field from which, against which my SELF had been constructed. I was as a leaf floating aimlessly in the wind, carried far from the tree. It was as though I wandered the earth homeless, clutching my possessions in a tiny knapsack while my entire family fortune had been stolen, denied, appropriated, and dispersed. Who was I? I was as nothing. Yet I knew that was not so. I felt deeply wronged, adrift, dazed, wandering vaguely in search of what was missing but I didn't know what it was until my foot touched the African continent and immediately I began to feel the truth rising up through my bones, charging my veins and arteries with vitality, with life itself.

Moment by momentous moment I awakened to my essence—to the selves awaiting my presence, my re-cognition, my re-knowing. It was all there. The origins of the Judeo-Christian myths which still structure our culture here in America. The myths, before the myths which set the piscean Christianity in motion were lived, were told, were created thousands of years before by MY ANCESTORS, by my own people. It is true that myth is sometimes more important than life—myth is greater than life—it gives life context. I had no real context—I was barely peripheral until I set foot on the African continent. There were the myths, the actors, and the principles, and the knowledge, the written observation of natural law—the Metu Neter, that which had first been observed, accorded and understood by my own people. Those whose genetic coding lives in my own cells. Those at whose feet the pagan Greeks went to study culture, those who observed and understood the universal laws of time, of geometry, of astronomy, of physics, of nature, of mysteries of life itself—those are MY people. I am of them. They are my family. I have found my ancestors, my archetypes, my home. I have place. I have reclaimed, re-membered myself.

Call

Audre Lorde

Holy ghost woman
stolen out of your name
Rainbow Serpent
whose faces have been forgotten
Mother loosen my tongue or adorn me
with a lighter burden
Aido Hwedo is coming.

On worn kitchen stools and tables
we are piercing our weapons together
scraps of different histories
do not let us shatter
any altar
she who scrubs the capitol toilets, listening
is our sister's youngest daughter
gnarled Harriet's anointed
you have not been without honor
even the young guerilla has chosen
yells as she fires into the thicket
Aido Hwedo is coming.

I have written your names on my cheekbone
dreamed your eyes   flesh my epiphany
most ancient goddesses   hear me
enter
I have not forgotten your worship
nor my sisters
nor the sons of my daughters
my children watch for your print

Aido Hwedo: The Rainbow Serpent; also a representation of all ancient divinities who must be worshipped but whose names and faces have been lost in time.

in their labors
and they say Aido Hwedo is coming.

I am a Black woman   turning
mouthing your name as a password
through seductions   self-slaughter
and I believe in the holy ghost
mother
in your flames beyond our vision
blown light through the fingers of women
enduring   warring
sometimes outside your name
we do not choose all our rituals
Thandi Modise   winged girl of Soweto
brought fire back home in the snout of a mortar
and passes the word from her prison cell whispering
Aido Hwedo is coming.

Rainbow Serpent who must not go
unspoken
I have offered up the safety of separations
sung the spirals of power
and what fills the spaces
before power unfolds or flounders
in desirable nonessentials
I am a Black woman   stripped down
and praying
my whole life has been an altar
worth its ending
and I say Aido Hwedo is coming.

I may be a weed in the garden
of women I have loved
who are still
trapped in their season

but even they shriek
as they rip burning gold from their skins
Aido Hwedo is coming.

We are learning by heart
what has never been taught
you are my given   fire-tongued
Oya   Seboulisa   Mawu   Afrekete
and now we are mourning our sisters
lost to the false hush of sorrow
to hardness and hatchets and childbirth
and we are shouting

Rosa Parks and Fannie Lou Hamer
Assata Shakur and Yaa Asantewa
my mother and Winnie Mandela are singing
in my throat
the holy ghosts' linguist
one iron silence broken
Aido Hwedo is calling
calling
your daughters are named
and conceiving
Mother   loosen my tongue
or adorn me
with a lighter burden
Aido Hwedo is coming.

Aido Hwedo is coming.

Aido Hwedo is coming.

P A 4 R T

Praying at Different Altars,

Singing Different Songs:

African-American Women Across

Denominations and Faiths

I am Nature, the universal Mother, mistress of all the elements, primordial
child of time, sovereign of all things, spiritual, queen of the dead, queen
also of the immortals, the single manifestation of all gods and goddesses
that are. My nod governs the shining heights of Heaven, the
wholesome sea-breezes, the lamentable silences of the world below.
—"PRAYER OF ISIS," from *Black Women in Antiquity*

I took myself to prayer and in every lonely place I found an altar.
—OLD ELIZABETH

I have been a Baptist, an atheist and a Muslim. I am now a Unitarian-
Universalist. This is an eclectic faith which encourages us to search for truth
and inspiration from any source that resonates spirituality. There is no
prescription for the way we worship or how we dress when we worship.
In blue jeans and in shorts if we desire. All that is asked of us is that
our prayers and our deeds be for social justice.
—QIYAMAH RAHMAN, 1994

This is the literal truth.
God can't be resisted or stopped, but can be shaped and focused. This means
God is not to be prayed to. Prayers only help the person doing the praying,
and then, only if they strengthen and focus that person's resolve. If they're
used that way, they can help us in our only real relationship with God. They
help us to shape God and to accept and work with the shapes that God
imposes on us. God is power, and in the end, God prevails.
But we can rig the game in our own favor if we understand that god
exists to be shaped, and will be shaped, with or without our
forethought, with or without our intent.
That's what I know.
—OCTAVIA BUTLER, from *The Parable of the Sower*

Descendant of slave and slave owner, I was empowered to minister the
sacrament of One in whom there is no north or south, no black or white,
no male or female—only the Spirit of love and reconciliation
drawing us all toward the goal of human wholeness.
—PAULI MURRAY, on her ordination as the first African-American
woman Episcopal priest, from *Song in a Weary Throat*

Walking in Eight Directions
on One Path

Thulani Davis

I consider my road to Buddhism the result of asking questions and getting answers full of laughter. Just before I married my husband, Joseph, he told me he wanted to have a Buddhist wedding. When I asked him what happened at a Buddhist wedding he said, "A lot of talking." I asked if there were vows involved, and he laughed and said, "A Buddhist only makes vows to herself." I said, fine, I could deal with that. Years later when, after being ordained, I called my Buddhist teacher and asked him how to conduct a Buddhist wedding, he laughed and said, "Well, you have to make it up."

He went on to explain to me that I must find the best way to give Buddhism the language of my experience, the language it needs to be spoken by my students. My *dharma* name connects me to Buddha's teaching through the practice of writing. This is my challenge, my job, my path within The Way. I don't ask as many questions now because the little that I know of Buddhism is that it is not a set of rites, though there are rites. It is a process—we call it "practice." It is a living, on-going, in-the-moment examination of self, of the experience of being. All questions are thrown back to the questioner. All questions and all answers are within our practice of being.

My experience with Buddhist teachers, who teach "one mind to one mind," through direct contact, one person at a time—who teach sometimes merely by being in the room with a student—has helped me to realize that "freedom" is impossible without freeing the mind of self-delusional garbage. We have to learn to check, side-step, or let go of the ego that puts one's self at the center of all universes, and let go of the demons of expectation—hopes that chain us down rather than move us forward. As a black woman I had considered having expectations a right I had not quite gained; as a Buddhist I realize they are the source of disappointment, the crutch that kept me from acting, from being responsible for self.

I have found myself challenged and freed in the way that I believe Jesus has made many feel challenged rather than merely consoled. I grew up in a world where Jesus was viewed as a balm, a consolation for suffering. Martin Luther King made me realize He offered challenge. The people of Albany, Georgia, who sang as they were packed into paddy wagons and trucks of every shape and size to fill the local jails, taught me Jesus meant challenge, self-examination, compassion. But I had lost the sound of that word over the years, the sight of that compassion. A series of unfathomable accidents, foolish questions, tough-guy martial arts teachers with crystalline unfettered minds, and mindful feasts with curious, happy (and always hungry) Buddhist priests brought me back to compassion, some shred of humility, a "faith" in life's lifeness and a "laying on of hands" in a centuries-old temple in Kyoto, Japan.

Practicing allows me to extend into my daily life the amazement and selflessness, the connection to life and beings that I have experienced in a few marvelous moments caught up in a mass of people with one joyful singing mind, or alone with one person to whom I'd bonded beyond speech, but most often when alone, writing. We are all enlightened in those moments when utterly unaware of "self," grasping for a mental description we come up with nothing and simply "let go," only breathing, and let the universe move through us. Bernice Reagon talks about it when she speaks of the power of group singing. I never fail to know it when on my knees chanting. It is the moment modern life mitigates against. The one we don't have time for. The moment when we first looked out a window and studied the stars, a moment often lost for a lifetime until a plane drops us off in a desert in Africa, or on a beach in the islands, or in Grandma's backyard in Tucson after a funeral or reunion. Sometime when we are "allowed" to be open, back in touch, like a child. Children have these moments every day; infants, every moment. They are not constrained from life by "knowing reality," they simply "know."

Practicing Buddhism, whether in sitting meditation, or by allowing myself to enjoy the wonder of life crossing the street in Brooklyn, two feet deep in snow, a chiseling wind moving with me in the street, the front door lock quite frozen, encourages moments of wonder, even as I continue to know, unlike the infant, the harshness around me. Practicing Buddhism is total commitment to right now. Not getting it together tomorrow. Being. Together. Now.

Whenever people ask me what is the how of the The Way I usually share the Eightfold Path.

1. *Right Views.* To keep ourselves free from prejudice, delusion, not being bound to any systems of thought, even Buddhist ones as absolute, but to use them as guides.

2. *Right Thoughts.* To turn from hypocrisy, negative attitudes, narrow-mindedness. Learning to realize change in the mind, to be open to others' views, to find truth through life.

3. *Right Conduct.* To see that our deeds are peaceful, benevolent, compassionate.

4. *Right Speech.* To refrain from pointless or harmful talk. To refrain from uttering words to cause division and hatred. To use words to resolve conflict. To refrain from saying anything untrue out of self-interest. Still, having the courage to speak out about injustice.

5. *Right Work.* To earn our living in a way that does not bring harmful consequences to humans and nature. To seek employment to which we can give our complete enthusiasm.

6. *Right Effort.* To direct our efforts continually to the overcoming of ignorance and the practice of compassion. Remain awake to the suffering in the world. Find whatever means to protect life.

7. *Right Mindfulness.* Stay awake, stay in the moment. Not to lose ourselves in anger, hatred, forgetfulness, drugs, escape. Mindfulness is a calm state of awareness from which we can act.

8. *Right Meditation.* To use the teachings of the Buddha and any and all meditation techniques to achieve mindfulness throughout daily life.

Spirituality, Sexuality, and Creativity: A Conversation with Margaret Walker-Alexander

Dilla Buckner

Dilla Buckner   As you know, spirituality is so central to scholarship on women's culture and women's literature that we can't discuss liberation or empowerment for women without also discussing women's spirituality. What does the word mean to you? How do you define it?

Margaret Walker-Alexander   Spirituality is a consciousness of God's presence within us. A consciousness that God is right here. Now. I remember my father telling me that if God isn't in you, then God isn't anywhere. I grew up believing that God is a part of me and I am a part of God. So spirituality for me means being centered in a consciousness of divinity within all the time.

Buckner   What we are finding in today's emphasis on women's spirituality is a new definition of God, or a rejection of God as he. How do you define God?

Walker   God is perfection. God is everything good. And God is everywhere in the Universe and, as I said, within me. Within all of us. For me, God is both female and male which is why I pray to Our Father-Mother God.

Buckner   Your religious background is the same as mine. We are both Baptists and your father was a Baptist minister, so I'm sure that you grew up hearing, as I did, the old saying, "Prayer changes things."

Walker   I grew up in a family that prayed daily and out loud. I don't always pray out loud, however. Sometimes I pray with pen and pencil and paper. I write out prayers. Other times I do a lot of mental praying. There's a very reflective side of me. It's been there since I was ten years of age. When I am working on a project I enter intense periods of meditation. I did that when I was working on *Jubilee*. I lie down and I reflect and I meditate for long periods

224

of time. Sometimes for days and weeks. And affirmations. I find that affirmations work for me. When I am having financial difficulty, I repeat the affirmation, "God is my source. God is my resource." If I am ill or if there is someone I can't get along with, I use affirmations and many of them come from Unity. I find that when I am angry, I can't do anything until I get the poison out of me, and I do that with affirmations. Many of them come from Unity. I have been reading *Daily Word* since I was seventeen. Affirmations work for me.

Buckner   Do you remember when you became spiritually aware?

Walker   I joined church when I was ten, but my spiritual awareness didn't come until I was seventeen. I remember wanting to know the presence of God. I remember the date; it was August of 1932. And I remember the Scripture of the sermon preached that day: "And sin shall have no dominion over you." I became very aware of the presence of God in me and because God was present in me, sin could have no dominion over me.

Buckner   Many women writing about spirituality say that it is not always experienced in an institutionalized church. In fact, they seem to imply that it can't be experienced in the church, in organized religion. That it is a very private and mystical experience.

Walker   Yes. I understand that. But I believe that spirituality is religious. I don't separate the two. I think once you have an experience which makes you aware of the presence of God within you, it doesn't matter whether you are Christian, Muslim, metaphysical, mystical . . . It doesn't matter. You are religious and spiritual, and I don't think you can ever turn your back on the meaning of the experience.

Buckner   Is that the case with you? Since your spiritual awakening at age seventeen, you have remained in the church? You've remained connected to that awareness?

Walker   No. I went through five years of bitterness and apostasy. I was disgusted with what I saw in the church and I simply wouldn't go. Didn't go to church. But I was brought to my knees by circumstances and I returned to the church. Let me add to something I said earlier about spirituality. I believe it is a strong force in women's lives, especially Black women's lives, and I believe spirituality and sexuality are the two strongest forces. Black women respond to these two forces more strongly than they do to anything else. I don't separate the two. Spirituality and sexuality. I don't separate the two.

Buckner Would you elaborate more on that, please?

Walker Well, I think women have a tendency to fight everything with these two forces. We don't think of sexuality when we talk about spirituality because of Freud's influence on our thinking. Freud limited sexuality entirely to the body and he believed that sexuality was the strongest force in the world. But sexuality isn't just about the body, or mainly about the body. It includes our spiritual selves, our spirituality.

Buckner Are you saying, then, that women are spiritual/sexual beings?

Walker Yes. I was reading an article the other day in which a young man said that he was interested in marrying a woman who was strongly influenced by spirituality. I knew at once that he was not separating spirituality from sexuality. He understood that the two go together. And that's the same with great literature and music and paintings. They are influenced as much by our spirituality as by our sexuality.

Buckner That in our creativity, we express who we are as spiritual/sexual beings. Is that what you are saying?

Walker Yes. Precisely. We create out of who we are, and we are both— not either/or, but *both*—spiritual and sexual. I recall some years ago doing a seminar on Richard Wright, and a student in the class asked what Wright's sexuality had to do with his writings. And I told him that if he had to ask that question, he didn't know very much about artists. About creativity. Sexuality is a strong force in creativity. It certainly works for me. It works *with* my spirituality, not apart from it.

Buckner Do you think Black women experience a unique spirituality?

Walker There is an earthiness to our spirituality and sexuality that comes from our African ancestry. The greatest art in Africa, particularly on the West Coast, was both sacred and secular, or spiritual and sexual. Isn't that true?

226

Buckner I quite agree with you. We can't, and shouldn't, always draw a line between the sacred and the secular. I certainly don't in my classes. The two are related. Most definitely.

Walker We see that in Black music. It is a rhythmic and organic art. It's about spirituality and sexuality. I like what a woman scholar said about Africans. She said they picked up the dust of Africa and carried it with them to the new world. They included it in their music. They believed their gods were in the dust, in the water, in the air, and everywhere. And to them, the gods were spirits. They were a spiritual people. Do you follow that?

Buckner Yes.

Walker They believed that they did not leave their gods in Africa, that they took them to the New World. And everything they did in the New World was controlled by what had been true in the Old World. They believed that dancing, singing, and drumming were all spiritual.

Buckner Are women inclined to be more spiritual than men?

Walker No, I don't think so. I think that in the New World we were told to be more inhibited and we became more inhibited. We lost some of the earthiness, the connection to nature that we had in Africa. The earthiness that we expressed in uninhibited movement and dance and song.

Buckner The earthiness that makes our spirituality unique?

Walker Yes. And we see it in our worship. In our rituals. I think there are certain religious groups that still share spiritual gifts. We see it in the dancing and the singing and the receiving of the Spirit. In an uninhibited way.

Buckner But you are not saying that we can experience spirituality only in church?

Walker Not at all. I experience spirituality mostly in a prayerful gathering of individuals or when I am alone with my thoughts and my meditations.

Buckner What would you like to say before we turn off the tape? I say turn off the tape because I know we will continue talking about spirituality.

Walker   That I am centered in a consciousness of divinity within all the time, and this is what spirituality means to me. God is a part of me and I am a part of God. That is my faith. My children will tell you that I believe I can make it with God. My faith is how I got ovah.

DreadPath/LockSpirit

Akasha (Gloria) Hull

Question: Why did I cut off (or, in Rastafarian parlance, "trim") a set of perfectly beautiful nine-year-old dreads only to commence locking again just one year later? The trimming actually began before that in October 1988, almost immediately after I had made a cross-country relocation and assumed a new job. I radically pruned my locks, but did not completely divest myself of them until 1989, shortly after my December 6th birthday. I suspect that the move and the mid-life birthday both contributed to a deeply felt sense of shedding the old and beginning anew. I was also extricating myself from a love relationship that was heavily associated with my hair: off with the hair, out with the lover! In general, this seems to have been a time to discard old, "locked-in" energy in order to make fresh starts. Just as clearly, though, I was loathe to give up—in one fell swoop—so many years of cultivated beauty and my elder lockswoman status. Yet, despite its fineness, this head of hair had reached—for me—a static state which was very different from the ever-changing dynamism which had helped attract me to dreadlocks in the first place. I have an even better understanding now of why people play around with various hairstyles "simply" for the sake of change.

After that one in-between year of no locks, I was eager to grow them again. I had spent those twelve months in total dissatisfaction with everything I did and did not do with my hair. The basic problem was that I could not make myself either comb it or cut it. Using the comb or pick was a laborious ordeal, and cutting it felt like a bloody amputation. So many years of not doing these things—fueled by the philosophies behind it—had thoroughly "ruined" me. Grooming my hair with my bare hands sufficed for quite a while, but when it grew beyond the shorter lengths, my black women friends wanted to know if I knew what I was doing with my hair, and one of them, Jamilah, volunteered to give me braids and a counseling session. This "neither fish nor fowl" state was obviously not working. With the well-earned relief

229

of someone who has given an experiment a dogged try, I let my understanding son barber me a soft Afro from which I could neatly begin my second dread in December 1990.

By this time, I knew that I would be gridding in new growth and power and a transformed sense of self. One indication was my determination to lock exactly as I believed it should be done. This meant following what "roots" people in the know had always counseled: to simply stop combing the hair and let it go. That easy, that simple. Just put away the paraphernalia and allow nature to take its course. No parting and twisting, no "glueing" and not washing, none of those make-it-happen, hairstyling, hair management instructions that currently pass as the correct information about how to have locks. If there is "kink" in the genes and the hair is chemical-free, it will (eventually) ravel itself together in some way(s). My first time, I had twisted a bit and had encouraged a pattern of small, symmetrical separations. This time, I would do nothing except keep the clumps divided into the aggregations they themselves made so that I would not end up with huge "kungas" on my head. This possible outcome was the only thing which was not okay with me, and this management the only manipulation which did not feel inconsistent with an extremely natural approach.

From my years of consciously absorbing dreads of all kinds (especially in Jamaica), I had really come to see that the healthiest, most beautiful sets of locks were those which evolved organically, growing out of the physicality and spirit of their individuals. I noticed the startling but always pleasing variety, the inexplicable resemblances to trees, roots, and other natural formations, the absolute rightness of each dread for its person—how the arch of the hair echoed the arch of the brows, eyes, or nose, or the thickness of lock paralleled the body's musculature, or the way texture and tint complemented the skin's own grain and tone. This, to me, was marvelous, magnificent—and I drank in these framed black faces with joy and appreciation. Yes, here was the way to truly have dreadlocks.

Unfortunately, preconceived notions about how a nice dread is supposed to look get in the way of this natural, laissez-faire approach. Most people seem to want to have (and see) locks which are thin and uniform, approximating as closely as possible the smooth regularity of braided styles, rather than deal with thick and/or thin, unpredictable organicism. And many prefer them long, still equating—for women—length with feminine attractiveness. When my first locks reached my shoulders, my mother finally accepted them, but told me—lovingly but baldly—that my new dread was "at that ugly stage." In similar fashion, Cheryl, a nationalist-minded, mid-30s friend, all but turned up her nose at my "stubby-looking" hair even as she shared that she was contemplating letting her (thin and regular eight-inch) plaits go into locks.

We are still being influenced by cosmetic—and commercial—standards of beauty, still buying into the system in the ostensible act of repudiating it. How hard it is to shed this programming! Defensive, a little hurt, a bit angry (but outwardly cool), I found myself explaining to Cheryl that the locks only looked stubby at the ends and would grow out with a different appearance. As opposed to maintaining a centered, serenely immune attitude, I was desiring her approval and positive response. This was the reversed version of the ambivalence I used to feel when accepting compliments for my locks from folks who said, "I like *yours*"—*mine* being the exception to those other wild-looking things they had seen on Bob Marley and MOVE members in Philadelphia. All of this is not to say that we lockswomen do not receive clear-eyed admiration. We do—quite often and sometimes from unexpected quarters—and it is immensely affirming.

Even though dreadlocks primarily assert a racial message and are basically free of stereotypical sex-role signification (although something could probably be made of a wild-irregular-powerful-masculine versus thin-groomed-feminine equation), they yet make an emphatic, gender-related statement. I wish I really knew, for instance, in what ways wearing long hair reflects a black man's self-concept and image projections. I do know that, for women, dreading is a rejection of a capitalistic, fetishized definition of female be-ing. Especially in the United States, strong, self-defining, and self-referenced women who have eschewed traditional notions of femininity—predominantly race/roots women and lesbians (often combined)—are the ones who dare to lock. Generally speaking, it still requires an ample measure of internal steadiness to walk this path of difference.

Dreading seems to also require at least a minimum level of comfort with the spiritual dimensions of existence. And, if one is going to lock in what I earlier described as the most natural way (though I am humble about prescriptiveness and the possible range of what is natural), spiritual issues become even more obvious: really, truly giving up control and "going with the flow"; trusting process/this process to yield what is appropriate and best; and having patience. I have learned the hard way (and am still learning—though with less hardness) that these three desiderata—faith, patience, and surrender—are major keystones of an evolving spiritual consciousness and approach to life. Having them on any level, in any arena is not easy. When trying to lock, one's patience is tested because it takes time, often a long time for the hair to aggregate and grow, not to mention its achieving full bloom. Faith waivers during those "ugly stages" and also when it looks as if what the hair is doing is headed in the wrong direction. Foregoing control is the hardest of all because one can so easily and summarily intervene (just reach up and twist or separate). The temptation to do so is also considerable, especially if one is susceptible to the ever-present pressure to always look "nice/good."

From this perspective, dreading can thus be viewed as a spiritual path/discipline. It can become a vehicle to enlightenment on an inner level comparable to the way it illuminates the external world via what we see/receive from wearing locks. If we are conscious and receptive, it functions as a full-time, built-in mirror that magnifies our realities. Having patience, faith, and the ability to surrender is an uplifting and liberating experience. Many of us women with locks say that we feel so "free." I believe this is not just because there is no combing, picking, teasing, styling, frying, fretting of our hair, but because there is likewise much less of that in our souls.

Related to this freedom is the opportunity that locking provides for a black woman to learn how she really feels about herself, to get in touch with her own true reaction to herself as she is. Here I mean internal feeling and not externally driven judgment or evaluation. Being so different forces us to really look at ourselves and ask/answer, "Hmm, what have we here?" Since the standard templates do not apply, it encourages the development of authentic/natural/original response. Regardless of what anybody says, I feel empowered to have discovered that I genuinely *love* the soft clumpings of hair at the base of my locks, or the tensile waviness of these tough, skinny ones, or the untamed way they all spring out when I am energized by sex or other fierce emotions.

Sometimes, though, I cannot be sure of how I feel. Sometimes I have to admit that I do not always like everything I see. At one point, I was wrapping my locks with scarves. This is because I did not relate well to the flatness of my hair when it was freshly washed, to its bangs-and-skullcap silhouette which called up for me unpleasant images of men and wet-look curls. However, this was my own not liking, my own unique and private quirkiness, emanating from some personal aesthetic inside myself and not adopted from the outside/others. I was wrapping because *I* felt prettier with locks and scarf. Of course, the social aspect of this was that I wanted to look good in public. But I was the one deciding about that "good."

Finally, locking can be healing—for any African woman who has internalized a negative dismissal of herself as ugly, particularly as this relates to hair and color issues. The almost formulaic epithet, "black and nappy-headed," has inflicted many a wound, for generations. In my case, this general experience was exacerbated by growing up with a light-skinned, "good-haired" sister with whom I was paired and compared. It was further amplified by the traumatic baby girl ordeal of having all my hair shaved off for medical reasons and suffering from the resulting rejections at an age when I could only feel but not understand. Once, without even knowing this story, a chiropractic healer performing craniopathy on me said that I/my head had never gotten enough holding. The psychic, emotional, and physical embracing of my locks helps cure this longstanding deficiency. And its power is somehow so deep and complete that it withstands society's sometimes still negative appraisals. This mojo is stronger than their bad medicine.

A Good Catholic Woman:
Reflections on Conflict
and Continuity in
the Nineties

Deborah James

It is the early 1990s and I am an African American woman, living in the South where I was born and raised and am raising my own children. By profession, I am a teacher at a small, liberal arts university. And, by many standards, I am a practicing Catholic. Yet I am a woman struggling to stay in a Church which seems, at times, to be seeking to rid itself of folks like me. My spiritual life, therefore, is a site at which the various aspects of my life often collide. I recognize in these collision points opportunities for my own growth through trying to come to terms with them. Besides that, I believe it is important to record our individual spiritual troubles as well as our triumphs. Otherwise, to those who come after, it might seem that having a developing, healthy spiritual life means that there are no struggles, something akin to how student writers see only final products. They are aware that their own work is so much messier and in the beginning, at least, much less. But these beginning writers, like those who are just beginning their spiritual journeys, need to know that it is possible that the messiness of the process contributes to the richness of the final product. So I want to record and explore my life as an African American Catholic woman in the nineties through looking at the models the Church seems to offer for being a "good Catholic woman." Those models raise the question for me: Is it possible to be a wife/mother, a teacher/writer, an African American woman, *and* a Catholic in the 1990s?

One model is embodied in a woman in my own parish. She is expecting her third set of twins, bringing the total of her children to nine—all under twelve. This seems to be a part of her Christian witness against abortion as well as her effort to obey the laws of the Church. It is a brave and moving one from some vantage points, especially because during her last pregnancy, also with twins, she was so ill that she was bedridden for the last weeks, and this pregnancy carries an even greater threat to her own health. Yet there is no hint that she is riddled with anxiety or frustration (not even the little jokes about her own fertility through which some women signal to each other their ambivalence in such cases). Moreover, when she is well enough, she and the children are part of the regular protest marches at the local "Abortuarium." She has a master's degree, homeschools her children, and concerns herself as she can with supporting the efforts of other people teaching the faith to their own children. She and her family present a well-scrubbed, shining witness to living a life of faith and obedience to the Church's precepts, regardless of the personal cost of such obedience. In many ways, her life appears to provide a true model of contemporary, Christian womanhood. Yet, there are some troubling aspects of this model, particularly for me as an African American woman.

Contemplating it and trying to reconstruct for myself what this woman's interior life must be like has become the occasion for some intensive soul searching on my own part. I wondered when I first heard about this latest pregnancy what obligation she has to her other children. Is it the aim of the Church to jeopardize the lives of the living children by encouraging the mother to risk her own health? That seems to me a problem of avoiding any type of birth control. I wonder also about the lives of her seven other children, particularly her oldest daughter. I watch the quiet intensity of her daughter's face during mass. At eleven, she will probably have to assume even greater responsibility for handling the younger children, particularly if her mother must go to bed during her pregnancy. And though I know that children even younger than she sometimes have greater responsibility with far less "backup," I wonder about consciously placing children in that position. Certainly this will give her an opportunity to grow, developing the skills to cope with real responsibilities. But it may also leave her a little needy, a little under-nurtured herself. Yet my personal faith says that "God will make a way out of no way." So if this is God's will for this family, somehow this will work. But is this level of jeopardy what is *required* of a "good Catholic woman"?

Pragmatically, I think also about the level of care this mother is able to provide as a result of her husband's success as a lawyer. She has hired help. Other women, however, particularly African American women and those less fortunate, who try to attend to her modeling or who are simply attempting to obey the letter and spirit of Church law might find themselves in a very different position. For one thing, they probably would have no outside help and would, therefore, need to find the resources within themselves to care for however many children they might have. Without another source of income or with nothing to equal a successful lawyer's income, there would be additional stresses and strains on nerves and relationships which this family model obscures. The most difficult thing about raising children seems to me finding the emotional and psychological resources to do a good job. The more kids, the more thinly spread those resources are. It is one thing to argue again that God will make a way, but what about what we already know or suspect about the level and pervasiveness of child abuse in this country? I know that *anyone* can become abusive and/or neglectful in circumstances where she simply runs out of economic, emotional, and psychological resources. Should we jeopardize ourselves and our children that way? Yet if we mean to be "good Catholic women," is there any other choice?

If being a "good Catholic woman" is limited to this model, I am forced to ask, is there a place for me as an African American woman who takes her intellectual/work life as seriously as she takes her spiritual life? My family is not all of my life; heresy, perhaps, but true. They are by far the largest part of my life (notice my defensiveness) but not the whole thing. Some of this is conscious choice; some seems to be simply the way I was made. Does the fact that my intellectual and work life are important to me mean that I should never have had children? Why did God allow me to complete this much of my education and find my teaching job if this is counter to His plan for me? Where does my academic interest come from? Since I have done all this work, am I not obligated to use these gifts in some way that serves Him? Does my interest in maintaining one aspect of my life preclude the other? With only one model held up to me by the priest and the Church, I think the answer is "Yes." Some people would argue that the purpose of both my education and my intellect is to raise my children and provide a stimulating home environment. I agree and that is a formidable task. But I am forced also to ask—is that all? And in this day and age, with prospects for African Americans so dim, can those of us with educations afford to keep whatever we have been fortunate enough to gain in our individual homes? Is volunteer community work the whole answer?

But perhaps the most disturbing aspect of being offered the "mother first" model is the message it gives to women in the Church. First, it points to motherhood multiplied as being the major role of women, the major way they can contribute to the life of the Church. It is even less clear how having more babies is connected to developing a deeper spiritual life except in the very important aspect of obedience to God's will. This seems to limit the development of a spiritual life to a biological function and not leave much of a place for women who are childless. What is a *woman's* spiritual life to consist of besides having babies if she is not a nun? For men, there are all kinds of opportunities to be more concretely connected to the church—from altar server to deacon. For women, particularly in the most conservative parishes, there are far fewer such opportunities and some resistance to allowing women to fulfill even the limited roles that are available. What is this refusal to value women's spiritual potential about? That leads to an even harder question: why would a woman of any race, especially an African American woman, be a Catholic?

Several women I know, women I respect and love, have turned away from the Church and some of them from religion altogether. They argue that the Church is uninterested in them as they are, that it is so politically corrupt, so intrinsically blind to its own centuries-long distaste for women sometimes disguised as adoration for the "Blessed Virgin" that it is impossible to stay in, impossible to raise daughters in, and a bad idea to expose sons to such ideas. And, in fact, when I listen to a priest get exercised about whether or not there could have been any blood at the birth of Christ, I admit that I wonder. I also wonder when I know that my daughter who is an open and wonderful nine-year-old would make a great altar server and her services are refused.

I wonder about less personal issues too. For example, when I listen to the priest talk about abortion, I wonder about the lives of the women who make that choice. For me it would be the wrong choice but even more wrong in the society which makes it often the lesser of several evils. So I don't have the same righteous indignation that the priest and the good members of our congregation seem to. I also think of all the children out there being abused, going hungry, being neglected, and I wonder about our obsession with the fetuses. I still believe that all life is sacred—*all* life. But why do we seem so preoccupied with fetal life? I also think, heretically probably, about birth control. I wonder about how and why available birth control as an issue is different

237

from whether or not to permit women to use painkillers during childbirth. The argument against using painkillers was rooted in scripture that said woman should bear her children in pain, the outcome of Adam and Eve's disobedience. But, though natural childbirth without drugs is the most favored way of giving birth today, almost everyone agrees that it would be foolish not to take careful advantage of whatever relief and help is available to us through modern science. It seems to me that birth control should be used like that—that is, people should be very careful and thoughtful about what would be best for the health and well-being of the whole family, then use it with discretion.

Yet it has been a blessing, in my case, to have the Church put the argument against abortion so strongly before me. It is really necessary for *someone* to raise the issues about ethics that the abortion argument brings up. In the same ways, it is important for me to continually be confronted with thinking about the implications of unlimited birth control. All of us individually and as a society need to carefully consider the consequences of "anything goes" as the moral dictum of a society. More importantly, all of us need to be pushed to consider what in this day and time makes abortion the only viable choice for so many people and whether the resources to raise children well should be reducible to disposable income.

And as for women in the Church, despite what seems in some places like an ever more restricted role, I know that one of the reasons I am a practicing Catholic today has much to do with the living models of African American Catholic womanhood I was blessed with in my youth. There were the Oblate Sisters of Providence. What did I learn from these models? Making a way out of no way was the very first one. Ours was a "missionary school" since there were so few African American Catholics, so few Catholics in North Carolina. Though I question some of the teaching practices of the sisters, I have been powerfully influenced by their example, especially by the examples of the best of them. These women never seemed subservient or reluctant to seek what they determined was necessary for the children in their care. They consistently struggled to provide new opportunities and challenges for us. That included everything from entering us in city-wide speaking and spelling contests to choral and basketball tournaments. And we were all supposed to share even down to our uniforms for the good of the group. When we were faced with a new challenge, we were simply expected to meet it (I did not know what an "Oratorical Contest" was until Mother Dolorosa entered me in it, but I knew I had to try to win and she and the whole class would help). These were not passive women, though they were prayerful. These were not retiring women, afraid of the world and so hiding out in a convent. These were not the charming, naive, simple souls of television and movie mythology. They not only lived in the neighborhood but were a part of it.

The greatest allies of these sisters were the women of that church, the women in my home parish, women who greet me even today with hugs and smiles and make me feel like I am coming home. They helped the sisters shame local merchants into providing whatever was needed for the children at the time; they sewed the costumes for the plays and fried the chicken and fish for the fund-raising dinners. When I think about the Catholic women I have had as models, they were all active and sometimes pushy women, demanding much from themselves and the children they deployed themselves to educate and protect. They made it their business to see that whatever work needed doing got done. And all of their examples taught me that when the way seemed unclear, prayer, and prayer unceasing, was the most powerful line of action. I have also watched them continuing their work faithfully, despite the personality of the various priests who have come and gone. Their example continues to teach me about commitment and faithfulness. Their lives have been complicated and they have had their full measure of difficulties and disappointments, but they are there like rock, solid and enduring. Their prayers continue.

So I am one woman who fights to stay in the Church because I believe that God went out of His way to get to me into it and I want to know what that is about and also because I do not believe that the Catholic Church nor any church belongs solely to the people who seem to be currently in power, just as I refuse to believe that the United States belongs only to the people who seem to be running the country. One of the messages I have received by being an African American, woman Catholic is that a spiritual life is not only a matter of what the Church provides but also of what one takes some trouble to provide for herself—reading, tapes, talks with other spiritual seekers. It is all too apparent, especially in my own parish, that *my* particular needs might not be addressed in the regular workings of the traditional parish. That means that I have to figure out how to address those needs myself. Sometimes I feel so alone, so heretical. Pushed by this sense of isolation and alienation, I have been reaching out to women of various faiths and finding strength and encouragement in unforeseen places. And, gradually, it has dawned on me that the truth of all our spiritual journeys is that although you may travel sometimes in company, ultimately you must keep seeking on your own.

Some of us find ourselves in opposition to some of the Institutional Church's practices and teachings simply by the accident of birth. Part of *our* journey will require that we not permit ourselves to be silenced. I am not seeking conflict but I do have real questions. In the last few years, in my parish at least, the notion has been put forward that if you question or oppose the Church's teachings or practices, you must get out of the Church. I don't believe that, quite simply because it was not a person who brought me into the Church. I was brought by Christ under the direction of the Holy Spirit. And it is right always to question practices that seem in conflict with the teachings and example of Christ Himself. Something in me tells me that there are others like me who simply feel silenced by the conservative voices that reign at the moment. But there is work to be done within the Church and we are all called to participate in that work. Part of that work is the very questioning I have engaged in here. A friend of mine who is Jewish shared with me a message from *Ethics of the Fathers*: you will not complete the work in your lifetime nor all alone, but you are not released from the obligation to keep working.

It seems to me that there is work to be done here in the contemporary Church and that the benefit of doing that work is in the enrichment of the Church and of the lives of our children. Those of us who have been called to that work, like Jonah, may try to go in the other direction, recognizing that the work itself is risky and, with only our own, personal power, impossible. Yet it is work that must be done and my faith says as I try to do the work put before me, I am never alone.

Laying on Hands: Women in
Imani Faith Temple

Catharine Goboldte

Manifestations of the Spirituality of African American Women

According to John Mbiti (pp. 59–76), an African historian and theologian, women played major roles in traditional African religions. African women were priestesses, queens, midwives, diviners, and herbalists. Also, there were female deities in the complex cosmologies of the different ethnic groups. For example, in Yoruba cosmology there are the women warrior *orixas*, Oshun, Yemoja, and Oya. In the forced migration from Africa to the Americas, the importance of the religious role of women was sustained and seen most clearly in the surviving African origin religions of South America and the Caribbean: Vodun, Yoruba, Santeria, and Cadomble, among others. The African influences survived in more indirect and sublimated forms in the United States where Protestant Christianity dominated. In African American Christian churches, while women make up the majority in the congregations, African American women are in the minority in positions of religious leadership (Lincoln and Mamiya, pp. 276–77). In the religions of African descent that survived or were reclaimed by African Americans in defiance of the imposition of Protestant Christianity, one finds women participating in traditional roles of spiritual leadership.

My focus in this study is on the role of African American women in a religious and spiritual community, and on the role of spirituality in the lives of African American women. I seek to contextualize the role of women in religion with an understanding of the role that religion plays in their lives in an effort to explore how their concept of spirituality affects their involvement in and beyond structures of religious institutions. Spirituality, that phenomenon so difficult to speak about or theorize and which is so often omitted from the

241

literature, may be a vital component in understanding the relationship of African American women and religion.

For African Americans, the reclamation of African-centered cultural perspectives and ethos is liberatory praxis. To determine ourselves Afrocentrically is to "literally place African ideals at the center of any analysis that involves African culture and behavior" (Asante, p. 6). My methodology, then, is an Afrocentric one. Ethnographic research methods are conducive to an Afrocentric methodology as they validate the subject's centered positionality and cultural context, and they require the explicit acknowledgment of the interaction between the researcher's own cultural template and the "culture" being studied. My method of data collection is Grant McCracken's model of the long interview complemented by participant observation and further triangulated by content analysis of transcripts of prayers, sacred texts, spiritual songs, sermons, institutional pamphlets, service programs, and other religious literature. In keeping with both the methodology and method, I allow the operationalization of the key concept, African American women's spirituality, and the categories of analysis to arise from the data collected. I have designed open-ended questions for my interviews because I am particularly interested in how the women would describe their experiences concerning: the structure and organization of their religious community; rituals and rites; ministry and education; concepts of the divine and spiritual symbols; discernment and divination; their involvement in issues of change in their faith communities; and the role of religion or spirituality in their lives. As a point of departure, I enter the field with a working definition of spirituality as provided by Dona Marimba Richards. According to Richards, "the essence of the Africa centered cosmos is a spirituality that gives force and energy to matter. Thus, humans are divine; the spirits manifest themselves in us (spirit possession) in the height of religious experience" (p. 211). This explication of spirituality is not unlike that found in the Bible, where spirituality is conceived as "love and devotion to God" (Deuteronomy 6:5; Joshua 22:5; 1 Kings 8:23; Psalms 1:2; 5:6) and as "produced by the indwelling of the Holy Spirit" (John 14:16,17; Romans 8:4). Richards contends that it is the "depth of African spirituality and humanism" that has ensured the survival of African Americans despite the dehumanizing holocaust of chattel enslavement.

Recognizing the diverse forms in which this spiritual ethos has survived among African Americans, especially women, I want to seek out the commonalities and contrasts within this religious communal setting. Thus I will look at the women of Imani Temple who come from diverse backgrounds—different religious communal settings, intellectual heritage, economic levels, and social situations.

Significance of the Study

This study is important because the African American Church tends to neglect the spirituality of African American women by legitimating the value of other cultures whose spiritual values may be based on power relationships which confuse the liberatory praxis of the spirituality of persons of African descent. This study will eliminate contradictions of spiritual power, and the spirituality of African American women may be used for the empowerment and liberation of our people to improve the everyday lives of African Americans. Terry Kershaw would call this "Emancipatory Knowledge" (p. 160): "The Afrocentricist speaks of research that is ultimately verifiable in the experiences of human beings, the final empirical authority" (Asante, p. 25).

The Case—Imani Temple, Philadelphia

While there have been ethnographic studies conducted on the African American church and women within those institutions, this case presents a unique situation of an African American congregation that comes out of a white church with no ordination of white or black women (Golden, pp. 273–78; Copeland, pp. 244–45; Davis, p. 90).

Imani Temple Church of Philadelphia, an African American Catholic congregation, was founded in 1989 by Rev. George Stallings, a Roman Catholic priest who formed his own congregation in protest of racism in the Catholic Church (Parker, p. 10). At Imani Temple Church of Philadelphia, I had an opportunity to look at the everyday life experiences of African American women, both lay women and a clergywoman, in a spiritual setting. The Imani Temple of Philadelphia is located in Southwest Philadelphia where it shares facilities with the Calvary United Methodist Church. I gained entry to the setting through a member with whom I have had a long-term friendship. She introduced me to Rev. Rose M. Vernell, the pastor of Imani Temple. My friend was anxious for her new pastor to meet other female clergy. My role as researcher was overt. Participant observation occurred during Sunday mass, as well as at special church services and functions such as an African fashion show/luncheon and church dinners. My role often included direct participation. For example, I was invited to preach during the Lenten season and on Good Friday.

On my first visit to Sunday service, I was greeted by friendly parishioners. At the door of the room prepared for worship, we were greeted by a courteous usher who gave us a bulletin that contained the order of worship with explanations of rites and symbols. The Imani Temple mass incorporates Roman Catholic sacraments and African rituals. The Mass includes prostration of the priest, pouring of libations, invocations of the saints and ancestors, African instruments, African American spiritual and gospel songs, and the Eucharist.

In the improvised worship setting, there was very little which resembled the chancels of the ornately decorated great Roman Catholic cathedrals; nor did the service resemble the highly formally structured and imperturbable Roman Catholic mass. The large rectangular room had a focal point along the horizontal front wall that was draped with Kente cloth. In front of the wall was a space enclosed by a curved kneeling rail. The choir sat in the enclosed area. Before the choir stood a portable altar covered by a Kente cloth from which the Holy Eucharist was blessed and served. To the left of the altar from the audience perspective stood the lectern from which libations were poured to the ancestors and the sermon was delivered. About 150 chairs for the parishioners were placed in a semicircle facing the altar. The piano and the pulpit area chairs rounded out the oval shape arrangement. Mass scheduled to begin at noon started about 12:30 and lasted until shortly after 2:00 P.M.

The liturgy began with the procession of worship service participants including the choir. They were accompanied by the music of drums, bells, and rattles. An explanation in the bulletin stated: "These are traditionally used in African ceremonies to call upon the Divine. Also, this heralded the arrival of an important personage; Here, Jesus who comes to feed us with his Body and Blood."

When the priest arrived at the altar, she lay prostrate upon the floor. "This act shows that [she] humbles herself completely before the glory of the Almighty Creator. This is a sign of greeting with the most profound respect."

The next act of worship was the Pouring of Libation, in honor of the Trinity. "This is a sign of communion, fellowship, and commemoration. It unites past, present, and future. It also prepares us for the Invocation of the saints." At this point in the service the congregation was asked to show pictures of loved ones while chanting "Be With Us" and names were added to a list of saints after the female cantor called the names of ancient Black biblical saints, saints from the early centuries of the Christian Era, and contemporary saints, for example, Martin Luther King, Jr. This ritual is explained in the bulletin: ". . . As we call upon the holy people of heaven and all of our ancestors to be present with us, we again show the unity of that which was, that which is, and that which is to come. It is expressive of the belief in African and African American spirituality that those who have gone before us are still present with us."

Service continued with the singing of the African American National Anthem, "Lift Every Voice and Sing," followed by prayer with the congregation's hands raised. Again, an explanation is found in the bulletin:

> Throughout the liturgy you will notice the Raising of Outstretched Hands. The basic gesture of praying with hands raised and outstretched, a natural posture expressing one's openness to help from a transient presence, was a gesture common among ancient Jews. When the posture was adopted by the Christians, they related it to Christ praying with outstretched arms on the Cross.

Tertullian, the distinguished Carthaginian theologian (who was Black) wrote: "We not only raise our hands, we also stretch them out, and copying thus the suffering of the Lord in prayer, we too confess to Christ."

Next was the "Liturgy of the Word." The readings are led each week by different members called "lecturers."

> The First Reading is taken from the Bible and the Second Reading is taken from the works of great African American spiritual leaders. This is in keeping with the efforts for enculturation inspired by Vatican II; local churches have incorporated into the liturgy readings from indigenous spiritual tradition.

Self-explanatory expressions of worship followed the Liturgy: the Gospel Acclamation and the Gospel Proclamation with the choir singing contemporary gospel music.

Visitors were asked to stand. A young lay woman expressed words of welcome. The pastor, joined by a congregant seated near the visitors, welcomed us individually with a handshake or hug. As is the custom in African American

Churches, the pastor invited me as an ordained minister to sit in the pulpit with her. However, I declined because I thought I could observe better from where I was sitting. The service continued with the Gifts of Love and Presentation of Gifts (offering plates were passed). After another selection by the choir came the Preaching moment.

The service continued with the Eucharist's liturgy and the communion service. An explication in the bulletin stated: "Some might be surprised by the intense level of vocal participation of the faithful in the Eucharist's Prayer; we draw attention to the following quotation:

> In areas such as North Africa, Egypt and Ethiopia, where the assembly's active participation in the liturgy was a cultural phenomenon, the Eucharist's prayer was structured so that it was a continual dialogue among the presider, the assembly, the deacon and the choir. For example, in the Coptic liturgy of Saint Basil, there developed as many as seventeen interventions of the people in the text of the institution alone.

This part of the service included the following rites: "The Lord's Prayer, the Breaking of the Bread and the Invitation to Communion." Regardless of denomination or church affiliation, everyone was invited to participate. After another choir selection, Remarks and Announcements were made. The service was concluded with a Prayer and Benediction by the Pastor.

About 85 percent of the people attending church this particular Sunday were women. About 95 percent of those who officially participate in the service are women. Women are involved in leading all of the rituals. From this body of worshipers, the pastor and five women were selected and agreed to give interviews. They ranged in age from twenty-five to seventy. Three were married. Occupations included pastor, homemakers, and retired and working professionals. Three were college graduates, and two other interviewees had some post-secondary education. Three interviewees were "cradle Catholics" which means they were baptized Roman Catholic as infants.

Spirituality as manifested by the women of Imani Temple is a liberating and empowering faith. This is observed in the syncretism of African and Christian spiritual practice, which I have described above, and is described by one of the women in this way: "The rituals are the same, yet they're different. Calling on the ancestors is different. We never heard that some of these saints were Black. The kiss of peace and the sacraments are the same." For many women, this syncretism is an infusion or reclamation of an African life-force. One said, "The Church is the center of my life. Through the study of the Bible and Afrocentricity, I feel like I am really alive now and not just existing in life . . . you know, not just going through the motions of life or religion for that matter." Another expressed it in this way: "I really want to be close to God. Now that I am studying the Bible, God speaks to me through the Bible. In the Roman Church, we never discussed the Bible. I feel closer to God and my culture when I hear the drums at worship." Thus, this reclamation of Afrocentricity, which then makes their faith more relevant to their lives, empowers the women of Imani Temple to conceive of a spirituality that places them in closer communion with God:

> I've been a Roman Catholic all my life and for the first time, my spiritual needs are being met through the preaching, singing and Black worship. I can feel God and the Holy Spirit in my life now. Rev. Rose is a strong believer in the Holy Spirit and she taught me so much that I didn't know before. I pray through the Holy Spirit myself now. Now I know what she is talking about. My faith in Jesus Christ and the trinity is stronger now.

Another member of Imani Temple experiences through this empowering and liberating spiritual faith a closer communion not only with her Christian God but also with her African and African American ancestors as well: "I came all the way from Minneapolis to visit Imani Temple in Washington, D.C. When I heard the drums at my first Mass, I just cried and cried just to think that I had lived this many years of my life and never felt the power of the Spirit in the same way that my ancestors felt it."

Another woman beautifully expressed her experience of the Divine within her: "Something goes all through me when I hear the drums and the calling of the saints like Moses the Black." The members are brought closer together as they share in the everyday factors of life. Several people commented on the communal make-up of the church that gives them opportunity to help each other.

> The make-up of our church is like most churches I suppose. More women, fewer men. My husband doesn't mind me going to church, but I can't get him to go. But we're like family at church—older women with their sons and grandsons. The younger women bring their boyfriends.

We don't have large families here like some churches do. There are parts of some families—two sisters, mother and daughters, a few husbands and wives with children. But we feel like family, I guess we are an extended family. We are the family of God.

The pastor is like the head of the family for God. We're like one big family. She is like the shepherd or shepherdess of the sheep. She's the overseer. God is neither male nor female. We sometimes use the expression Mother/Father God.

As an elder of the Church, I have to be close to God. So that I can assist the pastor on behalf of the people. I pray a lot for my pastor, the bishop, the people of my church and community.

For most women I interviewed, spiritual seeking resulted in satisfaction and their fulfillment in many ways. "Many have been looking for the same thing that I am looking for at Imani," said the Pastor, "and so we are testing the waters."

Conclusion

In this faith community, African American women exercise broad leadership. For these women, their involvement in mothering roles does not preclude them from filling positions of leadership that extend beyond the sphere of conventional women's work. The women in the diverse spiritual settings that I studied were of one accord on breadth of leadership. They described women heading faith communities, being involved in everything, having many roles, or not thinking of themselves in roles. I also observed women having roles that might not everywhere be identified with women. The chosen research setting included women who were formally ordained or initiated as responsible for setting rules and offering spiritual guidance. I observed women leading rituals and saw signs that they were appreciated for their inspiration.

Operating in economic spheres such as the marketplace, the treasury, and the administration were all positions of women's work as identified by participants and illustrated by these comments: "I am the administrator of the congregation. I was a cradle Catholic baptized as an infant, three weeks old, and never dreamed of being a part of the hierarchy of the Church. I'm an administrator on my job, so why shouldn't I be [an administrator] in the Church?"

Women's involvement in ministry in the settings studied included the ordained priest and pastor of the African American Catholic Congregation, and lay positions expressed by participants in terms of ministry and spiritual elevation.

> Women hold the key positions in our congregation. The moderator is a woman, the administrator is a woman and of course the pastor is a wonderful woman. She is always there for you. The heads of our ministries are mostly women.

> The key people in our church are: the Pastor who is a woman; the Elder who happens to be a woman. Mother Calvin, we affectionately call her. She counsels with us because of her wisdom and knowledge. She carries the incense, which symbolizes the cleansing of the Temple.

Along with this freedom that women used to characterize their woman leader, there was a sense that their spiritual community has allowed them to participate fully in a spiritual setting. In the words of one participant:

> What I like about the leadership at Imani Temple is that I can be anything. We now have women making decisions in everything and there are no secrets. In the Roman Church, men made decisions even for women and everything was a big secret or made so mysterious. When they asked about a woman, Rev. Rose, becoming our pastor, I said, "Why not?" She can do everything the male priest can do plus she is warm, charming and outgoing.

The breadth of involvement also is expressed in the openness to women as spiritual leaders, a recognition of the talents women bring, and a claiming of women as important in the lives of the women we interviewed and their communities. The recognition of women leaders was described in terms of personal qualities as well as acts:

> I had met Rev. Rose before she became our pastor; the fact that she was a woman never entered my mind. Her abilities and qualities were so fantastic, it didn't matter. I just knew I would like having such a down-to-earth person whom I felt comfortable with as my pastor. You know, warmer, and a person who would understand what I was facing in my daily life.

An explanation for the spiritual response of the women of Imani Temple to African religious rituals and rhythm may be found in the evidence presented by Dona Marimba Richards. Her evidence supports the view that ancient Africa survives in our spiritual make-up (Richards, p. 1). Richards illustrates how the message that she is trying to convey can be sung, danced, and understood by African American women. This communal experience was described by many women at Imani Temple in different ways, but I found to be true Richard's observation that the translation of that experience into an intellectualized language can never be accurate. The attempt results in reductionism (ibid., p. 3).

The evidence shows that African American women had a God consciousness before they had a Bible consciousness. However, scriptures such as John 14:16, 17, sanction the testimonies of the women of Imani Temple that spirituality is realized by the indwelling of the Holy Spirit: "And I will ask the [Creator], and [God] will give you another Advocate, to be with you forever. This is the Spirit of truth, whom the world cannot receive, because it neither sees [God] nor knows [God]. You know [God], because [God] abides with you, and [God] will be in you."

Katie G. Cannon, professor of Christian ethics at Temple University, attests to the essence of that liberating and empowering faith exhibited by the women of Imani Temple when she talks about her "inheritance from her Mother and ancestors," asserting that our life stories are an indispensable source of Black people's historical confidence and spiritual persistence despite all oppression: "In spite of every form of institutional constraint, racism, sexism and classism, African Americans have been able to exist in another world, a spiritual world, a counterculture within the white-defined world, complete with our own sacred texts, spirituals and religious practices" (Cannon, p. 84). Cannon sums up the legacy of the spirit of liberation and empowerment for the women of Imani Temple when she says, "My ancestors never surrendered their humanity or lost sight of a vision of freedom and justice they believed to be their due" (ibid.).

I recognize that the case study of Imani Temple does not focus on a conventional African American spiritual or religious setting. Thus, I shall not posit conclusions based on empirical generalizations. While the literature on African American women and religion does not capture my case, I by no means wish to suggest an absence of settings in which African American women are denied access to broad leadership. That the literature failed to address the experiences of the women I interviewed, I do, however, find to be a significant failing on the part of the current scholarship.

More work needs to be done that: (1) acknowledges the diverse expressions of spirituality within the African American population, particularly regarding women; and (2) incorporates the spiritual aspects of African American women's involvement in faith communities. Work such as this is particularly relevant in that it has implications for theoretical conceptions of power and leadership and notions of women's work. As Afrocentric scholars, clearly we cannot rely solely upon models of power and leadership and gender identity that come from outside of our lived experiences.

The voices of the women interviewed are particularly relevant to African American women in other contexts who may be seeking to exercise the same broad leadership, who may be seeking to actualize the divine in their lives. In the current scholarship on gender identity and female ideology, too often devalued or ignored are the voices of the women who exercise spiritual leadership. As one woman from the Church of the Advocate put it, "I don't think we've ever thought about it that way. I think we just feel so comfortable and sure of ourselves, I don't think there are roles, there is just a do what you have to do kind of thing."

This is the voice of a woman who has successfully dedicated her life to the work of lobbying the Pennsylvania government for funding to renovate and restore homes in the North Philadelphia area and provide decent housing for people. Thus, she asserts a female spiritual identity in defiance of the separation of nurturing roles from positions of leadership. Further research should seek to elaborate this conception of power and leadership that incorporates the capacity to nurture and the ability to lead. For there is no separation of the spiritual from the secular for African people.

For me, an Afrocentric researcher, this study has served as "Emancipatory Knowledge" in the sense described by Terry Kershaw. My future role will be to report back to the group of interest (the women of Imani Temple) and to become a participant of the group by utilizing my skills to help get rid of any contradiction and thus strengthen the group. This requires me to use this African American study on the spirituality of African American women as a tool for empowerment and liberation of our people (ibid., p. 84).

251

Works Cited

Asante, Molefi K. *Kemet, Afrocentricity and Knowledge.* Trenton, N.J.: African World Press, 1990.

Cannon, Katie G. "Surviving The Blight." Pp. 75–90 in *Inheriting Our Mothers' Gardens.* Ed. Letty Russell et al. Philadelphia: Westminster Press, 1988.

Copeland, Shawn M. "African American Catholics and Black Theology: An Interpretation." In *African American Religious Studies: An Interdisciplinary Anthology.* Ed. Gayraud Wilmore. Durham, N.C.: Duke University Press, 1989.

Davis, Cyprian, O.S.B. "Builders of Faith: Black Religious Women Before and After the Civil War" in *The History of Black Catholics in the United States* New York: Crossroads Publishers, 1990.

Golden, Michael, "The Vatican and the United Nations Decade for Women." *AFER: African Ecclesial Review* 27 (October, 1985): 273–78.

Kershaw, Terry. "Afrocentrism and the Afrocentric Method." *The Western Journal of Black Studies* 16, 3 (1992): 165.

Lincoln, C. Eric., and Lawrence H. Mamiya. *The Black Church in the African American Experience.* Durham, N.C. Duke University Press, 1991.

Mbiti, John. *African Religions and Philosophy* 2d ed.; London, England: Heinemann, 1990.

Parker, Anthony A. "We Can't Wait Any Longer": George Stallings' African-American Imani Temple Shakes the Catholic Church." *Sojourners* 18 (October 1989): 10–12.

Richards, Dona Marimba. *Let The Circle Be Unbroken: The Implications of African Spirituality in the Diaspora.* New York: Greenwood Press, 1985.

On Belonging as a Muslim Woman

Amina Wadud-Muhsin

Have We not opened up your heart
And lifted from you the burden
That had weighed so heavily on your back?
Behold, with every hardship comes ease . . .
with every hardship comes ease.
So, when you are freed (from distress)
remain steadfast
and unto your Sustainer turn your love.
— Qur'an 94: 1–8

As a little girl, I was afraid of thunderstorms: the raging winds, pouring rain, and roaring thunder. I shared a bed at night with my sister, and I would wrap myself within her warmth to shield me from the noise and turmoil. But in the day I found little refuge. Sometimes, I would hide myself in some corner or closet and try to decipher the message that I felt God was sending to me personally.

Then, there was my father. He used to hold me in his lap and remind me of the rainbow: the symbol that God gave of His promise never again to destroy the world by water. That was my first experience of the transcendent: tranquility in the midst of storm.

Much of my spiritual quest, from childhood on, has—although sometimes unconsciously—been to recapture that sense of transcendent tranquility in the midst of storm. Surely, the world rages on in torrents of thunderous rage as it rains confusion, destruction, hunger, chaos, and pain, and just as surely, within us all is the desire for the spirit of tranquility. Although I wish I could heal the many wounds of a wearied world—before its thunderous voracity—I often feel quite small.

This is my story. From the child of a disillusioned and disappointed Methodist minister, who died young, up to and through Islam. And, this is a woman's story, traversing paths in that journey that could never be glimpsed by my father. And with other dimensions that extend beyond the boundaries of what he taught me, to offer new parameters of meaning. Yet, while being different, my journey often attempts to reflect the same intense experience of his nurturing care and spiritual tranquility. Ultimately, I have felt challenged to transcend even the gifts he gave me in order to avoid his disappointments.

I wish I could say, this is a story of unending successes. But if I did, then perhaps it would not be a story of real life. As the Qur'an says, "Surely with every hardship there is ease"; but when it repeats itself, we see that the pattern of difficulty and ease is integral to life: and again, "with every hardship there is ease . . ."

This is the story of my spiritual quest as an African-American Muslim woman who labored to recapture the sense of tranquility I felt in the lap of my father. This is a quest of self-realization and belonging. Now, I wish to share a joy of Truth and an ecstasy of affirmed knowledge in fulfilling that quest.

Thunderstorm

We lived in semirural Maryland where my father, a young military man, had brought his fifteen-year-old bride. He had cleared a yard in front of a wooded area and built, with his own hands, the home of my childhood. Although many childhood memories are centered in my home—constructed with love and promise—it was the surrounding wild bush and forest that kept me in touch with my inner spirit and the spirit of God. I never tired of outdoor play on warm summer days. I roamed the woods with my sister and five brothers. I would linger so long in the woods that my mother had to come for me. She would whip me all the way home, stinging my bare legs with a fresh switch torn from one of the wood's own trees. "You are lazy and irresponsible," she would say. But my heart ever drove me back into the depth of the woods, to pick wild blackberries, or suck the sweet, tiny droplets from the honeysuckle bushes. There was so much to heal a hungry soul in those woods.

In the daylight there were no secrets, but after nightfall, the snakes would come out or the owl would hoot and my fear of the darker dimensions of the unknown would return in full force. I lived between the light of joy and the darkness of sorrow. As a Libra child, I suppose this meant I was ever weighing both sides of my experiences to balance the forces within my own soul. My father was the light for me, and my mother bore the threat of darkness. Between the two, I teetered out of control, trying to fathom some meaning out of a lively-lonely existence.

One day in early June, when I was nearly eleven years old, I skipped down the dirt roads between my school and our home, without a care in the world. I drank in the late spring greenery. The cherries were beginning to ripen and the apple trees were in bloom, preparing for their fall harvest. I knew all of these trees personally. I climbed them like a champion and munched the bitter-sweet fruit before it was fully ripened. After all, I thought, in two weeks I would once again be free to discover hidden wonders in the woods all day long, and to wade barefoot through small rivulets and streams within the dense, warm interior.

I walked through the small orchard diagonal from my house. Once I cleared the trees, I was in full view of my house. Something was dreadfully wrong! All of our possessions were piled haphazardly beyond the fence surrounding our yard. I climbed over the locked gate to run onto the porch. (Some hot summer nights, I would sit with my father on the wooden swing that swung lightly with the gentle push of his long legs.) This was my home. How could it be that I could not enter? A thick chain was wrapped around the screen door handle with a huge lock dangling from it. The wooden inside door had two small windows covered with frilly curtains. I could not see inside. Where was my mother?

"Ya'll been put out!" a neighborhood child taunted from beyond the gate. But this is the house my father built with his own hands. Only years later did I understand the technicalities over the leased land. The house might have been his (after annual taxes), but the land was mortgaged. Failure to pay the mortgage meant that we were evicted from the house my father had built with his own hands: the house of my tranquil childhood.

Homeless Wandering

For the next two weeks, we must have slept in my father's car. He took us to his job for a Saturday-night bath. A huge industrial tub elevated about two feet from the ground held the sweet, clean smell of Dial soap. For nearly a decade after that I unconsciously associated that smell with purity. It took me nearly three decades to regain the purity of lost childhood innocence. Between then and now, I dipped again and again below the brink of the chaos and confusion in a beleaguered world. Having surfaced again only recently, telling this story stirs deep memories.

When school was out, my father built a trailer for us to stay in. We still had dirt roads and access to some woods, but there was something stifling about our circumstance which brought the feeling of borrowed time. Since we did not remain at any one place for more than a month, I suppose I knew we did not belong.

I have no memory of seeing my mother over the next two months of summer—although I suppose we must have seen her for some brief moments. My father attempted to keep our lives normal. Mothering us two girls proved an overwhelming task. Neither my sister nor I could take care of my hair, and days would go by without getting it combed at all. But basic hygiene seemed the least of our worries.

One morning I woke to see my sister crying. She was sitting on her bed in a pool of blood. Since she did not die and was not even taken to the hospital, I guess I knew she was not ill. My brothers said something about the normalcy of this for women. All I could think was, "Where is the woman in our lives to comfort my sister and explain it all to her, and to me?" From betrayal there can never come trust.

In the City of Deceit

By the time the school year started my father had rented two rooms on the third floor of someone else's home. But this time, we were in the city: Washington, D.C. We lived in those two rooms for one year. This was not an uneventful year either. My sister became a stranger to me, a young woman with no time for me, a girl-child. I had no place to roam when I needed to feel the breath of life, so I became reclusive: a characteristic of my life in the city over the next four years, and one I would assume whenever I felt threatened.

I lived fully only in the small spaces I could find in which to hide. As a small child hiding, I used to take a doll with me. These days I was more likely to keep a book and live in the fantasies that unfolded on the pages. I was not fascinated so much with the story lines, saved damsels and handsome heroes, as I was intrigued with words which could unfold images and meaning. Worlds of words. Meanings through naming.

In the city I learned not to trust people with myself: not to tell them any secrets, nor to share with them my inner meanings. Most of all, I learned not to count on them to bring me joy. I learned that the intense reality of betrayal had a new name: survival. We cannot survive if we are true. This system does not want the real woman or the real man of African descent. So we must learn the skillful games of deception. But the games got played so well, we began to play them on ourselves. We could not distinguish between our survival in the sub-context of America and the resulting forfeit of our inner reality. I could not accept this mode of operation: deception for survival. It meant, of course, that I would struggle even harder for my survival. Since I was no good at the game, I played another: the game of hiding. But at this time no one came to seek.

But something else did. I was picked up in my life by a force greater than my own resistance and fear. At times along the way, I understood this force and would meet it joyfully. At other times, I resisted strongly and would misplace my trust, giving it to those so adept at playing the old game of deceptive survival, and then I would lose hope.

Education: A Path of Transition

The first and most significant experience with the force came when I was in junior high school. A significant manner in which the force activated itself in my life was in education. I clearly remember that at age four I couldn't wait to start school. I was enthusiastic about learning, studying, thinking, reading, computing. At six or seven when we would drive around town I would sound out street signs, store headings, and billboards. I remember when they began to come together and make sense: words. Combining the sounds of the letters together made something meaningful! I would occupy myself with this task, never noticing an otherwise tedious and boring car ride.

My immediate family and small circle of friends generated no interest in education, however. I was not read to. Our home contained no books, besides the Bible—which we were never encouraged to read. I didn't know there was a place where anyone with a card could borrow books for free: a public library. In my family, words are used as weapons to sting the emotions, not as instruments of wonder.

I had thought this was a Black thing because at the white school and in the homes of some of my white classmates I saw things differently. In third grade

I visited a friend who asked her mother for an after school treat by spelling out the word S-N-A-C-K. They seemed to possess a special membership in a secret world of wisdom. As I walked home that evening, I felt that my family didn't care because they didn't ask, "Have you done your homework?" or, "Do you understand the assignment?" let alone, "Can I help you with your lessons?"

When we moved to the city, I was in the sixth grade. I met other Black students who were interested in progress through education, but the focus was on doing better than others. I needed a competitive edge. After tests we would exchange and correct each other's papers. One girl befriended me and suggested that we correct each other's errors to achieve a better score. When she handed back my paper, I saw that she had made some of my correct answers wrong to lower my score and achieve the honor of being recognized for having the highest score.

Not long after this incident I was transferred to a school where a lack of interest in learning was complete. Although I made little effort and still achieved high marks in my academic subjects, I was given a "U" in behavior, for unsatisfactory. I internalized the meaning that learning was not important. By the time I reached junior high I was adept at passing my days in the classroom with little more than my body in attendance. My academic marks dropped to C's and D's and no one complained.

In the spring of my second year, a guidance counsellor noticed that despite my low grades I was scoring above the 95th percentile in the nationwide California Achievement Tests. She took it upon herself to find ways to pluck me out of an environment apparently ill-suited to my intellectual capabilities. Through a series of tests and small moves I eventually left my family at the age of fifteen—never to live with them again. Although I had escaped the oppression of feeling I did not belong in my immediate environment, I had not escaped the limitations enforced for being Black and female in America. New dimensions to this lesson had to be learned.

Living in Someone Else's Bubble

I spent my three senior high school years in an exclusive, all-white suburb of Boston. I was euphoric to be among the trees and I used to sing at the piano: a place of inner peace, the spirit of song. At times I felt: I belong here. In the long run, however, the cost of such thinking created an even greater personal displacement.

The high school years are used for learning the ropes of romantic exchange and understanding femaleness and maleness. Well, I couldn't be just "female." I was one of only two Blacks in the school.

I was a Black female. During those years I was never for a moment allowed to let my Blackness escape me. Aspects of my color and ethnicity were the points of entry and exit into many facets of my high school life. Privileges were given to me or withheld from me because of my race. In my first semester, I refused to stand for the pledge of allegiance. I was permitted to make my protest, but not to enter the classroom. So, for three years, I spent homeroom period wandering the halls. I was allowed to do this—although no one else ever was. In English class, one term, I refused to read a novel, because I found the language racially biased. I was excused. I was even excused from dissecting a frog on the day that Martin Luther King was shot. None of these favors was permitted to white students. In each case the affirmation was only that one set of rules applied for the whites and another set applied for me. No one ever knew that I simply didn't want to dissect the frog.

Even among those considered friends, there was sometimes a relegation of special terms, *because* I was Black. As a joke in junior year, they nominated me for the Daughters of the American Revolution Award—the implication being I couldn't possibly be a "daughter," because Blacks were not a significant part of the American Revolution (and of course, I didn't win!). In senior year the yearbook committee allowed us to arrange ourselves as we liked for group pictures. I stood over my kneeling friends holding up a fist in the symbol for Black power.

Being Black was a unique prize and a special curse. My first high school crush told me he couldn't kiss me because I was Black. I had no boyfriends because I was Black, or I had them out of curiosity or pity because I was Black. In short, at no juncture was I to forget that I was Black. So I never forgot.

It seemed to me that in my old neighborhood, since everyone was Black, color was not the major characteristic of consideration. They participated and were loved or hated because of personality or individual inclinations. At school my uniqueness was in being Black, little else mattered. Consequently, when I left high school, I had a distorted vision of my own special talents: I felt I didn't have any. All I had was Blackness.

When my high school days ended there was one further boon to being Black. In the late 1960s, universities and colleges responded favorably to my applications specifically because I was Black (but white educated!). In the end I chose the University of Pennsylvania, not because it was an Ivy League school, but because it offered the most substantial scholarship and I needed to be around more Black people—particularly males. My intellectual conformity could not be used again as an affirmation of liberal goodness. Such a situation had not allowed me to mold my unique identity from the core of my own soul. In high school that unique soul had been left to burn in a hell of loneliness and oddity.

During a recent visit to the suburban Boston town where I lived and went to high school, a young woman, now in her thirties who had been eight years old when I came to stay with her family, described living there as living in too much of a "bubble." In order to claim her unique self, she had to insist on a separation from the privileges the circumstances of her family had afforded her. To gain an independent sense of self, she had to break away from that "bubble" and face the elements of the world on her own terms. She asked if it had not also been too much of a "bubble" for me. I said, "No, because I was just passing through." I never belonged there.

To Belong to Someone: University Days

I didn't belong in the New England suburbs because I was Black. I didn't belong in my family because I was too bookish. When I came to the university, I tried one last miss-belonging, a major one as a Black woman: seeking to belong to a Black man.

Freshman year: everyone sizing up everyone else. Black females were subjected to an evaluation on the basis of looks, skin color, hair texture, body, clothes, social status, and to a slightly lesser degree, brains. Upper-class sisters were happy to tell me I had been ranked high on this scale, especially when I failed to live up to the standard because I wasn't selective about the brothers.

The brothers were supposed to be scrutinized and held at bay by similar trivial measures of worth. Since I hadn't been around Black men, I could not figure these measurements out and defend my status by demonstrating my selectivity. If they were human and friendly, I thought, "I can belong." It took me a while to recognize that too many of them were dogs waiting for us to put them on a short leash. This attitude seemed dehumanizing to me (and although afterwards, I chalked their behavior up to immaturity, nearly a quarter of a century later, I met a middle-aged version—so I guess it's not age-related after all).

In college I discovered another racial double standard: unlike rich white girls, we Black girls always had to be on our P's and Q's. If we participated too much—no matter how justified it was from the heart—we would be socially outcast. The unwritten standards and unspoken rules for the Black woman were rigid. Her acceptance or rejection in the community was based on how well she followed these standards. These rules were arbitrary, but they required familiarity—if one wanted to play the game. Soon I gave up on yet another game.

I had thought (or hoped) that in college I would automatically belong because I was Black—I expected the opposite from high school. But I learned that for a woman to belong, she had to be more than just Black, she had to get the rules of the game right. When I had ceased to play that game, I learned to choose friends on the basis of mutual interest in and communication about the deeper meaning of life.

It was also in college that I began in earnest to search for that deeper meaning within my own life. The most readily available assistance in this search was mind-altering drugs. But my days with drugs were short-lived. What my college mates got from drugs seemed to be fun. What I got was a venture into the deeper regions of the mind. I thought more about things and began to ask more questions. The existential quest took hold.

Are we put on the planet for a reason? How do we figure out that reason? What difference does knowing make? Do we live what we will or is life purely accidental? Looking over my past, I could not reconcile the accidents of meaning in my life course. Nor could I satisfy the sense of yearning I had always felt, or escape the great unhappiness and loneliness that accompanied it. Each time I hoped for an easy answer to my questions and for a feeling of belonging, I ended up disappointed. So I moved on, like a gypsy.

The summer after my freshman year, I took my first trip across the country. I drove with a cousin who worked for a truck company. I met his truck outside of Washington, D.C., at about ten o'clock at night. This was the beginning of a symbolic trend in my travel experiences for the next two decades: if I began my travels or arrived at my destination at night, that which I sought in the journey would elude me. The meaning that I sought would remain encased in mystery, and no matter how long I stayed or how far I traveled it would remain inaccessible. However, traveling through the south and entering California several days later widened my tiny life-circle and lent greater meaning to it.

The summer after sophomore year, I hitchhiked across country. This time I lingered here and there, rather than just passing through. Although now I find it foolhardy, at the time, I felt protected by the few rules I had worked out: Never be on the road after dark; find some place to stay until morning. Never get into a truck (since even my cousin had offered to seduce me, I was definitely against truck drivers). Always have travel fare for alternative transportation should luck fail me. It never did: a force greater than my limited common sense was with me.

In fact, after riding with friends to Missouri, I rode in only two cars. One belonged to an older Black couple who put me up in a hotel in Kansas, and the other belonged to a young white male who was going all the way to the west coast after stopping for a week in Colorado. I spent that week roaming the Rocky Mountains.

The night I arrived in Denver, it was raining. I stayed with some "Jesus freaks" (because they wouldn't solicit any sexual favors). But I felt unsure the next morning about my week-long plans, so I prepared to move on. I walked toward the east for about a half hour, feeling forlorn. When I stopped for breakfast I looked toward the west, for the first time: the rugged grays and majestic purples of the mountain peaks greeted me and urged me to try something more. I left the city and spent the next few days roaming through the mountains. I placed my hand back on the pulse of nature, but on more than just woods and trees, mountains, lakes, valleys, golden wheat fields and, later in California, the sun dropping into a raging ocean. All of God's kingdom was opened before me, and it was all here on earth.

That summer was important for my transformation. I learned two lessons about human meaning-making: (1) You make yourself out to be whoever you want to be, as if born anew each day. When I would meet people on the road, I could withhold any information about me I chose. I could be any parts of myself that suited the moment. I was freed from a form set by the past. (2) Each human is truly unique and their meaning unfolds as you exchange with them. You cannot prejudge what a person is like because of experiences with others in the past: each one deserves unconditional acceptance so that the wonders of each can be made manifest.

Islam, the Final Belonging: Belonging to Self

I have considered that the experiences of that summer opened my heart to new possibilities and meanings in my life. My acceptance of others was enhanced by the sheer good fortune of those whom I had chanced to meet along deserted walkways and busy sidewalks. The light-spirit of my childhood was rekindled with the gift of touching nature's magnitude. In the fall of 1972, that open heart received a message from the door of Islam.

There are actually many doors that lead to Islam. Coming up to a door in no way implies that one will necessarily pass through the threshold and enter into the depth of the experience within. Although many may choose from various doors, not all will venture deeply within. So, I never bother much over how someone initially stepped up to a door to Islam. I do pay close attention to whether they step boldly (or even timidly) into the room and peruse the quality of the core.

For the African-American woman one door that opens onto Islam continues to be Muslim men. It could be a particular brother, who then sets the parameter of her experience within, while she scarcely asks questions or seeks answers on her own. Or it could be the general sense of male-female which gives honor and legitimacy to women—against the white American defeminization and dehumanization. However, to personally experience the fullness of Islam—as with any religious experience—we must venture deeply into our own central core and ask those burning, yearning questions about being and meaning: Who am I? Why am I here? What has all this to do with me?

The convert in the modern African-American context has a particular concern with these questions, which those born into Islam often do not ask. Born Muslims often fail to make a personally affirmed *shahadah* (declaration of faith). Whatever has passed for "Islam" in their culture (and sometimes it is a big "whatever") is unquestionably accepted as the full meaning of Islam. No matter what they do, as a student once told me, they are 100 percent Muslim, while those of us who accept Islam with our hearts can never be. We strive even harder for a personally recognized, existentially realized meaning of Islam: a full at-one-ment. I hungered for a greater understanding of Islam and so was compelled to move into the depths of the room. It was a heavy gift.

> Have We not opened up your heart
> And lifted from you the burden
> That had weighed so heavily on your back?

Each of us can decide to follow the holy quest in a manner which makes our lives meaningful and which allows us the persistence and stamina to see it through the hard times. Often, we are inclined to give up. It's too difficult, Lord. Why don't I just take the easy road: that one that is nominal, ritual and social. Perhaps we can avoid the major sins, but often we also fail to have any major, life-altering discoveries about self, others, and the Holy Other.

It is of little consolation to hear this road often described as the one less traveled. Knowing ahead of time how little companionship one will find, one may turn away from the idea of unbearable loneliness. Perhaps it is better to hear this path expressed as the one which leads to radiant boons, including the ultimate boon: at-one-ment with the Ultimate, a harmonious synchronization with the greater cosmos.

My door into Islam was accidental. During my sophomore and junior years in college, I began to change my lifestyle. I wore long clothes, cut my already natural hair back very short, and eventually kept it covered. I also became more conscientious about my diet: with no meat and more wholesome foods. These things I began as celebrations of the honor of my being. Life is a gift that we must live with honor—not by random standards imposed on us by an exploitive environment.

I pronounced my *shahadah* on Thanksgiving Day, 1972. A few months after the declaration of my Islam, another accident occurred which proved important: someone gave me a copy of the Qur'an. In reading the Qur'an, I relived my childhood sense of worlds of meaning through words. Sometimes, very simple statements move me to tears and awe. Sometimes the complexities quench my thirst for deeper understanding. I come away from the

Qur'an—to which I have dedicated all of my professional energies, up to my Ph.D., in learning to interpret—with the sense that all the questions I have asked can be clarified there. Not literally "answered," as some would say, implying that only the Qur'an has the Truth, or that all Truth is in it. Rather, the Qur'an establishes a vision of the world, and beyond, with meanings and possibilities for self that lead to certainty.

With this sense of self-honor, and meaning through learning, I must conclude with a description of the sense of belonging to Al-Lah (the God) and His universe. In Islam, the image of the creation of humankind includes the special gift of the very spirit of God which is blown into humans above all the rest of creation. Thus, each of us represents a significant and intentional part of the cosmic order. Within the core of my being I know the truth of all answers—because they attest to the harmony of the universe, of which my own personal harmony is an integral part.

My self is intentional, having a unique connection with the Creator and the creation. I belong to Allah, whose domination extends over the heavens and the earth. Looking toward the light within, I see a reflection of the divine light without. Finally, that self is purposeful in creation. The test of the meaning of my being is in activating the divine light in all that I do. There are no gaps in this vision, only greater and deeper challenges of meaning. It is not a simple task that can one day be completed, but an ever-moving process of completion. I belong in my wholeness of self, in my relations to others, and in my faith in Allah.

The Sacred Journey:
The Gift of Hajj

Daa'iyah Taha

———

It was 1993, during the month of Ramadan, the month of fasting, that I first knew I would be making Hajj, the Pilgrimage to Mecca. It is an act of love and devotion that every Muslim must make, at least once in their life. At that time, I had neither the money nor the means to even consider such a long and expensive journey. But through the days of prayer and contemplation that fasting had provided for me, I had come to realize that Hajj was no longer something that I could casually put off as a mere eventuality, deferring it to my previously laid plans, my lack of means, my fear of the unknown or anything else. I had become anxious, spiritually restless, knowing that something within me needed to change, needed to grow. I wanted to be closer to God. Something in my *soul* needed Hajj. So I prayed to God to allow me to visit His House.

In an effort to raise money for the trip, I spent the year marketing a self-published specialty book and selling women's clothing out of my home. I was working hard and saving what I could. But at the pace I was going, I realized that my efforts alone would not be enough to secure arrangements for me to make the Pilgrimage that year. Hajj was now only three months away. I had resolved to keep on working and saving, but reality was telling me that if I would make Hajj that year, it would be solely by the Grace of God. And it was.

I was home one evening with my family, ready to settle down with a snack and a good movie when the phone rang.

"How you doin', Baby?" I didn't recognize the voice on the other end of the line. I could tell it was an older African-American woman by the sweetness and the gentle tremor in her voice.

"I'm fine. Who is this?"

"This is Wincie."

My mind went into search mode. Wincie? Oh yes, Wincie, the hairdresser, my mother's old friend. She had known me since my childhood days of impatiently squirming in the beautyshop chair, waiting for her to be done with my mother's hair. Over the years, we had seen each other only now and then at mosque functions, the last time being several years ago. Why was she calling me now? I listened curiously as she asked about the family and remembered everyone fondly. Then she remarked, "I saw an ad in the paper for your book. Can you mail me a copy?"

"Oh, yes," I replied, honored that she would even ask, thinking that I had discovered the reason for her unexpected call. I took down her address and promised to mail her a book right away. We chatted on a few minutes more, and then she said, "I'd like to ask you something."

"Yes?"

"Have you made Hajj yet?"

My heart began to race because I now knew exactly what this call was about. I answered slowly, "No, ma'am, I haven't."

"Good!" she said excitedly, "Cause I want to send you to Hajj! It was such a beautiful experience for me! I have been saving this money and trying to decide what to do with it. I'm so happy God blessed me to think of you. I just know you'll come back with so much that you can share in your writing."

I don't remember what we said next, or even hanging up the phone when we were through. I only remember the tears streaming down my face and the incredible feelings of both gratitude and unworthiness in my soul. This was the answer to my prayer. Through her generous gift, I was going to make Hajj!

I don't recall much of what transpired in the weeks before I left, except that my days were filled with hurry, each melting into the next, each bringing me closer to the moment when I would board that jumbo Saudia jet, headed for Hajj. And when I did finally lift off over the Atlantic, I remember a feeling of panic pushing up through my throat, making my body stiffen as the jet roared upward. I just could not believe that I was actually headed for Mecca, to Hajj, to the Holy Ka'bah, to see the sacred precincts toward which I had prayed every prayer for the last twenty years. I would be there in less than twelve hours.

I rested for most of the flight, waking periodically to the soft buzz of quiet conversation. And then the announcement came, about an hour before the plane touched down in Jeddah. It was time for everyone to assume the ritual Hajj garment. For the men, two pieces of seamless white cloth, one draped over the shoulders, the other wrapped around the waist. For the women, any garment affording them modesty and comfort. Once in pilgrim garb, I began the ritual chant, "Here I am, O God! At your service! Here I am!" And the anticipation swelled within me as I realized that Mecca would soon be just a short bus ride away.

It was about three o'clock in the morning when we rolled into the Holy City. I peered into the darkness, through the bus window, looking for a sign that the Ka'bah was near. And then I heard it—this voice, ringing through the morning air like a sweet, melodious siren. It was the call to prayer, sounding out from the Sacred Mosque. I knew then that the Ka'bah was ever so near. At last, I would begin the rites of Hajj.

I stepped through the doors of the Mosque into a maze of gray-and-white-swirled marble columns, each flowering into delicately carved arches which framed the structure. It was seemingly round, the arches symmetrically repeating themselves in a harmonious curve to the right and to the left of me. The light was muted, hovering in those hollowed arches, softening the heat against us. There were pilgrims everywhere, some standing, some sitting, and some lying down on their sides. I fastened hands with other pilgrims and zigzagged through the crowds that carpeted the mosque floor. My heart raced with anticipation as I made my way toward the courtyard. Hurrying down steps that my feet have no memory of touching, I glanced up to see the corner of the Ka'bah peeking through the rows of arches in front of me. I clasped my hand against my mouth, trying to hold in the outpouring of emotion that burst forth from my heart. My shoulders shook as I stepped into the splendor of the full sight!

There it stood, like a majestic black jewel, rising out of the center of a lake of cool white marble—the Ka'bah, more magnificent than my imagination could ever have fathomed. Head turned upward, my hungry eyes reverently canvassed the holy edifice. A simple cubic structure, solid and upright, its noble shoulders solemnly draped in gold-trimmed black cloth. To the west of the Ka'bah, encased in glass, are the imprints in stone of the feet of its builder, Prophet Abraham. Still further west is a short arched wall, which guards the grave of the woman at whose breast the noble Prophet Ishmael was fed, and at whose skirt he was taught the love of God. She is Hagar, an African woman, the only woman buried in these holy precincts. I momentarily closed my eyes against the sun, offering a prayer of thanks to be standing on such sacred ground.

Gracing the eastern corner of the Ka'bah, suspended within a silver casing, is a special stone. It marks the starting point for encircling the hallowed House, its shiny meteoric blackness calling to mind the undeniable innocence and colorlessness of our common human nature. It was here, at the Black Stone, that I began to move—slowly, thoughtfully, incredulously, tearfully, lovingly, prayerfully. Around the Sacred House. Seven times, counterclockwise in a slow human whirlpool, against time and place and lines that divide one human soul from another. Around the Sacred House. Shoulder to shoulder, tear to tear, hope to hope, we all toiled in a teeming, rotating cycle of Oneness. Around the Sacred House. Past Abraham's footprints, past Hagar's skirt, multitudes of men and women, rich and poor, Arab and non-Arab, black and white, from every corner of the globe. Around the Sacred House. Now somehow all an equal part of this Divine human equation, forging forward toward the promise of God's forgiveness. Around the Sacred House. With the simplest words and the deepest devotion, in every human tongue, in one grateful human voice we answered God's Call as we made the sacred circle a final time. Around the Sacred House. When the seventh circuit was complete, I performed the commemorative prayers near the Station of Abraham. I felt connected to humanity in a way that I had not known was possible. My soul was so joyful, so thankful, and so thirsty for more. And it was now ready for the Sacred Waters of Zamzam.

I descended the stairs which lead down beneath the courtyard floor into the area of the Well of Zamzam. I passed streams of women with containers of Zamzam water gripped tightly in their hands or balanced perfectly on their heads, carefully carrying them away for safekeeping until they returned to their respective homes. Of all the gifts that a returning pilgrim can bring to their loved ones, Zamzam water is the most requested and the most beloved gift of all. The Well is enclosed behind marble walls. Its waters pour forth from faucets and is savored from silver cups loosely chained to the faucet handles. As I patiently waited in line for my turn to drink, I savored in my mind the history of the Sacred Well's beginnings.

It is reported that God ordered Abraham to take his wife Hagar and their infant son Ishmael to a desolate place in a desert valley and to leave them there. With only a few dates and a bucket of water from which to drink, he left them, praying to God for their protection and safety. As Hagar watched him walk away, she cried out, "How can you leave us here? We will soon have nothing to eat or drink!" She repeated her question to him many times. He did not answer her. Finally, she thoughtfully inquired, "Is this God's will, or is it your own decision?" "It is God's command," he confirmed. And with remarkable faith she replied, "Then God will not neglect us!"

She drank the water and ate the dates, nursing her son with the nourishment they provided. But soon the provisions were gone. Hagar's heart ached at the sound of her son's thirsty cries. Knowing full well the symbionic relationship between faith and work (God helps those who help themselves), Hagar knew that she had to get busy. In an act of unconditional faith, she left her child, there on the floor of that lifeless valley, and began her quest.

Back and forth, back and forth, seven times between the hills of Safa and Marwa, she ran—searching, groping, scanning, seeking to find whatever help she could to relieve her thirsty child. But there was not a bird, nor a blade of grass, nor any living thing in sight that could give them any aid. There was only the hot sun on that lonely silent wasteland. When she returned to Ishmael, he lay there on his barren desert bed, kicking his feet in the sand. As his tiny toes pierced the dry earth, a small cool spring began to bubble up from the ground. Feverishly, Hagar dug her hands into the sand, corralling the water, keeping it from dissipating. She then drank from it and suckled her child, praising and thanking God for His infinite Grace. This marked the beginning of the Well, and the beginning of the City of Mecca, to which her husband would one day return, and with the aid of Ishmael, construct the Holy Ka'bah. And it is here, at the endless, life-giving waters of this ancient well, that every pilgrim must lovingly and gratefully remember Hagar—the black slave woman, the beloved wife of Prophet Abraham, and the devoted mother of Prophet Ishmael, a model of faith for all of humanity.

It was with love and gratitude that I took my first sip of the ancient water. It was cool and fresh, almost thick, its mineral-laden richness lying heavy on the tongue. I drank my fill, remembering Hagar, and praying that I would one day be as faithful.

From the relief of the Well I ascended the stairs, back into the heat of the day. Continuing the rites of Hajj, I made my way through the mosque, up the sloping mount, to the site of Hagar's ancient drama. It was now time to perform the ritual search between the two hills in the same faithful manner as she had done. The crowd stretched into two throbbing human streams, slowly plodding forward to the distant mount ahead, then diligently laboring back. I locked arms with other pilgrims and melted into the masses starting down Mount Safa. There I was, among the throngs of men and women moving forward, in unavoidable closeness, in inescapable discomfort, pressing, pushing forward, onward to Mount Marwa. Sometimes it was not even in our view. Only the sides and backs of pilgrims sweating, surging forward. It was such a struggle—back and forth between the hills, seven times. Just as Hagar had done alone, in search of help for her crying son, we now did en masse, in search of peace for our crying souls. And the Divine relief was near, but not before she had exerted and exhausted all of her own human resources. She had lived what we were now clearly learning, as we struggled on.

After descending Mount Marwa for the last time, we spilled out, one by one, onto the pavement outside the doors. Realizing that we had triumphantly completed the first rites of Hajj, we instinctively raised our hands and slapped each other five in our own ritualistic touch of victory. I cried and praised God out loud through my smiles and tears. Although I couldn't put it all together then, I knew that I had experienced something that would change me inside forever. I couldn't have known then how I would live that experience every day for the rest of my life. With every challenge I now face, I am again at Safa, ready to struggle through to Marwa, knowing that the relief of Zamzam is near. With every prayer I again face the Ka'bah, knowing that I stand shoulder to shoulder with human beings everywhere, forming one solid circle of praise around the Sacred House. Because of Hajj, I would never again desire to be held above or accept to be held behind another human being. I stand gratefully beside humanity in the dignity of the Circle. This is what my soul was longing for. This gift my soul received at Hajj.

From the House of Yemanja:
The Goddess Heritage of
Black Women

Sabrina Sojourner

It is difficult, if not impossible, to be raised in the United States without hav-ing Christian value judgments invade one's life. Until recent times, it was doubly hard for Black Americans to escape this intrusion because of the in-trinsic political and social, as well as religious, role the Black church has played in our community. It was only as late as my parents' generation that countless Black women and men began leaving the church, no longer be-lieving in the salvation offered by a white god and savior. Now many women of my own generation are discovering that God is not only not white, She has never even been considered male until relatively recently!

Reclaiming Our Spiritual Mother

The lack of information about Black Goddesses in most works on Goddess worship might lead one to believe that such information does not exist. This simply is not so! We of African descent have a rich Goddess and matrifocal heritage. While it is true that many tribes maintained a kingship for centuries before the notion of written history, more often than not, the king received his legitimacy from a magic-sacerdotal female clan. In other instances, the power of the king was channeled through the figure of a "dowager queen" or wifely queen. With some tribes, the kingship was not a position desired by most men because the king was ritually murdered every six months to a year.[1]

The information I have gathered about African Goddesses, heroines, and Amazons is a synthesis of bits and pieces of information from a variety of sources. The following profiles are taken primarily from the works of three women: Merlin Stone,[2] Audre Lorde,[3] and Helen Diner.[4]

Yemanja is the mother Goddess of the Orisha and, as such, is related to Mawu. Yemanja is the Goddess of the oceans; rivers are said to flow from Her breasts. River-smoothed stones are Her symbol. The sea is sacred to Her followers. In Brazil She is worshipped as Iamanja and is honored on the eve of Summer Solstice.

Mawu is known as the creator of the universe. As mother of the Vodu, She is related to Yemanja. Another form of Mawu is that of Mawulisa (Mawu-Lisa), the inseparable twins of the universe. For the Dahomean people, Mawulisa is the female-male, sky goddess-god principle, also represented as west-east, night-day, moon-sun. Where She is known as Mawu, Lisa is called either Her first son/consort or Her twin brother. Other manifestations of Mawu are Seboulisa and Sogbo.

Ala is a goddess of the Ibo people of Nigeria. She is called the provider of life and the mother who receives again in death. It is Ala who proclaims the law that is the basis for all moral human behavior. It is a Nigerian custom to have life-size images of Ala sitting on the porch of a small wooden house in the village visible to all who pass by.

Jezanna is the Goddess of the Moshona people of Zimbabwe. Her symbol is the moon and Her high priestess is Her primary representative.

Songi is the Great Mother of the Bantu people of central and southern Africa. A sacred legend holds that Nsomeka, a young woman, met Mother Songi in the forest one day. Songi notched Nsomeka's teeth. That evening, from the notches sprang forth livestock, fruit trees, houses, and shade trees. When the men of the village beat their wives for not producing these things for them, Nsomeka gathered all the women in her field and notched their teeth. None of the men could join them until they had promised to treat the women with respect.

Mboze is the First Mother of the Woyo people of Zaire. Her sacred story expresses women's attempts to keep tradition in the face of betrayal. Mboze has a daughter, Bunzi, by Her son/lover, Makanga. When Her husband, Kuitilkuitl (who had changed his black skin for white), learns that Makanga is the father, he beats Mboze to death. Bunzi grows older to do the work Her mother had once done, rewarding the faithful with bountiful rains and harvests.

Mbaba Mwana Waresa is the Goddess of the Zulu people of Natal. Among Her gifts, this holy Rain Goddess of the Heavens also gave Her people beer so that they might better celebrate their joyous times.

Tji-Wara (or *Chi-Wara*) is said to have introduced agriculture to the Bambara people. A good harvest is assured through pleasing Her.

African Amazons of the Goddess Lands

As with Amazon cultures of Goddess-oriented Anatolia, much of what we know about the Amazons of Libya (a term that once referred to all of Africa) centers around their fierceness as warriors. Through legend, mythology, and historical facts, we know of Merina,[5] for instance, and her peaceful march east through Egypt. Once in Syria, she conquered the Arabs, settlement after settlement. She led her Amazon troops through Phrygia and up the coast of the Mediterranean. In their path of triumph, they founded towns and colonies. Lesbos and other eastern Mediterranean islands are said to have fallen to Merina. Cast ashore at Samothrace after a terrific storm, Merina named the island and erected a temple to the Mother-Goddess (probably Neith), celebrated mysteries in Her honor, built altars, and made sacrifices. These were all in accordance with a vow she had taken during her hour of peril.[6]

The trek to Samothrace had been long and arduous. Their exhaustion benefited Greek forces led by Mompsus, a Thracian, and Sypylus, a Scythian. At their hands Merina was defeated and killed, ending the ferocious nation of Libyan Amazons. Most of her followers returned to North Africa. There they continued to honor Neith. The Libyan Amazons also worshiped Pallas Athena and Pallas Promochos, the Vanguard Goddess, as their goddess. As before the death of Merina, women were expected to remain virgins (unmarried) while in active service.[7]

Revival of Yoruban Theology among Black American Women

The African belief in a pantheon of goddesses and gods did not die when the Africans were brought to the "New World"; it merely changed. Traces of Yoruban culture survive in the West Indies, the United States, and South America. In the late sixties, transmitters of this tradition began to be sought out by Black intellectuals wanting to reclaim a lost part of their spiritual heritage. Now a third group has emerged: women who are challenging the present patriarchal structure of the religion. It is their belief that half-truths and false taboos have been imposed on them and on the Yoruban manifes-

274

tations of the Goddess, that undue power has been placed in the hands of men, and that it is their duty as the daughters of Yemanja, Oshun, and Oya to restore their mothers as the heads of the House and regain respect for women.

Two such women are Luisah Teish and Robin Pearson. Teish has lived in the San Francisco Bay area since 1971. She was not born into the Yoruban culture, but does not approach it completely as an outsider; during her childhood in the Delta region of Louisiana, remnants of it were all around her. Her formal interest began in the mid-sixties when she began dancing with Katherine Dunham. Upon her arrival in the Bay area, Teish started teaching Afro-Haitian dance. Since much of the dance is rooted in religion, Teish also provided her classes with information about the religious culture. In 1977 she started teaching classes on the Yoruban goddesses, mostly to women.

Teish believes that Oshun, the Yoruban goddess of love, beauty, and female power, has been wronged by contemporary patriarchs of the Yoruban culture. "Oshun is usually depicted as the very delicate, very conceited, and jealous female," observes Teish; but many aspects of this goddess are kept hidden. For instance, Teish explains, "We are told that Oshun's bird is the peacock whose only value is its outward appearance. However, if you listen carefully, you may also hear Her associated with the vulture." Teish adds with a sly smile, "And we all know how powerful the jaws and the claws of a vulture are."

Robin Pearson lives in Jamaica Plains, Massachusetts. Like Teish, Pearson was not born into the Yoruban culture. She joined a communal house in the mid-seventies that is oriented toward female spirituality. Pearson has since left the strictly ordered house and is working on her own. Both she and Teish hope to become priestesses; the complex ceremony of initiation can span five years. Because the initiators have tremendous influence over the outcome, both women hope to go to Africa, make contact with women who keep the old ways, and return to this country to open feminist Yoruba houses, centers that again will honor the Mother and Her daughters.

Redefining Our Spiritual Heritage

The Africans who adopted Christianity maintained their African spiritual sensibilities. Thus, with their conversion began the tapestry of Black theology and folk religion, comprised of threads of African religions and culture, Western civilization, and Christianity. It is colored with the practices, rituals, and philosophies of white, Christian theology and the African tradition that religion permeates all aspects of life with no final distinctions between what is secular and what is sacred.[8]

It is the latter aspect that accounts for the spiritual aspect of Black art, theater, music, and literature. This is why, even though raised outside the Church, there is rarely a Black individual who does not understand the Church's significance to the Black culture and community. Black theology and folk religion, like traditional African religions, seeks the power or the spirit of God (Divine Energy) in all times and places and things; without that power, one is helpless.[9] Because the Church has succeeded in providing for its community a "heaven on earth"—a sense of joy in the face of adversity—it has maintained its central position. By attuning yourself to the Spirit, or its manifestations, you become one with that power. Thus, when Black Christians talk about putting themselves in the hands of God, they are generally referring to their need, desire, or ability to tap into a divine source of energy and utilize that energy to push/pull themselves through a situation. This is not much different from the Pagan process of channeling energy, which many women are reviving today.

Perhaps the Amazons who rode into Europe from the Russian steppes were fierce, blonde, blue-eyed women. My Amazons have always been dark. It is not easy growing up in a society whose language and laws fear, despise, and dehumanize the rainbow of people who are of darker hues. It is not easy trusting alliances with women who continue a *status quo* negation of one's racial/cultural/ethnic/class background. The dark-skinned women who rode, thousands strong, across the African continent and through the Arab world are my reminder that I am the ancestral daughter/sister of a powerful nation of women. Whether their battles were merely for the sport and spoils of war or for the preservation of Mother Right is immaterial. It is their fight and strength that I cling to. For me, this image has been an amazing source of courage, conviction, and freedom.

The works of Diner and Stone are a very helpful and encouraging beginning, but there is much more that needs to be uncovered. Black women must tend to this cultural history; because it is our own, we are more likely to intuit the threads of truth that join the surviving facts. Several Black women writers have already begun to explore the mythical/spiritual realm of our existence: Zora Neal Hurston in *Their Eyes Were Watching God* and *Of Mules and Men*, as well as in most of her anthropological writings; Marita Bonner in her play *The Purple Flower*; Audre Lorde in "Uses of the Erotic: The Erotic as Power," *The Black Unicorn*, *Coal*, and more than can be named here; Toni Cade Bambara in *The Salt Eaters*; Ntozake Shange in *for colored girls who have considered suicide/when the rainbow is enuf*, the short story "Sassafrass," and numerous poems, Pam Parker in *Movement in Black*; and Joyce Carol Thomas in her play *Ambrosia*, a powerful tale of spiritual reincarnation.

The chasm that exists between the matrifocal cultures of yesterday and the brutal subjugation of our African sisters today, which includes widespread genital mutilation, is treacherously deep. Numerous institutions and individuals have been complicit in leading us to believe that the latter is the "natural" way things have always been. What they try to ignore and we often fail to remember is that patriarchal religion and cultural mores are only a few thousand years old—hardly worthy of the term "forever"! Improving the quality of women's lives around the world requires more than economic and/ or political theory. It is my hope that as more and more Third World women read Diner, Stone, Lorde, and others, they will begin to fill in the names, rituals, and deeds—the realities—of the Goddess-worshipping and woman-honoring cultures of our ancestors. I long for a discussion of spiritual, as well as economic and political, structures among Third World women, among all women.

Notes

1. Helen Diner, *Mother and Amazons: The First Feminine History of Culture* (Garden City, N.Y.: Anchor Press/Doubleday, 1973), pp. 177–181.
2. Merlin Stone, *When God Was a Woman* (New York: The Dial Press, 1976) and *Ancient Mirrors of Womanhood: Our Goddess and Heroine Heritage* (New York: New Sibylline Books, 1979/80).
3. Audre Lorde, *The Black Unicorn* (New York: W. W. Norton & Company, 1978).
4. Helen Diner, *Mother and Amazons*.
5. Merina is most widely known as Myrine, her Greek name, but the former is her Libyan name.

277

6. Guy Cadogan Rothery, *The Amazons in Antiquity and Modern Times* (London: Francis Griffiths, 1910), p. 113.

7. See ibid., p. 113, and Diner, *Mother and Amazons*, pp. 108–9.

8. Joseph R. Washington, Jr., *Black Sects and Cults* (Garden City, N.Y.: Anchor Press/Doubleday, 1973), p. 20.

9. Ibid.

She Who Whispers

Luisah Teish

They think they frighten me
Those people must be crazy
They don't see their misfortune
Or else they must be drunk.

I, the voodoo Queen,
With my lovely handkerchief
Am not afraid of tomcat shrieks,
I drink serpent venom!

I walk on pins
I walk on needles,
I walk on gilded splinters
I want to see what they can do!

They think they have pride
With their big malice,
But when they see a coffin
They're as frightened as prairie birds.

I'm going to put gris-gris
All over their front steps
And make them shake
Until they stutter!
—*JESSIE GASTON MULIRA*, "The Case of Voodoo
in New Orleans," about Marie Laveau

There had been winters before. Cold, windful winters of frost-bitten hunger and snowcapped loneliness. But this winter it was deep, deep desolation that cut and mashed the spirit of the woman. Inside was lacking. No amount of heat thawed the chill, no warm broth and conversation satisfied the aching sense of loss, failure, and worthlessness. All because inside was lacking.

She looked through her self's mirror image and saw gold that had some-how turned to rust, love gone to stale lovelessness, and knowledge degener-ated into meaningless facts; and decided her birth, her very existence had been an error, a freak occurrence took place when Mother Nature batted her watchful eyelid.

Determined not to tolerate such an existence, the woman set her mind on suicide. She removed the clothing from her body and remembered how once she had a love of sewing, but had lost it somehow. En route to the bed, she passed her books and hoped maybe in the guise of poetry, they would bring some moment of exhilaration, to her sister. She said goodbye to her music collection, the universal magic that now failed, for the first time in her life, to bring her any semblance of joy. All these golden gifts bestowed on her had somehow betrayed, or been betrayed by her.

So she laid herself down in that lost lonely nakedness and implored Life to remove itself from her young but weary body. And, my God, it happened! An occurrence so bizarre that she thought herself engrossed in a grisly occult novel, such as she had been so fond of reading in that life. A paper-thin image of herself rose, floating out of the carcass, and rested itself somewhere on the stark white ceiling.

Her perception changed, and she viewed the world from the eye of the im-age. The image watched quietly as the body adopted a grayish hue; the eyes grew cloudy; and the lips sealed themselves one to the other.

The chest no longer heaved up and down with the breath of life, and the heart ceased to pound out the terrifying drum rhythms. Instead there was a musical silence that no instrument would imitate.

From her view on the ceiling, the image saw the figure of a young girl come and touch the body, trying to arouse it, but receiving no answer, assumed it to be in deep sleep. And—tired herself—the young girl muttered, "She's really tired, I'll ask her in the morning." This kindness initiated a struggle within the carcass. A struggle to somehow explain to the loved that there would be no tomorrow; to make her understand why; to give what last moment of aid one could give; to scream out loud a plea to forgive this act of doubt, of fear, of unamendable cowardice. But too quickly the girl vanished.

Without warning, a voice—quite her own, yet more lovely—rose from the breast of the carcass and spoke, saying, "Get back in yo' body, Girl, you have work to do."

No sooner had the command been given than a thin blue light appeared, streaming between body and soul. It flowed painlessly until they were one again, and the chest began to ebb and flow with a fresh spring air.

Not needing the use of a mouth, the woman called her own name aloud, asking, "What is my purpose?" The room then seemed to have lost its dimensions, being free of top, bottom, sides, and contents. Yet it was filled with bold white letters traced in black; words of instruction, each accompanied by a picture of the task to be performed, each task giving-birth to a feeling of power and of peace. The woman fancied for a moment that she was lying in a great, gentle stream of warm, crystal-blue water; that the sun rising outside her bedroom window slowly filled every pore with gold; that strength and beauty lifted the sealed eyelids and gave them new clarity.

Then there was rest.

That morning, the woman watered her plants to the inner rhythm of Bata drums and gold-brown biscuits. Her younger sister came into the kitchen rubbing her eyes and yawning. "Ain't you bright and chipper this morning? You slept so hard last night, Girl, I thought you were dead. Tried to wake you but I figured you musta' been real tired, so I just let you alone."

"Really," the woman answered, feeling somewhat strange, "What did you want?"

The young girl wrinkled her brow. "Funny, I can't remember now, but I wanted you to do something . . . hunh. Oh well, it'll come back."

They sat down to a breakfast of biscuits, coffee, and laughter. That's all there was . . . that cold needy winter.

I call this experience my nervous breakthrough. Prior to it I was literally out of my mind. For a month I was quiet as a church mouse all day, and I screamed all night that I was a captive on this planet and didn't want to be here. I was strung out on *doctor-prescribed* dope and poison and under the influence of people who themselves were frightened and powerless. Like many others, I made the mistake of judging my worth by the paper in my pocket and arrogantly rejected the beauty of the flowers.

I wanted to be an asset to my community, to contemplate the meaning of existence and produce beauty. But literally everything in the society told me I was a useless nigger wench. I was someone who was best forgotten and destined to be destroyed. I was caught between my soul's desires and society's dictates.

Thank Goddess my sister, Safi, was confident that I would come through it, so she did not call "the man" in the white coat.

Since then I have worked as a mental patient's advocate, and I maintain that many people in our state institutions are really in spiritual crises. The addition of mind-melting drugs makes their breakdown almost inevitable.

Sister, if you are caught between the devil and the deep blues, let go of your present thought patterns. Release your grip on what you've been taught is reality, and invoke for a breakthrough. You won't regret it.

This experience pushed me to go to a Voudou priest for my first reading from the oracle. The oracle is a system of divining using sixteen cowrie shells. Through it a priest can read your past, present, and future and name your personal deity. From the moment the priest announced that I was the daughter of *Oshun*, I began to think of myself in a different, more positive way. *Oshun* is the Goddess of love, art, and sensuality. She is a temperamental coquette with much magic up her sleeve. She was the *me* I hid from the world.

The priest opened many doors for me and showed me that I should yield completely to my spiritual urgings. Among the things he suggested were many I had been considering. He said my Goddess wanted me to read Tarot cards for other people. I'd already bought and studied Tarot but restricted the readings only to myself. He said I should call myself a spiritualist and teach what I learned to others. In the past I'd restricted my teaching to the spiritual significance of the dance. In short, he said that my Goddess was speaking *to* and *through* me and that I should "listen to my head" and do whatever She told me to do. He told me that I had "smiling enemies" and that I should change my circle of friends. And in fact, my attempts to change myself brought heavy criticism down on me from the people who had come to depend on my remaining the same. I wrote the following poem to crystalize this experience:

Friends

Once I was a real nice girl
with smiles for all, you hear?
Until that still small voice
began to whisper in my ear.

She said, "If you will listen
you will find, in fact
that others too are whispering,
Babe, but it's behind yo' back."

So then I got real quiet
(just to check it out)
and listening to my friends
brought second thoughts and doubts.

Willie says I'm skinny.
May says much too fat,
but when I serve them dinner,
Child, I'm really where it's at.

Betty wants to cut my hair,
and then dye it black,
While Lilly says that modesty
is what I really lack.

Frank, he calls me egghead
because I like to read,
and Sally Jo, my shy friend,
offers scag, coke, and speed.

Prudence G., my white friend,
says politically I'm wild.
My black friend calls me Uncle Tom
because I like to smile.

Helen says, "Stop singing,
Girl, I can't stand your range."
Still small voice says,
"Go on, Girl, you know
that's got to change."

Now I do less crying,
it seems I get more done.
Whatever my dear friends now say,
I take as lightweight fun.

When feeling really rotten
and things come to bad ends,
if you think you have no enemies
better look among yo' friends.

Learn from my mistakes, my friend,
you'll come out better by far.
Your true friends will help
you change,
but accept you as you are.

Now I began, almost magically, to meet older women who were spiritualists in various traditions. They entrusted me with the shopping for their occult supplies. In exchange they taught me their charms. I met a root woman from New Orleans, who taught me how to make lucky hands for financial gain and to work John the Conquer Root.*

One day while sitting at a bus stop in Berkeley I saw a woman in a brightly embroidered tunic and turban and thought I knew her. I waved, but she did not see me. I sat down and forgot about it. Moments later she came running over to me, crying, hugging me, and calling "Marguerite, I'm so glad I've found you!" She thought I was her cousin whom she had last seen running to safety from an earthquake in Guatemala. We became fast friends. She gave me readings, took me on herb hunts, and performed a "bath of fire" with me.

*The John the Conquer—a root used for luck and protection.

Much to my amazement the flames caressed my body, but—as she had commanded—I was not burned.

The teachings of these older women reinforced those of the Fahamme temple. These women called God by various names and invoked spirits unknown to me, but demonstrated that the *power* of the spirit is all there is in the universe.

In 1977 I got a CETA job with a Berkeley Neighborhood Arts program. I wrote and directed *The DeerWoman of Owo*, a play based on a Yoruba folktale. In time I was asked to teach a workshop on African Goddesses at the Berkeley Women's Center. The women who attended my workshops were enthusiastic and supportive. We shared our knowledge of various Goddesses and marveled at the similarities.

At a seance one night I was told to go home to New Orleans to visit my mother, because my ancestors were dissatisfied. This is when I discovered that my paternal grandmother's house (for whom I had been named), where I'd floated out of my body, sat on the site of the former home of Mam'zelle Marie Laveau, the Voudou Queen of New Orleans.

Homegrown Juju Dolls: An Interview with Artist Riua Akinshegun

Gail Hanlon

Riua Akinshegun is an artist who is exploring how to turn pain into a creative and motivational force. In 1971, as a member of the organization, The Republic of New Africa, she was shot in the spine by another member of the group and was not expected to live. Says Riua, "I became a paraplegic and was in constant pain for seventeen years. I was not a functioning person. But art saved my life. It brought me peace when I was in severe pain." Riua's sculpture, ceramic masks, traditional batik, and African wrap dolls[1] began to gain recognition as she continued to create art to channel her pain.

In 1989, Riua had an operation on her spine that released her from her pain, and a whole world opened up to her. In June 1990, she traveled to Mali, where she had a show at the National Museum; to Lagos, where she had an exhibit at the Ayota Museum; and to Senegal. "Homegrown Juju Dolls—A Series on Chronic Pain and Healing"[2] was her latest show. She recently finished her autobiography, *The Seed of My Soul*, a work coauthored with novelist Odie Hawkins.

It is Riua's hope to teach people how to manage both spiritual and physical pain, in order to reach their full potential whatever their present circumstances. To do this, Riua draws upon her near-death experience as a result of the shooting, her subsequent suffering, and the resulting near-homelessness and continual poverty she experienced while trying to survive on Social Security payments. "Everybody has some sort of pain," she explains, "whether it is physical, mental, or spiritual. I teach people how to channel their pain through art as a creative force."

woman of power   You have used the word "channel" in connection with your work. Do you feel that your work is channeled?

This interview first appeared in *Woman of Power* (Fall 1991), where interviewer Gail Hanlon is identified as "woman of power."

Riua   Yes. You see, I was in serious pain for seventeen years and there were three things I could do to get out of pain. One was astral projection, or going internal. The second thing I could do to get out of pain was my art. The third was making love. Astral projection for me takes two forms—in and out of the body. The first time I experienced going out of my body was on the operating table after the shooting. When I experienced that first astral projection, I could look down at my body on the operating table and I saw the intravenous tubes and all the other tubes that were keeping me alive. I floated out into the hallway and went down the hallway and everyone was in the waiting room crying—my students and my family and everyone. And I was getting ready to go out the door but I kept thinking about everyone in the waiting room so I went back to comfort them.

My art could also get me some relief from my pain. When I go into my work, things just start happening. I incorporated the wrapping technique that was carried over from slavery here into my dolls because I wanted to put a little bit of history into the pieces. I'm just beginning to understand my last series of work. It's just coming to me now what I did, whom I created. I created three dolls in my last series, "Homegrown Juju Dolls: A Series on Chronic Pain and Healing," and it's been just recently that I've understood that one of my dolls, "Wisdom Past and Future," did all of my woeing, all of my nonverbal crying and mourning, for me. "The High Priestess" was for protection, and "Earth Mother" kept me grounded and in tune with nature.

I have arguments with the dolls as I'm creating. They want me to do something and I don't want to do it; I'm stubborn and I don't want to listen. And then finally I'll say, "Okay, I'll try it." And when I try it, it just fits. I don't even understand what I'm creating. It's been a year since I created them, and I'm just beginning to understand them. That's why I have a hard time releasing them and selling them, because I don't even know them yet. When they're ready to be released, they'll let me release them. It's very difficult right now because they're still talking to me, still telling me things.

I have also made some sculptures. I think I'm getting ready to merge my dolls and sculptures together, and do some larger pieces. I'm not quite sure what the medium will be, whether ceramic or even wood, it could be anything. Because I work in mixed media, I'm not restricted to anything.

woman of power   Did you begin to work out of the African tradition after you went there? Do you feel that you've reclaimed or somehow reshaped
those spiritual traditions into your own personal tradition?

Riua   Oh, yes. When I went there, I was not trying to deal with the religions
of the African people. I was just going for art and culture, thinking somehow
it was separate. But one of the goddesses, Oshun,[3] the goddess of fertility, the
goddess who protects women and children, just claimed me. I have never
been claimed like that before. I became a daughter of Oshun. I would go to
her shrine and talk to her a lot. I was very affected by how the people incor-
porate all the gods into everything. I met Ogun,[4] Shango,[5] all of them.

After a while, I understood that the African people were trying to be in
tune with everything around them. And I find that if I can be balanced with
nature, then things will work around me pretty well. Knowledge opens up
for me. I try to listen to the Earth. I try to listen to the wind. I try to acknowledge everything respectfully, because everything has power. Rocks, seeds,
everything.

When I was there, I had no idea about going into my body. My pain got so
bad when I was in Africa that I had to withdraw, what I call "ignoring pain."
So what I learned to do there was to go inside my body. I just started listening
to my pain so that it would release me. I tried to make a friend out of it.
Whatever I was doing, I would go inside.

These days, since the operation, my world seems so chaotic because when
I was in pain I was so much in my body, so much in the physical world, that
I tuned everything else out. The rest of my life was done through a veil,
through a haze. The pain taught me to live in the immediate world, and I still
do that because once the door is open it doesn't have to be closed. Now that I
no longer have to spend so much energy on the pain, my concentration seems
effortless, especially for my artwork. I can work for hours on end. While I was
inside my body, sometimes for two or three hours, I couldn't respond to anything around me. People would be in my room; they'd be talking; I could hear
them; I could follow the conversation; I could see; but if I acknowledged any
of it or responded, the pain would just attack me. So I would just withdraw,
and when I was withdrawn I got to understand my organs. I would review my
day, and I learned to take time to do that every night. What that allows me

to do is immediately take out nonsense, things that keep me unbalanced, or things that I said that were not quite correct. This daily withdrawal keeps me really balanced. And that's where I get my power and my spirituality.

woman of power How do you think your work helps to empower women in particular?

Riua I wanted to do something to put an end to seventeen years of chronic pain. And when I got ready to go into the studio to work, I kept thinking about chronic pain, chronic pain, and nothing would come.

So I looked at my life. And I saw that I tried not to live my life as a sufferer. I thought about what carried me through these seventeen years, and that was the healing aspect of it. So I changed the title of my show from "Chronic Pain" to "Chronic Pain and Healing." Most of my pieces focus on how to channel your energy. For example, my sculptures are sitting on pouches and inside the pouches are healing objects. These are woman guardian pieces called "The Guardian Woman I and II," "Malakia," even "Oshun." Those are some of the images of spirituality I pulled on to carry me through. So I did workshops with the Guardian Woman series for women. We all came together and talked about things in our lives that we wanted to focus on changing, and things that would motivate us in other ways.

For example, one woman lost her child in a fire. She was forty before she even had her first child, and she lost her. So we talked about how happy the child was, and that helped us to see that the important thing was to make the mother happy, because the child was fine. We said, "We've got to work on us." So she created a piece of sculpture that was so whimsical that every time she saw it she had to smile. And inside the pouch she put different things that had belonged to her daughter, so that she'd remember that her daughter wants to see her smiling.

woman of power How do you think women can celebrate our spiritual selves?

Riua By acknowledging it. By understanding it. By getting into it. Most women don't even know the power we have. If women would just look back at history and see how we've evolved, we could know that. But unfortunately, many women don't know that.

I think women need to unite among ourselves. Somehow the African woman is not being pulled into the feminist movement. I think that when we talk about feminism, if we can include the whole picture, that will help us to draw in African women. One of the problems is that during the sixties, when the Black movement became separate from the white movement, when the feminists became separate, and the disabled became separate, even though many of the techniques were borrowed from the Black movement, somehow feminism didn't pull in Black women.

Even so, African people are not yet strong enough to separate out as women. I can't separate and leave my child alone. Or leave the whole race alone. We're dying as a race. I think that we can start being a total vision and yet understand the need to pull together for that reinforcement.

How do we celebrate ourselves? By following our intuitive nature instead of pushing it back. If we can learn to listen to our inner selves and not worry about society's interpretation of things, that will free us up. Spirituality can't be separated from breath, let alone art. I don't pray; however, I try to live my life as a prayer.

Notes

1. African wrap dolls are made in the style used in the U.S. during slavery times. Bits of cloth are wound around wood or wire.
2. Juju means magic.
3. Oshun is the Yoruba Goddess of love, healing, and female energy, Queen of the River.
4. Ogun is the Yoruba wild man of the woods; a blacksmith.
5. Shango is the Yoruba lightning and thunder god.

at karnak temple

ginger floyd

i had to come
alone
to this special place
karnak temple
egyptian city of the gods
sacred ground

i had to come
alone
to be alone
with my god
and my innerself
and in the cosmic universe of spirits
to merge with life before
and life yet to come.

prayer calls
donkeys braying
birds singing
shadows of temple columns
being chased away by the arrival of dawn

i sit
alone
at karnak temple
on sacred ground
humbled by its glory
and giving thanks
for the miracle of morning.

P A **5** R T

Invoking the Spirit:
The Healing Power of Affirmations
and Rituals

I looked at my hands and they looked new
I looked at my feet and they did too.
—*FROM A NEGRO SPIRITUAL*

When we perform rituals as our ancestors did, we become our ancestors,
and so transcend the boundaries of ordinary space and time, and the
limitations of separation that they impose. When we call the spirits
and they enter our bodies we symbolize in our being the joining
of, and therefore communication between, two spheres of
the universe: "heaven" and the "earth."
—*DONA MARIMBA RICHARDS*, from *Let the Circle Be Unbroken*

Herein dwells the still small voice to which my spiritual self is attuned. I find,
also, that I am equally sensitive to any outside obstructions that would mar
this harmony or destroy this fortress. These inspirational vibrations are
known to me as my inner voice. Therefore, as I come face to face with
tremendous problems and issues, I am geared immediately to these spiritual
vibrations and they never fail me. The response is satisfying, though the
demand may call for great courage and sacrifice.
This power of faith which is my spiritual strength is so intimately a
part of my mental and emotional life that I find integration and
harmony ever present within me . . . and my happiness within
is a fortress against doubt and fear and uncertainty.
—*MARY MCLEOD BETHUNE*

Meditate and learn to be alone without being lonely. . . . Learn to be quiet
enough to hear the sound of the genuine within yourself so that you can hear
it in other people. . . . A few minutes every hour, a half hour every day, a
day a month, a week a year—in dedicated silence—is a goal to pursue.
—*MARIAN WRIGHT EDELMAN,*
from *The Measure of Our Success*

From *I, Tituba*

Maryse Condé

As for me, I was driven off the plantation by Darnell at the tender age of seven. I would probably have died if it hadn't been for that almost sacred tradition of solidarity among slaves.

An old woman took me in. As she had seen her man and two sons tortured to death for instigating a slave revolt, she seemed to act deranged. In fact, she was hardly of this world and lived constantly in their company. She had cultivated to a fine art the ability to communicate with the invisible. She was not an Ashanti like my mother and Yao, but a Nago from the coast, whose name, Yetunde, had been creolized into Mama Yaya. People were afraid of her, but they came from far and wide because of her powers.

She started off by giving me a bath of foul-smelling roots, letting the water run over my arms and legs. Then she had me drink a potion of her own concoction and tied a string of little red stones around my neck. "You will suffer during your life. A lot. A lot." She uttered these terrifying words perfectly calmly, almost with a smile. "But you'll survive." That was not very reassuring! But the hunched and wrinkled figure of Mama Yaya gave off such an air of authority that I did not dare protest.

Mama Yaya taught me about herbs. Those for inducing sleep. Those for healing wounds and ulcers. Those for loosening the tongues of thieves. Those that calm epileptics and plunge them into blissful rest. Those that put words of hope on the lips of the angry, the desperate, and the suicidal.

Mama Yaya taught me to listen to the wind rising and to measure its force as it swirled above the cabins it had the power to crush.

Mama Yaya taught me the sea, the mountains, and the hills. She taught me that everything lives, has a soul, and breathes. That everything must be respected. That man is not the master riding through his kingdom on horseback.

One day I fell asleep in the middle of the afternoon. It was the dry season.

The slaves were chanting plaintively as they hoed and cut in the stifling heat. Then I saw my mother. Not the disjointed, tormented puppet swinging round and round among the leaves, but decked out in the colors of Yao's love.

"Mother!" I cried.

She came and took me in her arms. God! How sweet her lips were! "Forgive me for thinking I didn't love you. Now I know I'll never leave you," she said.

"And Yao? Where is Yao?" I cried out in happiness.

She turned around. "He's here too." And Yao appeared.

I ran to tell my dream to Mama Yaya, who was peeling the tubers for the evening meal. She smiled knowingly. "Do you really think it was a dream?" I remained dumbfounded.

From that moment on Mama Yaya initiated me into the upper spheres of knowledge. The dead only die if they die in our hearts. They live on if we cherish them and honor their memory, if we place their favorite delicacies in life on their graves, and if we kneel down regularly to commune with them. They are all around us, eager for attention, eager for affection. A few words are enough to conjure them back and to have their invisible bodies pressed against ours in their eagerness to make themselves useful. But beware of irritating them, for they never forgive and they pursue with implacable hatred those who have offended them, even in error. Mama Yaya taught me the prayers, the rites, and the propitiatory gestures. She taught me how to change myself into a bird on a branch, into an insect in the dry grass or a frog croaking in the mud of the River Ormond whenever I was tired of the shape I had been given at birth. And then she taught me the sacrifices. Blood and milk, the essential liquids. Alas! shortly after my fourteenth birthday her body followed the law of nature. I did not cry when I buried her. I knew I was not alone and that three spirits were now watching over me.

It was at this juncture that Darnell sold the plantation. A few years earlier his wife, Jennifer, had died leaving him a frail, pale baby son, who was periodically shaken with fever. Despite the copious milk he received from a slave, who had been forced to give up nursing her own son, he seemed destined for the grave. Darnell's paternal instinct was aroused for his only white offspring and he decided to return to England to try and cure him.

The new master bought the land without the slaves, which was not at all the custom. With their feet in chains and a rope around their necks, they were taken to Bridgetown to find a buyer. Then they were scattered to the four corners of the island, father separated from son and mother from daughter. Since I no longer belonged to Darnell and was a squatter on the plantation, I was not part of the sad procession that set off for the slave market. I knew a spot on the edge of the River Ormond where nobody ever went because the soil was marshy and not suitable for growing sugarcane. With the strength of my own hands I managed to build a cabin on stilts. I patiently grafted strips of earth and laid out a garden where soon all sorts of plants were growing, placed in the ground with ritual respect for the sun and air.

Today I realize that these were the happiest moments of my life. I was never alone, because my invisible spirits were all around me, yet they never oppressed me with their presence.

Mama Yaya put the finishing touches to her lessons about herbs. Under her guidance I attempted bold hybrids, cross-breeding the *passiflorinde* with the *prune taureau*, the poisonous *pomme cythère* with the surette, and the *azalée-des-azalées* with the *persulfureuse*. I devised drugs and potions whose powers I strengthened with incantations.

In the evening the violet sky of the island stretched above my head like a huge handkerchief against which the stars sparkled one by one. In the morning the sun cupped its hand in front of its mouth and called for me to roam in its company. I was far from men, and especially white men. I was happy. Alas! all that was to change.

One day a great gust of wind blew down the chicken house and I had to set off in search of my hens and handsome scarlet-necked rooster, straying far from the boundaries I had set for myself.

At a crossroads I met some slaves taking a cart of sugarcane to the mill. What a sorry sight! Haggard faces, mud-colored rags, arms and legs worn to the bone, and hair reddened from malnutrition. Helping his father drive the oxen was a boy of ten, as somber and taciturn as an adult who has lost faith in everything.

The minute they saw me, everybody jumped into the grass and knelt down, while half a dozen pairs of respectful, yet terrified eyes looked up at me. I was taken aback. What stories had they woven about me? Why did they seem to be afraid of me? I should have thought they would have felt sorry for me instead, me the daughter of a hanged woman and a recluse who lived alone on the edge of a pond. I realized that they were mainly thinking about my connection with Mama Yaya, whom they had feared. But hadn't Mama Yaya used her powers to do good? Again and again? The terror of these people seemed like an injustice to me. They should have greeted me with shouts of joy and welcome and presented me with a list of illnesses that I would have tried my utmost to cure. I was born to heal, not to frighten.

I went home sadly, with no further thought for my hens and my rooster, who by now must have been crowing in the grass along the highway. This meeting was to have lasting consequences. From that day on I drew closer to the plantations so that my true self could be known. Tituba must be loved! To think that I scared people; I who felt inside me nothing but tenderness and compassion. Oh yes, I should have liked to unleash the wind like a dog from his kennel so that the white Great Houses of the masters would be blown away over the horizon, to order a fire to kindle and fan its flames so that the whole island would be purified and devastated. But I didn't have such powers. I only knew how to offer consolation.

Gradually the slaves got used to seeing me and came up to me, at first shyly, then with more confidence. I visited the cabins and comforted the sick and dying.

From *The Salt Eaters*

Toni Cade Bambara

Are you sure, sweetheart, that you want to be well?"
Velma Henry turned stiffly on the stool, the gown ties tight across her back, the knots hard. So taut for so long, she could not swivel. Neck, back, hip joints dry, stiff. Face frozen. She could not glower, suck her teeth, roll her eyes, do any of the Velma-things by way of answering Minnie Ransom, who sat before her humming lazily up and down the scales, making a big to-do of draping her silky shawl, handling it as though it were a cape she'd swirl any minute over Velma's head in a wipe-out veronica, or as though it were a bath towel she was drying her back within the privacy of her bathroom.

Minnie Ransom herself, the fabled healer of the district, her bright-red flouncy dress drawn in at the waist with two different strips of kenti cloth, up to her elbows in a minor fortune of gold, brass and silver bangles, the silken fringe of the shawl shimmying at her armpits. Her head, wrapped in some juicy hot-pink gelee, was tucked way back into her neck, eyes peering down her nose at Velma as though old-timey spectacles perched there were slipping down.

Velma blinked. Was ole Minnie trying to hypnotize her, mesmerize her? Minnie Ransom, the legendary spinster of Claybourne, Georgia, spinning out a song, drawing *her* of all people up. Velma the swift; Velma the elusive; Velma who had never mastered the kicks, punches and defense blocks, but who had down cold the art of being not there when the blow came. Velma caught, caught up, in the weave of the song Minnie was humming, of the shawl, of the threads, of the silvery tendrils that extended from the healer's neck and hands and disappeared into the sheen of the sunlight. The glistening bangles, the metallic threads, the dancing fringe, the humming like bees. And was the ole swamphag actually sitting there dressed for days, legs crossed, one foot swinging gently against the table where she'd stacked the tapes and records? Sitting there flashing her bridgework and asking some stupid damn question like that, blind to Velma's exasperation, her pain, her humiliation?

Velma could see herself: hair matted and dusty, bandages unraveled and curled at the foot of the stool like a sleeping snake, the hospital gown huge in front, but tied up too tight in back, the breeze from the window billowing out the rough white muslin and widening the opening in the back. She could not focus enough to remember whether she had panties on or not. And Minnie Ransom perched on her stool actually waiting on an answer, drawling out her hummingsong, unconcerned that any minute she might strike the very note that could shatter Velma's bones.

"I like to caution folks, that's all." said Minnie, interrupting her own humming to sigh and say it, the song somehow buzzing right on. "No sense us wasting each other's time, sweetheart." The song running its own course up under the words, up under Velma's hospital gown, notes pressing against her skin and Velma steeling herself against intrusion. "A lot of weight when you're well. Now, you just hold that thought."

Velma didn't know how she was to do that. She could barely manage to hold on to herself, hold on to the stingy stool, be there all of a piece and resist the buzzing bee tune coming at her. Now her whole purpose was surface, to go smooth, be sealed and inviolate.

She tried to withdraw as she'd been doing for weeks and weeks. Withdraw the self to a safe place where husband, lover, teacher, workers, no one could follow, probe. Withdraw her self and prop up a borderguard to negotiate with would-be intruders. She'd been a borderguard all her childhood, so she knew something about it. She was the one sent to the front door to stand off the landlord, the insurance man, the green-grocer, the fishpeddler, to insure Mama Mae one more bit of peace. And at her godmother's, it was Smitty who sent her to the front door to misdirect the posse. No, no one of that name lived here. No, this was not where the note from the principal should be delivered.

She wasn't sure how to move away from Minnie Ransom and from the music, where to throw up the barrier and place the borderguard. She wasn't sure whether she'd been hearing music anyway. Was certain, though, that she didn't know what she was supposed to say or do on that stool. Wasn't even sure whether it was time to breathe in or breathe out. Everything was off, out of whack, the relentless logic she'd lived by sprung. And here she was in Minnie Ransom's hands in the Southwest Community Infirmary. Anything could happen. She could roll off the stool like a ball of wax and melt right through the floor, or sail out of the window, stool and all, and become some new kind of UFO. Anything could happen. And hadn't Ole Minnie been nattering away about just that before the session had begun, before she had wiped down the stools and set them out just so? "In the last quarter, sweetheart, anything can happen. And will," she'd said. Last quarter? Of the moon, of the century, of some damn basketball game? Velma had been, still was, too messed around to figure it out.

"You just hold that thought," Minnie was saying again, leaning forward, the balls of three fingers pressed suddenly, warm and fragrant, against Velma's forehead, the left hand catching her in the back of her head, cupping gently the two stony portions of the temporal bone. And Velma was inhaling in gasps, and exhaling shudderingly. She felt aglow, her eyebrows drawing in toward the touch as if to ward off the invading fingers that were threatening to penetrate her skull. And then the hands went away quickly, and Velma felt she was losing her eyes.

"Hold on now," she heard. It was said the way Mama Mae would say it, leaving her bent in the sink while she went to get a washcloth to wipe the shampoo from her eyes. Velma held on to herself. Her pocketbook on the rungs below, the backless stool in the middle of the room, the hospital gown bunched up now in the back—there was nothing but herself and some dim belief in the reliability of stools to hold on to. But then the old crone had had a few choice words to say about that too, earlier, rearing back on her heels and pressing her knees against the stereo while Velma perched uneasily on the edge of her stool trying to listen, trying to wait patiently for the woman to sit down and get on with it, trying to follow her drift, scrambling to piece together key bits of high school physics, freshman philo, and lessons M'Dear Sophie and Mama Mae had tried to impart. The reliability of stools? Solids, liquids, gases, the dance of atoms, the bounce and race of molecules, ethers, electrical charges. The eyes and habits of illusion. Retinal images, bogus images, traveling to the brain. The pupils trying to tell the truth to the inner eye. The eye of the heart. The eye of the head. The eye of the mind. All seeing differently.

Velma gazed out over the old woman's head and through the window, feeling totally out of it, her eyes cutting easily through panes and panes and panes of glass and other substances, it seemed, until she slammed into the bark of the tree in the Infirmary yard and recoiled, was back on the stool, breathing in and out in almost a regular rhythm, wondering if it was worth it, submitting herself to this ordeal.

It would have been more restful to have simply slept it off; said no when the nurse had wakened her, no she didn't want to see Miz Minnie; no she didn't want to be bothered right now, but could someone call her husband, her sister, her godmother, somebody, anybody to come sign her out in the morning. But what a rough shock it would have been for the family to see her like that. Obie, Palma, M'Dear Sophie or her son Lil James. Rougher still to be seen. She wasn't meant for these scenes, wasn't meant to be sitting up there in the Southwest Community Infirmary with her ass out, in the middle of the day, and strangers cluttering up the treatment room, ogling her in her misery. She wasn't meant for any of it. But then M'Dear Sophie always said, "Find meaning where you're put, Vee." So she exhaled deeply and tried to relax and stick it out and pay attention.

Rumor was these sessions never lasted more than ten or fifteen minutes anyway. It wouldn't kill her to go along with the thing. Wouldn't kill her. She almost laughed. She might have died. *I might have died.* It was an incredible thought now. She sat there holding on to *that* thought, waiting for Minnie Ransom to quit playing to the gallery and get on with it. Sat there, every cell flooded with the light of that idea, with the rhythm of her own breathing, with the sensation of having not died at all at any time, not on the attic stairs, not at the kitchen drawer, not in the ambulance, not on the operating table, not in that other place where the mud mothers were painting the walls of the cave and calling to her, not in the sheets she thrashed out in strangling her legs, her rib cage, fighting off the woman with snakes in her hair, the crowds that moved in and out of each other around the bed trying to tell her about the difference between snakes and serpents, the difference between eating salt as an antidote to snakebite and turning into salt, succumbing to the serpent.

"Folks come in here," Minnie Ransom was saying, "moaning and carrying on and *say* they wanna be well. Don't know what in heaven and hell they want." She had uncrossed her legs, had spread her legs out and was resting on the heels of her T-strap, beige suedes, the black soles up and visible. And she was leaning forward toward Velma, poking yards of dress down between her knees. She looked like a farmer in a Halston, a snuff dipper in a Givenchy.

"Just this morning, fore they rolled you in with your veins open and your face bloated, this great big overgrown woman came in here tearing at her clothes, clawing at her hair, wailing to beat the band, asking for some pills. Wanted a pill cause she was in pain, felt bad, wanted to feel good. You ready?"

Velma studied the woman's posture, the rope veins in the back of her hands, the purple shadows in the folds of her dress spilling over the stool edge, draping down toward the floor. Velma tried not to get lost in the reds and purples. She understood she was being invited to play straight man in a routine she hadn't rehearsed.

"So I say, 'Sweetheart, what's the matter?' And she says, 'My mama died and I feel so bad, I can't go on' and dah dah dah. Her mama died, she's *supposed* to feel bad. Expect to feel good when ya mama's gone! Climbed right into my lap," she was nudging Velma to check out the skimp of her lap. "Two hundred pounds of grief and heft if she was one-fifty. Bless her heart, just a babe of the times. Wants to be smiling and feeling good all the time. Smooth sailing as they lower the mama into the ground. Then there's you. What's your story?"

Velma clutched the sides of the stool and wondered what she was supposed to say at this point. What she wanted to do was go away, be somewhere, anywhere, else. But where was there to go? Far as most folks knew, she was at work or out of town.

"As I said, folks come in here moaning and carrying on and *say* they want to be healed. But like the wisdom warns, 'Doan letcha mouf gitcha in what ya backbone caint stand.'" This the old woman said loud enough for the others to hear.

The Infirmary staff, lounging in the rear of the treatment room, leaned away from the walls to grunt approval, though many privately thought this was one helluva way to conduct a healing. Others, who had witnessed the miracle of Minnie Ransom's laying on the hands over the years, were worried. It wasn't like her to be talking on and on, taking so long a time to get started. But then the whole day's program that Doc Serge had arranged for the visitors had been slapdash and sloppy.

The visiting interns, nurses and technicians stood by in crisp white jackets and listened, some in disbelief, others with amusement. Others scratched around in their starchy pockets skeptical, most shifted from foot to foot embarrassed just to be there. And it looked as though the session would run overtime at the rate things were going. There'd never be enough time to get through the day's itinerary. And the bus wasn't going to wait. The driver had made that quite plain. He would be pulling in at 3:08 from his regular run, taking a dinner break, then pulling out sharply with the charter bus at 5:30. That too had been printed up on the itinerary, but the Infirmary hosts did not seem to be alert to the demands of time.

The staff, asprawl behind the visitors on chairs, carts, table corners, swinging their legs and doing manicures with the edges of matchbooks, seemed to be content to watch the show for hours. But less than fifteen minutes ago they'd actually been on the front steps making bets, actually making cash bets with patients and various passers-by, that the healing session would take no more than five or ten minutes. And here it was already going on 3:00 with what could hardly be called an auspicious beginning. The administrator, Dr. Serge, had strolled out, various and sundry folk had come strolling in. The healer had sat there for the longest time playing with her bottom lip, jangling her bracelets, fiddling with the straps of the patient's gown. And now she was goofing around, deliberately, it seemed, exasperating the patient. There seemed to be, many of the visitors concluded, a blatant lack of discipline at the Southwest Community Infirmary that made suspect the reputation it enjoyed in radical medical circles.

"Just so's you're sure, sweetheart, and ready to be healed, cause wholeness is no trifling matter. A lot of weight when you're well."

"Be Healed": A Black Woman's Sermon on Healing through Touch

Monya Aletha Stubbs

*"You need a miracle," the doctor told me. He didn't think my husband
would make it through the night. I could not see my husband's face or arms
or hands. His entire body was wrapped in gauze, a mummy wrap the nurses
called it, which kept him warm, so fast his body temperature was dropping.
Only his feet were visible and accessible to my touch. I held them in my
hands. I stroked them with love and although my husband was unconscious
I felt that he knew I was there. I held my husband's feet in my hands
and I prayed long and hard for a miracle, never for a moment doubting
that he would fully recover. I can witness to the power of prayer.*
—*GLORIA SCOTT*

Pus-filled sores covered my scalp, my right earlobe, and part of my nose.
I was thirteen years old, infected with a severe case of impetigo. A friend
yelled at the school lunch table, "Hey, doesn't Monya remind you of a mangy
dog?" He said it jokingly. Everyone laughed. I smiled to hide my sadness.

The doctor said the disease was highly contagious. I would have to stay out
of school a few days to allow the antibiotics to work. The nurse warned me
not to touch the sores without washing my hands immediately. She told me
to be careful, or I might spread the infection to other parts of my body. The
doctor told my mother, "Mrs. Stubbs, use gloves, gently wash your daughter's sores every night, and base them with the medicated salve that I pre-
scribe." But my mother never used gloves. For three weeks, each night, her
bare hands bathed my infection.

My mother always held a prayer service as her hands washed my head and
face. I was never certain of what she said; she talked under her breath. Between mumbles, she moaned old church hymns. Sometimes, though, in the
midst of her mumbles and moans, I could hear the words, "Heal her." I was
afraid to talk to my mother as she cared for me. Her steady intonations produced a sacred rhythm and the mere thought of disturbing her hallowed

groove caused the sores on my head to sting. Nevertheless, about a week or so into our healing ritual, very concerned about her becoming infected, I finally asked if she were not worried about catching the disease. She responded: "Yes. But there is more at stake than drying up your sores. Each day you go to school; you go into the world, feeling and looking ashamed. I see in your eyes that it hurts you. Your self-esteem is being shattered; your spirit is troubled. In order to heal you, I must touch you, I must feel you. I can't use gloves." My mother was never infected. My sores disappeared. My self-confidence was restored.

I am sure my mother was confident that the antibiotics eventually would kill the bacteria and heal the sores on my body; but she also understood that the sores were tragically affecting my psyche, my spirit as well as my body. Healing, to my mother, was a very basic concept: the spiritual and mental effects of the illness had to be cured along with the physical symptoms. Healing had to reach the damaged spirit and mind—the side effects of physical illness—or consequences just as detrimental as the physical sickness, if not more so, could occur. Healing, then, not only includes the physical; it also includes the psychological and the spiritual. An appropriate term for my mother's philosophy is "Holistic-healing": a healing of the body, mind and spirit.

When remembering my mother's insistence on touching me I am reminded of biblical stories about the healing ministry of Jesus. It is fascinating to note how those who sought healing felt the need to touch Jesus: "And the whole multitude sought to touch him: for there went virtue out of him and healed them all" (Luke 6:19 OAB).* Jesus often used touching as part of healing and restoring ill persons to health. Seldom did he merely speak deliverance without some form of physical contact. Jesus touched the leper and healed him (Mat. 8:3). The woman who suffered with internal bleeding for twelve years was healed after touching a tassel of his robe (Mat. 9:19–20 OAB). Jesus touched the eyes of two blind men and restored their sight (Mat. 9:29 OAB). Jesus took Jairus' daughter by the hand and raised her from the dead (Mat. 9:18–26 OAB). Physical connection, whether initiated by Jesus or those needing to be cured, was a notable part of the healing ministry of Jesus.

*Oxford Annotated Bible. Other references are to the *King James Version* unless otherwise noted.

In observing this touching by Jesus, I do not seek to establish touching as a requirement for healing. I simply offer some thoughts about touching as part of healing those who are sick, with the only objective being that my thoughts may inspire the thoughts of others. The inspiration for my insights comes primarily from my mother and the lives of other Black women I have encountered, either personally or through the narratives of elders. Friends and neighbors also function as sources of inspiration. I want to compare the healing through touch ministry of Black women I know and the biblical accounts of healing by Jesus.

I believe that healing through touch, "HTT," serves three significant functions: it meets, it rejects, and it empowers. HTT provides both the healer and the sick an opportunity to meet at the place of affliction. Next, HTT rejects societal condemnation of the ill. Finally, HTT encourages, if not compels, the sick to accept further responsibility beyond the healing of their physical symptoms.

Meeting at the Center

We observe Jesus touching and healing, but when we consider the awesome powers attributed to him we must ask: Did Jesus really have to touch the sick, or did the sick need to be touched? There are biblical accounts where Jesus simply spoke and the sick received deliverance. Luke 7:2–10 describes such an instance where spoken words alone from Jesus restored a centurion's slave to health, after the centurion requested that Jesus simply "speak the word." By my analysis, this spoken word of Jesus compares with the antibiotics that the doctor prescribed for my childhood infection. Though sufficient in the healing of the physical sickness, the spoken word alone, however, does not heal the mental and spiritual effects of the illness. The expressions of my mother to me during my childhood encounter with impetigo explained that the physical distortions of illness create a brokenness of one's self-worth and spiritual well-being. Insecurity and self-hatred mocked the leper throughout his daily life. Loneliness and fear, for twelve years, tortured the woman who suffered with an issue of blood. The blind and the lame must have felt incomplete and isolated. Therefore, I suggest that the spoken word of Jesus could heal physical symptoms; but he had encounters that required more than verbal antibiotics—encounters that required him to address the psychological

307

and spiritual brokenness that accompanied the physical ailment. Some had to touch or be touched to be made whole.

Healing through touch provides both the healer and the sick the opportunity to meet at the center of affliction. The center of affliction is not a physical place, but a place where the mind and spirit converge. A moment when understanding, need and the desire to help become focused. The instance when the sick acknowledge their sickness and the healer responds in reaching out to heal. Luke 6:19 (OAB) describes the general psychological and spiritual condition of the sick as they sought Jesus: "And all in the crowd were trying to touch him: for power came out of him and healed all of them." The physical ailments differed, but the afflicted had a common desire for physical contact with Jesus. In responding, Jesus did not place himself in a pharisaic tower and demand the sick to meet him in the "upper-room." Instead, symbolized by his touch and willingness to be touched, Jesus shared the space of sorrow of the sick—and then he guided them, hand in hand, to the "upper-room," their moment of healing. Jesus understood that speaking deliverance did not meet the needs of the crowds that wanted to experience physical contact with him. He reached out and touched the sick, met them at the center of their affliction, not only where their bodies were, but where their troubled minds and spirits were also.

Status Quo Sensitivity

While some may be willing to touch the sick, too often the rule of our society is to touch only if you can remain emotionally distant and spiritually unattached—what I call "status quo sensitivity," a response that does not allow one to feel/empathize with the inward grief of others, their despondent state of mind, or their physical anguish. "Feeling" is the virtue that empowers touching to restore and transform. The act of touch is incomplete without the capacity to feel. Touching without feeling is like hearing without listening. When we do not listen to the words of another we escape responsibility for reacting or responding. Similarly, those who touch without feeling/empathizing may ignore or even condemn the problem or sickness rather than engage in solving the problem or healing the sickness. Status quo sensitivity is unacceptable to holistic healers because it does not transcend "self." Status quo sensitivity never asks "How would I feel if it were me?" Instead, it proclaims, "Thank God it's not me." The question "How would I feel if it were me?" raises holistic healers above condemnation and complacency to a level of divine understanding and resolution.

Jesus rejected society's cruelty toward those who were "the least of these." He recognized that acknowledgment of one's humanness, in spite of one's illness, restored self-confidence and self-worth. Jesus' touching/feeling/healing ministry symbolized his persistent commitment to mending the shattered minds and spirits of those doubly victimized, first by society's castigation and then by their own self-imposed criticism. Moreover, Jesus by his touch provided the spiritual thread that bound the ill person's fragmented self, while simultaneously charging them to be mindful of their responsibility to serve others.

My mother faithfully parted my hair with her hands. She moved slowly and carefully to avoid irritating the inflammations on my scalp. Unlike Mother's compassionate touch, my experience at school had been especially difficult. The stares of my classmates had been piercing. My ex-best friend's new best friend had occupied my usual seat at the lunch table. The "mangy-dog" joke had produced hordes of laughter. As I remembered those awful school days, I touched my mother's arm gently and my heart cried out, "Thank you mother for touching me, for feeling me, no one else would." I returned to school strengthened by the loving, healing touch of my mother.

The love mother expressed through her touch did not produce impudence. It helped me to share the gift of love with others who suffered from broken bones, broken hearts, and broken spirits. My experience inspired me to devote energy to noticing the frustration in those voices that heard the bitter reality of sounds of hopelessness. It drove me to befriend those whose eyes only perceived the idea of impossibility, yet strained to behold the truth of miracles. I rose to a level not governed by status quo sensitivity. "How would I feel if it were me?" became a compelling mandatory question. My healing made me seek to become a holistic healer. I received a calling to responsibility beyond my physical healing.

"Be Healed"

The biblical text, Mark 5:25–34, describes a woman who suffered from hemorrhages. She exhausted all her funds on physicians; but her condition only worsened. She was alone—no sign of friends, children or husband. Weak and feeble from her steady loss of blood, the hemorrhaging woman was immersed in an enormous crowd of people, all eager to be nearest to Jesus. Nevertheless, this sickly woman, exploited by physicians and dismissed by society, decided to act for herself to transform her despondent condition. With persistence she made her way through the pressing crowd, reached, and "touches the hem of his garment." She did not grab, snatch, clutch, grasp, or grip his robe; she was too frightened of being noticed. She was too humble, the crowd too massive, her body too frail. Hence, she just gently reaches out and "touches" Jesus. Immediately upon her touching his garment the bleeding stopped. Something powerful happened, something divine that defied the finite logic of the human mind, something to do with touching and healing. Jesus, knowing that power had gone from him, stopped in the midst of the crowd and asked, "Who touched me?"

In this instance of healing through touch, Jesus did not touch the woman. Rather, she reached out and touched him. The sick one touched the healer. Jesus was moved to respond, to acknowledge her touch. As must happen sometimes, the sick one somehow found the energy to impose her need upon the agenda of the healer. The rigors of living and trying to survive, the circumstances of the moment, the historical events that brought us to our present predicament, are sometimes so overwhelming, so oppressive that they stifle our articulation of pain and grief. Sometimes pain and grief can be so piercing that it devastates the mind and breaks the heart. Therefore, like the woman with the issue of blood, whose reality was fogged by the "idea of impossibility," yet whose spirit strained to "behold the truth of miracles," we can only reach out to touch one another, and believe that the "power to behold" in one will connect with the "desire to heal" in another. The power to behold the truth of miracles is an initial source of healing, the innate spiritual gift of knowing one's present condition is not necessarily one's permanent truth.

At this point it is important to give close attention to the last two statements Jesus made to the woman, after the initial touch and healing: "Daughter, *your faith has made you well*, go in peace, and *be healed* of your disease" (Mark 5:34, emphasis added). Thus, Jesus acknowledged that it was not his power alone that healed the woman. He gave credit and recognition to her deliberate mental, physical and spiritual efforts to actualize her healing.

Through her touch of the hem of his garment, the woman who encountered Jesus expressed herself humbly, without words, "I'm hurting. I need help." Issues of embarrassment and humility can muffle cries of despair: but touch can express emotions and become a silent voice that empowers the sick to communicate feelings that are often ineffable. It can give them a sense of pride and responsibility in their healing. Because touch brings attention to the problem, it ultimately serves as the current that connects the sick person's power to behold the truth of miracles with the healer's "desire to heal." This union produces the state Jesus calls *"be healed."*

The text explains that upon touching the robe of Jesus, the woman's hemorrhage healed immediately. Both she and Jesus knew that her bleeding had stopped. Therefore, when Jesus said "be healed" he was not simply speaking of the woman's physical condition. He was also addressing her mental and spiritual state of fear and uncertainty. The physical ramifications of her illness had been solved before this commission, as evident when Jesus said: "Daughter, your faith has made you well." Jesus, however, did not end his remarks with a mere confirmation of her physical deliverance. Instead, he also charged her to "be healed," a phrase that suggested assurance in the healing of the damaging mental and spiritual effects of her sickness—but, even more than that, a phrase that identified a responsibility that went beyond the concerns that the woman had for herself.

I suggest that the phrase "be healed" told the woman not only to acknowledge her physical healing, and remain confident in her mental and spiritual healing, but it also implied that she had the ability to assume the role of a holistic healer. The power passed from Jesus to the woman endowed her with the spiritual energy and the duty to serve humanity just as effectively as Jesus. One may rightly assume that if power went out of Jesus and healed the woman, then the woman now possessed the power that Jesus transmitted to her by touch. What she received, she too could impart.

In extolling the divinity of Jesus, we often forget that he never proclaimed himself as a unique, one-of-a-kind, divine/human encounter. Quite the contrary, he spent the whole of his ministry inviting others to do what he did. He said, "Take up [your] cross daily, and follow me" (Luke 9:23). Of his miracles, for those who believed, he said "Greater works than these shall [you] do" (John 14:12). Of his perfection he said, "Be ye therefore perfect as your [Creator] which is in heaven is perfect" (Mat. 5:48). Of the power of the universe itself, he said, "For, behold, the kingdom of God is within you" (Luke 17:21). Over and over Jesus made clear that others could exercise the power of God incarnate in the world. God reveals Godself in the energy of love that is expressed through touch from one to another. The person Jesus was not present when the hideous appearance and rotten smell of my scalp caused the oppression of my spirit. Yet, it was comforted and liberated by a divine presence that revealed Itself through the loving touch of my mother. Hence, the life of Jesus serves as a guide, as symbolized through touch, for people to experience "other manifestations and incarnations of God present within different contexts of oppression."* Sickness is one of many kinds of oppression that holds humankind in physical and mental bondage. The Christ, the incarnation of God's divine love/energy, must be respected and revered as it was revealed in the person of Jesus, and as it is presently evidenced through the healing touch of those seeking to restore harmony and wholeness to the world. Ultimately, healing through touch functions as a tool of empowerment and encouragement that enables and demands those who benefit from its transforming energy to share with others the gifts of renewed life and existence. The healed are commanded to "be healed" beyond their physical ailments and to share the spiritual power of their healing with others.

She Touched Me

As I further reflect on my mother's touch, the lives of other Black women flood my thoughts. Women, who throughout the centuries, nurtured and sustained generations with their firm soothing voices, their courageous loving eyes, and their gentle healing hands. As I reflect on my mother's touch, I see an old midwife, not in a hospital, but in a one-room shack, aiding in the healthy birth of a young Black child. As I reflect on my mother's touch, I notice, in my mind's eye, a woman rubbing salve on the back of a beaten slave;

*Brown-Douglass. *Third World Theologies: Commonalities and Divergences*, ed. K. C. Abraham (Maryknoll, N.Y.: Orbis Books, 1990).

I focus more closely, and I see another woman, sitting on a porch, in the bitter cold of winter with her asthmatic son in her arms, wrapped in a blanket, praying that the fresh air will help him breathe more easily. I see women holding their sisters and brothers, comforting them through unrealized dreams and unforeseen misfortunes. As I reflect on my mother's touch, I am humbled, honored by the millions of lives that flash before my eyes, lives of Black women who have dedicated themselves, who continue to dedicate their energies to the holistic healing of themselves, to the holistic healing of their race, and to the holistic healing of humanity.

One song writer wrote, "Shackled by a heavy burden, beneath a load of guilt and shame. And then the hand of Jesus touched me, and now I am no longer the same." Today, I sing, as I am certain many sing: "I was shackled by a heavy burden, beneath a load of guilt and shame. And then the hand of my mother, my godmother, my grandmother, my sister, my sister-friend . . . *touched* me, and now I am no longer the same."

Healing from Afar with Your Mind

Sharifa Saa

The natural inclination of our spirit
is to make what is not whole,
whole again.
And if we find dis-ease, we must return the ease.

It is the spirituality of women—African, African-American, and of the African Diaspora—that has kept the earth from devouring itself. It is the healing power of these women that has healed the people of the earth forever. These women, our light-bearing ancestors, and we always chose to use our healing power until we began to see that we and our power was being misused. And so, for a short moment in time, the world was allowed to indulge itself in its madness, until we decided to take things in hand again. We're back, world, ready this time to make what is not whole, whole again, to return the ease. We shall return not only the earth to its wholesome self again, but also ourselves to our wholesome selves and reclaim our position as queens of the universe, beginning with the new millennium, year 2000, European time.

To begin the reclamation and hold the healing in place, we first must be reclaimed and healed. We must pay attention to our spiritual and body energy centers/*chakras*. We must first clean them often with breath exercises, crystal balancing, healthy food, spiritual bathing for releasing, and physical exercising. We will begin by cleaning one *chakra* at a time, moving from the root to the spleen to the solar plexus to the heart to the throat to the brow to the crown. When we feel discouraged, we will say: "Goddess power is always available, completely reliable, and never out of touch with me."

The colors and crystals associated with the *chakras* are as follows:

Root (between the legs)—red/ruby, obsidian, tourmalinated quartz

Spleen (between pubic hair and bottom of navel)—orange/tiger eye, carnelian, gold

Solar plexus (navel to waist)—yellow/amber, citrine, pyrite

Note: In the original manuscript, all solidi are reversed.

314

Heart (heart area and lungs)—green/rose quartz, moonstone, adventurine, malachite

Throat (throat and neck)—blue/lapis and turquoise (favorites of Kemites), celestine, chrysocolla, sapphire

Brow/third eye (eyebrows to hair line)—indigo/sodalite, onyx (dark), kyanite, sugalite, blue topaz

Crown (top of head)—violet/amethyst, selenite, gold

Some crystals and stones are effective on all the *chakras*: quartz crystal (clear), diamond, rutilated quartz, herkimer diamond, jasper, hyacinth (zircon). Copper and silver are excellent conductors of energy, so we can use them to help transport energy from *chakra* to *chakra* and spiritual level to spiritual level. We know which *chakra* to work on because each center is connected to both physical and spiritual aspects:

Root—physical vitality, rebuilding of body when open and flowing, sexual health/ and spiritual attraction

Spleen—eliminative system, colon, liver, spleen/ and spiritual cleansing of resentment, anger, and confusion allowing for clear thought

Solar plexus—digestion, circulation, nervous systems/ and spiritual intuition center, Divine inspiration

Heart—regeneration of tissue as oxygen circulates with the blood, growth/ and spiritual growth, health, prosperity, seat of the "soul," one aspect of the spiritual being

Throat—sound communication, thyroid and thymus centers/ and spiritual creative force, elimination of worn out thoughts and conditions

Brow/third eye—eyes, ears, sinuses, pineal gland (producer of melanin)/ and spiritual connector between consciousness and higher consciousness, spirit contact, "ESP"

Crown—pituitary gland, master gland of body/ and spiritual center of cosmic energy flow, can permit attainment of the mystic experience

To continue the healing, we will eat the proper diet containing as much raw food as possible. We will stay away from meat of all kinds and especially dairy foods, which cause us in particular to suffer with "female problems." We will be careful to eliminate sweets as much as possible, and we will never take in caffeine, nicotine, or any other drug, as the latter weaken our astral bodies and allow our strength to slip away.

Finally, we will exercise with African *yo-ka*, now called "yoga," to balance our spirit, mind, and emotions, and to rejuvenate the physical body. We will be ageless, wise, fun loving, determined, strong, flexible, and not resentful. Only we can make whole again what is not whole. When we arise and become women, our men can arise and become men. We will demand it; they will demand it.

We can heal each other by using our mind/God/Goddess power. When we know a sister needs help, we concentrate our mind on her as a perfect being in the eyes of the God/Goddess. We see her in Grace, doing what is perfect for her and for us. There are many techniques to accomplish "mind healing." Let me share two.

With technique one, you'll need a picture of the subject. A picture allows you to visualize her again very easily. Prepare a meditation space where you will concentrate on the subject and nothing else. Hold her picture in your hands or set the picture directly in front of where you are sitting. If you are holding a picture in your hand, put the left hand on the bottom and the right hand on the top of the picture. Use the fingertips of your right hand to cover the picture completely. Picture violet energy entering your mind, and then gradually see the energy moving into your fingertips and into the picture. If the picture is in front of you, see the energy flowing from your eyes into the picture. Allow no other thoughts to enter your mind except positive affirmations about healing the subject such as: "Sister, you are perfect." "Sister, you are healed." "Sister, the Force is with you." "Sister, the Goddess is with you." "Sister, arise and take your divine place." "Sister, I love you." Make up affirmations to suit the subject if you know her well enough. Remember that the energy you send returns to you with the same or greater intensity. Have fun and do your task with great joy.

With technique two, you don't need a picture of the person. All you need is the *name* of the one to be healed. This technique really requires your best concentration. If the healing involves a part of the body, find a picture of that part of the body and picture yourself cleaning it. If no other information is available except the name, you will need to focus your mind like a laser beam. Sometimes it helps to use a candle, which is placed in front of the place you sit to meditate. You must chant the healing into the candle. For example, you might say, "Eshe, Eshe, Eshe, Eshe, Eshe, Eshe, Eshe, you are perfect in the

Light, you are perfect in the Light, you are perfect in the Light." Repeat the name seven times; the healing affirmation three times. Pause. Do another set of seven and three and continue until you have completed at least ten sets. You should be able to tell if the subject is healed by the way *you* feel, your divine inspiration (solar plexus) will "tell" you. If you don't feel right, continue until you know that everything is fine. You will "know" if you are concentrating properly. You may have to practice concentration until you can focus your mind without difficulty; however, this ability will spill over into the rest of your life, and you will find that you get things done more quickly. Remember that the energy you send returns to you in the same or greater intensity. Have fun and improve your life while you are healing another.

Your natural spiritual inclination is to make what is not whole, whole again. This time, let's do it again with Goddess/God consciousness . . . for the love of it.

A Womanist Litany

Imani-Sheila Newsome-McLaughlin

When and where we enter
all our sisters come
a cloud of witnesses
singing our name

How many times can I tell you
this story?
Familiar phrases strung together
like cheap beads scattered
before we know their beauty

When and where we enter
all our sisters come
a cloud of witnesses
singing our name

They say "We've come this far
by faith."
When we come forward
it is not just faith that
propels us forward
it is the echoes of prayers
of whitedress women and
Sunday School teachers

When and where we enter
all our sisters come
a cloud of witnesses
singing our name

And if there is a wall
a fire around me I
can call on that
praying/singing
place it in my mouth

and from the womb of
my spirit
comes healing for my
daughters

and my sons

Walking on water or
sand or shattered
hearts
God is with us
Running forward to mercy
We can carry others
along
The Spirit leading
through storm
and wind
through empty myths
and secret sin

For when and where we enter
our sisters and
brothers
our sons and our daughters
our neighbors

our repentant now knowing
enemies
all come
singing our names
in praise of God

Litany for the Blessing of a House

Toi Derricotte

For Mary Helen Washington

Speaker: What is the house
but a roof over infinite solitude?
What is it
but a leaning out into the void?
What is it
but a starry ear listening?
What is it
but a tilting precipice?
What is it
but a cup of wind?

Call: With nourishing quiet

Response: *Bless this house.*

Call: With changing seasons

Response: *Bless this house.*

Call: With loyal friends

Response: *Bless this house.*

Call: With joyful conversations

Response: *Bless this house.*

Call: With unexpected comings

Response: *Bless this house.*

Call: With timely leavings

Response: *Bless this house.*

Call: With spontaneous dinners

Response: *Bless this house.*

Call: With bread fresh from the bakery

Response: *Bless this house.*

Call: Joyful helpers

Response: *Bless this house.*

Call: Arguments of sincere and loving friends

Response: *Bless this house.*

Call: Resolutions after struggle

Response: *Bless this house.*

Call: Deep ripenings of summer

Response: *Bless this house.*

Call: Bright relinquishments of fall

Response: *Bless this house.*

Call: Early darknesses of winter

Response: *Bless this house.*

Call: Silence of unexpected snows

Response: *Bless this house.*

Call: Tub of infinite water

Response: *Bless this house.*

Call: Stove of renewable fire

Response: *Bless this house.*

Call: Table of endless yield

Response: *Bless this house.*

Call: Mirror of continuing beauty

Response: *Bless this house.*

Call: Bed, palm of comfort

Response: *Bless this house.*

Blessing for the Body of the House, the Female Interior

Call: Irrepressible truth

Response: *Bless this house.*

Call: Beauty without self-consciousness

Response: *Bless this house.*

Call: Courage of everyday acts

Response: *Bless this house.*

Call: Discourse of desire

Response: *Bless this house.*

Call: Hunger and replenishment

Response: *Bless this house.*

Call: Joyful solitude

Response: *Bless this house.*

Call: Peaceful joining of opposites

Response: *Bless this house.*

Call: All of you holy mothers and daughters

Response: *Bless this house.*

Call: All of you holy fathers and sons

Response: *Bless this house.*

Speaker: Will all of you present please call out your special requests for the blessing of this house. (*Each call is followed by the group response, "Bless this house."*)

Prayer (given by Speaker)

Grant, Mother God,
who has given us all the blessings of this earth,
who has given us each other,
who has brought us our beloved friend, . . . (*name of person whose home is being blessed*)

Grant an ever deepening understanding
of our purpose in this life,
and since you have blessed us
with this good and singular friend,
we ask you make her house a place of comfort,
and that the daily rituals of its care
will tie her to flesh and body.

May this house be a symbol of your protection,
as we are all connected under the roof of your heaven.
Grant that we will be led to tolerance
by accepting our own gifts and limits,
and that we will learn to truly love.

Ritual to Invoke the
Goddess Isis

Nancy Thompson

Isis, the dark-skinned goddess from Africa, is revered as the Universal Goddess—Mother Goddess—Moon Goddess. She is the primordial great goddess of Egypt, the first daughter of the Great Sky Goddess Nut. Originally Isis's name was Au Set which means exceeding queen or "spirit." Isis was the wife and sister to Osiris who was killed by his brother Set. Set dismembered Osiris's body and scattered his body parts throughout the land. Isis found and gathered up all of Osiris's parts and performed a magical rite that brought Osiris back to life. With the revived Osiris, Isis conceived and brought forth a child—the Sun God Horus.

We, as descendants of African people, are innately ritualistic. Ritual is a sacred ceremony that allows us the space to tap into an ageless and timeless wisdom. Invoking Isis in ritual allows her to lead us through the mysteries of death and renewal, taking us through the darkness to a place that goes beyond our fears, failures, and frustrations to connect with a deep source of transcendent understanding and creative inspiration. Through this process we gain the ability to transform, renew, and empower ourselves and others.

To invoke Isis in ritual is to reconnect to the Goddess within. To seek our Goddess within is to heal and affirm ourselves.

This ritual can be performed alone or by a group of women. If done as a group, everybody can be involved in planning the ritual. However, one woman should be designated to lead it. Make sure the ritual takes place in a space that will be free from outside distractions for two to three hours.

One of the most important elements for any ritual is an altar. The altar serves as a focal point for the ritual. Items for your altar include an altar cloth, candles, flowers, and sacred objects. It is also good to include symbols for the four elements. For example:

Earth: Crystals, potted plants

Air: Incense, feathers

Water: Chalice/cup, seashells

Fire: Candles

Ritual Structure

Purify space   Purification can be accomplished by smudging, sprinkling saltwater, or by using a feather. It is done to clear the ritual space of negative energy and to allow participants to let go of outside worries and concerns in order to fully enter into the ritual.

Light candles   Candlelight creates a serene atmosphere and is a signal to the Goddess that something sacred is about to take place.

Casting the circle   A circle is cast by invoking the four elements of earth, fire, air, and water; invoking the four directions—north, south, east, and west; and invoking the Goddess. The circle creates a safe space for participants to be in the presence of the Goddess and to feel completely protected and loved.

Suggested Invocation:

"I invoke and invite the four elements and four directions to be with us now. I invite you into this circle."

"East, Element of Air, Power of the Mind and Intellect: Be with us now."

"West, Element of Water, Feelings and Emotions: Join us in this circle."

"North, Element of Earth, Groundedness in the Body: Be with us now."

"South, Element of Fire, Creative Energy and Power: I invite you into our circle."

"Goddess Isis, Great Mother of All: Be with us in this ritual."

Repeat:

"The circle is cast. We are between the worlds. The Goddess welcomes her women. Blessed Be."

Share special objects Bring items that represent your creative power and ability or that have special significance for you. Share what they symbolize for you and then place them on the altar.

State intention of ritual To invoke the presence of the Goddess Isis and to ask for and receive her blessing.

Read Call from Isis

I am nature, the universal mother, mistress of all the elements, primordial child of time, sovereign of all things spiritual, queen of the dead, queen also of the immortals, the single manifestation of all gods and goddesses that are.

Though I am worshiped in many aspects, known by countless names, and exalted with all manner of different rites, yet the whole round earth venerates me. Both races of Ethiopians, whose lands the morning sun first shines upon, and the Egyptians who excel in ancient learning and worship me with ceremonies proper to my godhead, call me by my true name, namely Queen Isis.

(Apuleius, 2d century C.E.)

Ritual Meditation Do a relaxation meditation that focuses on releasing tension by relaxing specific parts of the body. Start by focusing on your breathing. Then focus on releasing tension and relaxing your feet, legs, thighs, pelvis, stomach, back, chest, shoulders, arms, neck, throat, head, face, and scalp. After you are in a completely relaxed state, take the following journey:

Visualize yourself facing a door. You open the door and walk down the hallway in search of a place that is safe and healing for you.

This safe place may be out in nature—near water or in a grove of trees.

It may be inside—a special room, a nice quiet spot in your house, anywhere you feel completely safe and comfortable.

Now wherever you are, visualize yourself to be, find a comfortable place to sit or lie down.

As you sit or lie down feel the Goddess Isis's presence in the room with you.

Acknowledge her presence and ask her to reveal herself to you.

Spend a few minutes now just allowing Isis's presence to be there with you.

She may come as an image, a sound, or a feeling. However she chooses to come to you just be there with her.

Now take a minute to allow your need to arise, whatever it is you want Isis to assist you with. It may be a physical healing, guidance, help with finances, problems with a relationship, whatever it is bring it up now.

Now ask Isis for assistance in meeting this need. Allow yourself to relax and be open to receive her assistance.

Be quiet and still for a moment as you feel Isis blessing you and giving you what you need.

Be open to receive her blessing.

Now make that blessing into a symbol, something you can refer to in the coming weeks that will symbolize what you received from Isis. Take a few moments to come up with that symbol.

Now, holding that symbol in your hands, thank Isis for the blessing you just received.

Make a commitment to do whatever you are led to do over the next week to help manifest this blessing into your life.

Once you have made that commitment, say goodbye to Isis and thank her again for the time the two of you have spent together.

Now get up from where you have been sitting or lying and visualize yourself walking back toward the hallway and down the hallway back to the shared ritual space.

As you are walking back down the hallway become more aware of returning to the shared ritual space.

As the ritual leader counts backward from ten to one, return completely to the present and be alert.

Open your eyes when you are ready as you have now returned to the shared ritual space.

If the ritual is performed alone, the sole participant may want to prerecord the guided relaxation. If working with a group, the ritual leader should pace the various components of the meditation so that participants have enough time to do their inner work but not so much time that they get bored or distracted. An excellent source to use for guided meditations is Margo Adair's *Working Inside Out: Tools for Change*.

Share your experience   If the ritual is done with others, share what occurred for you during the meditation. If done alone, reflect on what occurred for you. You may want to write something down or speak aloud. Good questions to ask include:

Where was your safe place?

How did Isis come to you?

What did you ask for assistance with?

How did Isis respond?

What symbol did you choose for Isis's blessing?

What is it that you want to manifest in your life? (Affirm that it has been manifested. If doing the ritual with a group, ask for and receive affirmation from members of the group.)

Raise energy   Energy can be raised playing taped music, singing, chanting, or drumming during the ritual.

Ground the energy Energy can be grounded during the ritual by becoming silent, bending over, and touching the floor with the palms of your hands for a few seconds.

Open circle Thank the four elements, four directions, and the Goddess Isis for being with you during the ritual and ask that they remain with you as you return to your daily activities.

Repeat:

"The circle is open but unbroken. May the peace of the Goddess be with you. Merry meet and merry part and merry meet again. So Mote It Be."

Personal Reflections

As a result of creating and leading this ritual, I have gained a heightened awareness of my power as an African-American woman. I am more focused and clear on what I want to accomplish creatively, and the right people, opportunities, and resources have started to come my way. I am able to move forward with a sense of clarity and purpose.

Doing the ritual with other women has shown me the healing power of collective feminine energy. Women who were strangers to each other came together and were able to connect and support one another in a very deep and profound way. Here are some of the insights these women have gained as a result of opening up and sharing their ritual experiences:

"This was my first introduction to the concept of Goddess rather than God. The thought of a feminine Higher Power was very empowering for me."

"I was able to expand my vision of what is possible."

"I am able to be more comfortable living in the now."

"By entering into the darkness within, I felt a major shift take place on a very deep level."

"I experienced an increased awareness of my ability to change negative circumstances in my life just by changing how I think about and approach a situation."

In writing this ritual, it is my wish that more and more women will become aware of their Goddess within and allow the Goddess to heal, transform, renew, and empower them.

Suggested Readings

Adair, Margo. *Working Inside Out: Tools for Change.* Berkeley: Wingbow Press, 1984.

Beck, Renee, and Sydney Barbara Metrick. *The Art of Ritual: A Guide to Creating and Performing Your Own Rituals for Growth and Change.* Berkeley: Celestial Arts, 1990.

Stein, Diane. *Casting the Circle.* Freedom, Calif.: Crossing Press, 1990.

Teish, Luisah. *Jambalaya: The Natural Woman's Book.* San Francisco: Harper and Row, 1985.

Vanzant, Iyanla. *Tapping the Power Within: A Path to Self-Empowerment for Black Women.* New York: Writers and Readers Publishing, 1992.

Guardian Spirits

Iyanla Vanzant

Every living being has a God-appointed guardian spirit which walks through life with you. This good spirit unites with you at the moment you are born. Some refer to it as "guardian angel" or "protector spirit." In African culture, guardian spirits are called, "Egun." It is the duty of your Egun to assist you on your life path. Like the spirit of your head (Ori), the Egun waits for acknowledgment and recognition. It will not interfere with the choices or decisions of your conscious mind. However, in times of need or danger, this spirit will give guidance and insight in the form of thoughts or presentiments. When you follow the direction given by your Egun, also called "your first thought," you can overcome many challenges and obstacles.

A guardian spirit may be an ancestral spirit or some other benevolent force whose spiritual evolution is dedicated to assisting living beings. While ancestral spirits have a vested interest in the survival of their descendants, they are not always guardians for their living family line. A guardian spirit may be an acquaintance from a previous life existence or a highly evolved soul who is appointed to assist in your care. Unlike your Ori, the guardian exists outside of your physical body. However, it is within your "spiritual reach" at all times.

Guardian spirits may or may not have names. You may call it "my guardian," "Egun," "my protector," or any common name you choose. In a state of relaxation and meditation, you can ask the spirit for its name. The response will be in the form of a thought. You may have a dream in which you see a person who is familiar but you cannot remember his or her name. Chances are it was your guardian spirit. Males may have female guardians; females may have male guardians. They are appointed based upon their past life experiences and your present life mission. Consequently, your Egun, or guardian spirit, is most probably of the same race and ethnic background as you are.

In addition to your principal guardian spirit, there are other benevolent spirits who assist you in life. Those of the Catholic faith refer to them as

Saints. Others may acknowledge universal spirits or earth spirits. These highly evolved, sympathetic forces unite with your guardian at various times to assist you in confronting your challenges. You may experience it as a burst of energy, or an onslaught of information or opportunities. The key is to become focused and centered, and ask your Egun for clarity and guidance.

To contact or communicate with your guardian spirit, you must simply be open and willing to do so. Your guardian spirit remains with you whether or not you recognize its presence. However, recognition, praise, and thanksgiving of your guardian spirit will strengthen its presence and influence in your life. Guardian spirits are ministers and messengers of the Creator. They provide another valuable link to universal intelligence and divine power. They walk with you, stand beside you, and care for you throughout life.

Prayer is the best method of communication with your Egun. You may want to erect an altar for your guardian spirit to assist you in maintaining constant contact and recognition. To set up an altar you need:

1. A small table covered with white cloth.
2. A large vessel of water (to purify the channels of spiritual communication).
3. White flowers (nature's gift of beauty, birth, and love).
4. A white candle (to foster energy and communication).

This basic set-up brings the four power elements of the universe together—air, water, fire, and earth—and provides a source of concentrated energy.

The key to any spiritual process is your mind. You must be willing to surrender your ego to a higher spiritual force. As a living being, you are linked to the power of all spirits. Through your Ori, you have the keys and secrets to your unique mission. Your challenge is to surrender what you think to what you are intuitively told to do. This is not an easy task. You must overcome years of conditioning, the influences of your environment, and the desire to be in control. You cannot receive spiritual consciousness with reasoning or intelligence. Focus. Trust. Have unquestioning faith. Recognizing ancestral spirits, guardian spirits, and the spirit of your head is the foundation of spiritual evolution according to African culture. For African American women, it is a process by which we can overcome all physical limitations and live a life of service and healing. It does not matter what religious path a woman chooses.

What will determine our destiny is the degree to which we strive to bring forth the essence of spirit. At the spiritual level, a woman is the divine expression of love. She is co-creator with God, capable of bringing forth new life. A spiritual woman is a healer, teacher, and nurturer of life, because it is her ability to love that will soothe all who come into contact with her. The following is an ageless prayer dedicated to universal guardian spirits.* Daily repetitions will provide spiritual strength and guidance.

Prayer for Guardian Spirits

Prudent and benevolent spirits,
Messenger of God (the Creator, Divine Spirit).
Your mission is to assist me and guide me by the good path.
I thank you for your support.
Help me to endure the tests of this life and accept them without complaint.
Deviate from me all negative thoughts.
Please do not let me give access to dark spirits who intend to make me fail in the progress of love for myself and all fellow beings.
Take from my eyes the veil of pride which prevents me from seeing my own defects and from confessing them to myself.
Above all my guardian spirit, I know you are the one who protects me and takes an interest in me.
You know my necessities. Please guide me and assist me in accordance to the will and in the grace of the Creator.
I welcome your presence, your guidance and your assistance.
Thank you pure spirit.

*Adapted from Alan Kardec, *Collection of Selected Prayers*.

Your Inner Voice

Susan L. Taylor

There have been times when confused about my life—the direction to take, the moves to make—I've given up my power. Given in to panic, to anger, fear. Or I've turned to others for my answers. We know that when asked, most folks will gladly tell us about ourselves: who we are, what we're feeling, and where we should be heading. And if we don't honor ourselves by listening to our lives, we'll believe them.

No one knows what's best for us better than we do. No one cares about us or has our interests at heart more than we do. There is no one outside of ourselves who can tell us who we are and the meaning of our lives. Listening inwardly to our interior world and learning what our happiness requires is our most important task. Otherwise, we negate the essence of who we are and ours becomes a feeble and halting existence because we haven't considered what makes us feel whole.

When our elder sisters talk about their lives, I listen. Many elderly Black women speak with deep regret about not having lived their dreams, not having had a plan to move their own lives forward. They say they were raised to put their own needs on hold while they supported others. These women gave selflessly to uplift their families and the race. They made our lives possible. And most say that while they would make many personal sacrifices again, they wouldn't be as long-suffering. They say they lived for others beyond the point that was healthy or necessary and that it wore them down.

The lives of the women who came before us should remind us that while we are created to serve each other, we are meant to fulfill ourselves as well. We don't have an eternity to realize our dreams. Only the time we are here. In the autumn of our lives, we don't want to regret having been unfaithful to our needs. And we don't want to die with our music locked inside us.

Be for others, but be for yourself too. Our choices must be for mental, physical, and spiritual well-being. We must attend whole-heartedly to our wholeness. Choosing what nourishes you may at times seem selfish, but it never is. It's smart, because when we continually subordinate our feelings and needs we lose touch with our reality, and we become disillusioned and depressed. What you do for yourself takes nothing away from anyone else; what's good for you is good for your family and good for the community. Honoring your needs makes you stronger, happier, more willing and able to serve.

Who am I? What does my happiness require? Am I growing, moving my life forward? We must continually ask and answer these life-supporting questions. If we'd take time to explore our interior world and listen to our inner voice, we'd master ourselves and our lives. Then we wouldn't feel overwhelmed or out of harmony. We wouldn't settle for nonsupportive relationships when understanding and support are what we need most; we wouldn't find ourselves doing tedious work when our creative spirit needs to soar, or having children before we're emotionally or financially prepared. Not listening to your inner voice cuts you off from your truth, from your greatest support: the wisdom of the spirit.

Listening to ourselves doesn't mean accepting as gospel the first thing that comes to mind. Knowing who we are and what fulfills us demands self-examination. It requires quiet introspective time. Talk to yourself, to your spirit, as you would to a wise best friend. Debate with yourself. Weigh your pros and cons. Articulate in your own mind what it is you really feel and believe. The more you talk to your spirit, the more you'll come to understand the wisdom within. The more you'll trust your inner voice.

By heeding our inner voice we affirm our self-worth. We feel centered and happy because we are spending time doing what is needed to live a balanced, wholistic life. Now we are in agreement with ourselves and the big questions in our lives are answered. We are in alignment with our life's purpose and can use wisely God's many blessings that we often take for granted—like life, breath, and our ability to think and create a better world.

Staying in touch with the wisdom within us doesn't mean that we won't suffer or struggle. As long as we live, there will be challenges in our lives. We are forever *growing* through something. That's life. But when we are in touch with the divinity within us, we see the larger spiritual cycles that are always at work—even in what may seem like the worst of times. When we take time to listen inwardly and take our difficulties to the altar within, the Holy Spirit always reveals the lessons we must learn and how we can use the challenge at hand as an opportunity to grow and develop a more trusting relationship with God.

We want inner peace and assurance and must seek them within ourselves. Only there can we discover that still, small place where truth resides. Life is an inner experience. Money, possessions, even our most meaningful relationships and good health can be here today and gone tomorrow. When we are connected to the Living Spirit within us, we are divinely guided, so even when we cannot see the light, we will not lose our way.

Life doesn't vanquish us when we use all that God supplies, when each day we make a habit of taking time to get still and listen inwardly. Then we will have the faith to hold fast to this truth: The wisdom and strength within us are always greater than any chaos in the world.

The Power of Affirmations

Marita Golden

I have been composing and utilizing my own affirmations for the past five years as a form of prayer. Unlike some who see affirmations as distinctly different in intent and nature than the ritual of prayer, for me affirmations are simply another form or type of prayer. Like prayers, affirmations are an invitation for the world to manifest in benevolent ways. I use affirmations not so much to try to control reality (which is impossible anyway), as to feel and tap into the power of love and to feel a connectedness with the Ultimate Power. Affirmations allow me to acknowledge that I am not alone, even in moments of crisis, doubt, or confusion, that I can and do believe in my value and in God's benevolence. Affirmations state in a powerful, totally fulfilling way that I am God's eyes, hands, ears, legs, and mind on earth, and lead me always, relentlessly, and certainly back to love, forgiveness, and understanding of myself and others. But affirmations possess their unique power in tandem with the organic, whole nature and personality of one's life. Affirmations must echo and reflect the choices and decisions made and sought during the mundane, often trying minutes, hours, days, and weeks of everyday life. Whatever power affirmations possess is acquired through weaving their spirit throughout the texture of one's dreams and desires and yearnings, consciously and unconsciously. Affirmations have helped me to change my life and shape new values, have given me courage and led me to peace of mind.

Several years ago when I was seeking a reconciliation with my former husband, hoping to positively reunite him with our son, I wrote the following affirmation. I chanted/recited/spoke it each morning seven times during my period of meditation, and the door to a healthy future for my son with his father was opened. My affirmation, which longs so sincerely for healing and reunion, calmed my fears, put my son ahead of past hurts and anguish, and allowed me to find more courage and forgiveness than I knew I possessed. The affirmation did not reunite my son and his father; rather, it allowed me to *imagine* such a reunion, openly, cleanly, and generously, and it melded with forces already at work in the universe.

In the infinity of life where I am
all is perfect, whole, and complete
I am one with the Power that created me
I possess the positive will to reunite
my son and his father
I move away from bad memories
of the past, fear of the future
in this quest
I assume, with God's blessing
and help, a happy future for my child
I send out love and generosity
into the universe in order to receive
for my son love and generosity
I feel my son's father moving closer
to Michael with love and pride
other positive men, male role models
and friends fill my son's life
As his parent I am understanding
patient with an open heart
shaped by God.

Each morning as I said these words I visualized my son and his father in a room together, dared to imagine my son's father's face smiling and pleased gazing at Michael and at me. These were images and feelings that had been suppressed so long I was amazed that I could conjure them. That I could do so proved that forgiveness grows even beneath the thickest covering of pain. Six months after I began saying these words each day, my son and his father were reunited. I not only said this affirmation but worked in concrete ways to bring father and son together. And a year and a half after I began saying these words I met the man I would marry, who with his family (of four brothers and one sister) have extended to my son and me the kind of shelter and love that I know is a gift from God.

I recite the following affirmation each day as a way of staying centered on the essentials of life and fighting off the onslaught of invasive, dangerous distractions that blind you sometimes to who you really are and what you really do possess.

Everyday I am blessed
Each day brings me joy
God, family, friends, work
are my network, my saving grace
I am a child of God
I am where I am supposed to be
My life is full and complete.

I say these words even when I feel empty, betrayed, and deserted by God. That is when I say them loudest and most fervently.

Postscript. I have begun incorporating at the end of my morning meditation period the reading of something that is laugh-out-loud-roll-on-the-floor funny. I get to use facial muscles and parts of my brain and spirit that might not get used that way during the day, if it turns out to be *one of those days*. God wants us to be good, She/He also wants us to feel joy.

Walking in the Spirit

bell hooks

From Sisters of the Yam

Writing was always a sanctuary for me in my wounded childhood, a place of confession, where nothing had to be hidden or kept secret. It has always been one of the healing places in my life. At the end of William Goyen's essay "Recovering," he states, "It is clear that writing—recovering life—for me is a spiritual task." Like Goyen, I believe that writing is "the work of the spirit." Lately, when I am asked to talk about what has sustained me in my struggle for self-recovery, I have been more willing to talk openly about a life lived in the spirit than in the past. In part, I have responded to the urgency and need I have witnessed in younger black females who speak with grave uncertainty and fear as they ponder whether or not they will be able to survive life's difficulties. And I have wanted to tell them the truth, that I am sustained by spiritual life, by my belief in divine spirits, what other folks often call "higher powers."

Spirituality sustains most black women I know who are engaged in recovery processes. For some of us, spiritual life is linked to traditional Christian faith. Others of us expand our horizons as we seek to give expression to our faith in gods, goddesses, or in higher powers. In *Feel the Fear and Do It Anyway*, Susan Jeffers acknowledges that many nonreligious folks are uncomfortable with the idea of the spiritual. Describing in a clear manner what is meant by this term, she explains, "When I speak of the spiritual, I speak of the Higher Self, the place within that is loving, kind, abundant, joyful . . ." Throughout our history in this country, black women have relied on spirituality to sustain us, to renew our hope, to strengthen our faith. This spirituality has often had a narrow dimension wherein we have internalized without question dogmatic views of religious life informed by intense participation in patriarchal religious institutions. My purpose here is not to critique more conventional expressions of religious life. Indeed, the spiritual and the religious are not necessarily one and the same. My intent is to share the insight that cultivating spiritual life can enhance the self-recovery process and enable the healing of wounds. Jeffers suggests:

> Too many of us seem to be searching for something "out there" to make our lives complete. We feel alienated, lonely and empty. No matter what we do or have, we never feel fulfilled. This feeling of emptiness or intense loneliness is our clue that we are off course, and that we need to correct our direction. Often we think that the correction lies in a new mate, house, car, job, or whatever. Not so. I believe what all of us are really searching for is this divine essence within ourselves.

In fiction by contemporary black women writers, healing takes place only when black female characters find the divine spirit within and nurture it. This is true for Avey in *Praisesong for the Widow*, for Celie in *The Color Purple*, for Baby Suggs in *Beloved*, for Indigo in *Sassafrass, Cypress and Indigo*, and countless other characters. For some of these characters, spirituality is linked to Christian faith, for others, African and Caribbean religious traditions. And in some cases, like that of Shug in *The Color Purple*, a break must occur with Christianity in order for a new spirituality to emerge. Jeffers suggests that unless we "consciously or unconsciously tap that spiritual part within" ourselves, "we will experience perpetual discontent." This same message is conveyed in black women's fiction. However, black women seeking healing want to know how we can actualize divine essence in our everyday lives.

Living a life in the spirit, a life where our habits of being enable us to hear our inner voices, to comprehend reality with both our hearts and our minds, puts us in touch with divine essence. Practicing the art of loving is one way we sustain contact with our "higher self." In Linell Cady's essay "A Feminist Christian Vision," she suggests that the divine is not a being but rather the *unifying of being*:

> The divine spirit of love motivates and empowers humans to see more clearly and to act more justly by identifying the self with that which lies beyond its narrow borders. Notice the correlation between the self and the divine in this theological vision. From this perspective the self is not a substantial entity, complete and defined, but a reality always in the process of being created through the dynamic of love, which continually alters its boundaries and identity. Similarly, the divine is not perfected and completed being but processes that seek to expand and perfect being.

In Zora Neale Hurston's novel *Their Eyes Were Watching God*, Janie is able to experience her divine essence first through union with nature and then through the experience of erotic love. Yet, she ultimately fashions a life in the spirit that is fundamentally rooted in her understanding of the value of human life and intersubjective communion where she experiences the unity of all life.

Taking time to experience ourselves in solitude is one way that we can regain a sense of the divine that can feel the spirit moving in our lives. Solitude is essential to the spiritual for it is there that we can not only commune with divine spirits but also listen to our inner voice. One way to transform the lonely feeling that overwhelms some of us is to enter that lonely place and find there a stillness that enables us to hear the soul speak. Henri Nouwen, in *Out of Solitude*, reminds us to attend to our need for solitude: "Somewhere we know that without a lonely place our lives are in danger. Somewhere we know that without silence words lose their meaning, that without listening speaking no longer heals. Somewhere we know that without a lonely place our actions quickly become empty gestures."

Black women have not focused sufficiently on our need for contemplative spaces. We are often "too busy" to find time for solitude. And yet it is in the stillness that we also learn how to be with ourselves in a spirit of acceptance and peace. Then when we reenter community, we are able to extend this acceptance to others. Without knowing how to be alone, we cannot know how to be with others and sustain the necessary autonomy. Yet, many of us live in fear of being alone. To meditate, to go into solitude and silence, we find a way to be empowered by aloneness. It is helpful to have days of silence, times that allow us to practice what Thich Nhat Hanh calls "the miracle of mindfulness." He uses the term mindfulness to "refer to keeping one's consciousness alive to the present reality." Worry and stress often keep us fixated on the future, so that we lose sight of the present, of what it means to be here and now. Mindfulness helps us find a way back to the present. Black women's lives are enriched when we are able to be fully aware, to be mindful. Meditation enhances our capacity to practice mindfulness and should not be dismissed.

Black women who are more engaged with conventional religious life may find it helpful to engage both in silent and spoken prayer. In his essay "Pray for Your Own Discovery," Thomas Merton suggests that we "seek God perfectly" when we "entertain silence" in our hearts and "listen for the voice of God." Prayer allows the individual to speak directly with God, with spirits and angels. In the act of prayer, individual black women who may have tremendous difficulty baring their soul can find a space to speak, to pour out their hearts' longing and, in the act of praying, gain a sense of direction. Prayers often guide, leading us into fuller awareness of who we are and what we are meant to do.

Dreams can also serve as guides to the spirits. Black women have had long traditions of dream interpretation, passing these skills from generation to generation. I grew up in a world of black women who were serious about the interpretation of dreams, who knew that dreams not only tell us what we need to know about the self but guide us when we are lost. Yet when I went to college, I abandoned the practice of giving close attention to my dream life. I have returned to that practice, recognizing it to be a space of empowerment. When we are in need of greater self-understanding or guidance, it can be helpful to keep a dream book, a notebook where we write down our dreams and our reflections and thoughts about them.

Living a life in the spirit, whatever our practices, can help black women sustain ourselves as we chart new life journeys. Many of us have lifeways very different from those any other generation of black women have known. Madonna Kolbenschlag suggests in *Lost in the Land of Oz* that all women today will know seasons of loneliness unlike those experienced by previous generations: "Women, more so than men, are trying out a new myth. They have no role models or generational anchors to lean on in trying out a new story, and so it is scary and lonely. . . . The orphaned woman has broken with many of the old codes of normality, but has not yet found what will take its place." Nurturing our spiritual selves we can find within the courage to sustain new journeys and the will to invent new ways to live and view the world. In *The Feminist Mystic*, Mary Giles invites us to celebrate this positionality, where we are poised between the old and the new, and urges us to be guided by a dynamic love:

> To live and to love and to create are one. In living, loving, and creating we move
> in mystery, alert to possibility bereft of models from the past and without hint of
> one to come. In the absence of models we experience absolute freedom, and in

freedom, risk, responsibility and the joy of being opened to whatever the moment
may bring forth in us.

Certainly black women seeking self-recovery are charting new journeys. Although I have read countless self-help books, the vast majority do not even
acknowledge the existence of black people. It is a new journey for black
women to begin to write and talk more openly about aspects of our reality
that are not talked about.

At times I found writing about some of the issues in this book very sad-
dening. And I would say to Tanya, my play daughter and comrade, that I felt
writing this book would "break my heart." We talked often about why individuals who suffer intensely often cannot find ways to give their anguish
words. To speak about certain pains is also to remember them. And in the act
of remembering we are called to relive, to know again much that we would
suppress and forget. This book hardly speaks to all that needs to be said. And
yet so much of it was hard to say. And sisters have asked me: "Aren't you
afraid that black people will punish you for saying things about black experience they feel should not be said?" I gain courage from my spiritual life, from
the sense that I am called in writing to give testimony, that it is my spiritual
vocation. I call to mind the biblical passage from Romans that says: "Do not
be conformed to this world but be ye transformed by the renewing of your
mind, that you may know what the will of God is." Reading inspirational
writing is an essential part of self-recovery. We are sustained by one another's
testimony when we find ourselves faltering or falling into despair.

Although, I had been thinking for years that I would write this book, it
never came. Thoughts, ideas, and memories were inside me but they did not
manifest themselves in words. Suddenly, in the past months, black women
were asking me where they could find the Sisters of the Yam book. And there
would be such disappointment when I would say that it had not yet been
written. Again it was the sense of urgency I felt from sister comrades that
made me think "now is the time." Yet as the writing progressed, I began to
feel depressed and frustrated that other plans had fallen through. One evening as I sat in stillness, I heard an inner voice telling me that I was meant to
be here in my house doing this book right now. And I felt peaceful and calm.
This to me is a manifestation of the power that comes from living a life in the

spirit. In his essay "Healing the Heart of Justice," Victor Lewis shares the insight that it is a necessity for us to move against fear and despair to embrace healing visions:

> To value ourselves rightly, infinitely, released from shame and self-rejection, implies knowing that we are claimed by the totality of life. To share in a loving community and vision that magnifies our strength and banishes fear and despair, here, we find the solid ground from which justice can flow like a mighty stream. Here, we find the fire that burns away the confusion that oppression heaped upon us during our childhood weakness. Here, we can see what needs to be done and find the strength to do it. To value ourselves rightly. To love one another. This is to heal the heart of justice.

The purpose of this writing was to add to that growing body of literature that hopes to enable us to value ourselves, rightly, fully.

In spiritual solidarity, black women have the potential to be a community of faith that acts collectively to transform our world. When we heal the woundedness inside us, when we attend to the inner love-seeking, love-starved child, we make ourselves ready to enter more fully into community. We can experience the totality of life because we have become fully life-affirming. Like our ancestors using our powers to the fullest, we share the secrets of healing and come to know sustained joy.

Epilogue:
Remembering
Roseann Pope Bell

Gloria Wade-Gayles

You lifted the veil and put on the caul. Seer, sage, scholar, sisterspirit, pioneer/prophet you were, seeing our future with internal eyes. Madwoman with a vision you were, preaching liberation. Always liberation. For the people. For women. For the planet. And for the academy. You never used the words—"a new canon"—but you conceived it and you bore the labor pains in silence.

With Beverly Guy-Sheftall and Bettye Parker-Smith—and preached on by Toni Cade Bambara—you produced a manuscript that would change the color, gender, and soul of literary studies. You carried it from publisher to publisher, and each time you exited through revolving doors that rejections turned like straw-stuffed scarecrows in a strong wind, you stiffened your back and held to your resolve. Like Harriet, you returned again and again to the wilderness, determined to lead us out of darkness. Like Sojourner, whose color, height, and penetrating eyes you wore, you preached about being a woman Black and a scholar, too. And like Anna J. Cooper, you lectured about "the wobbling gait" and promised rejoicing for the "darkened eye restored." Marie Brown entered, and the rejoicing began: You, Bettye, and Beverly had given birth to *Sturdy Black Bridges*, the first serious study of Black women's literature, the seed from which sturdy oaks now grow.

Tales Sistren Tell would have been another seed, making you twice again a pioneer. To birth it, you traveled throughout the Diaspora recording the words of sisters who remembered mothers, who celebrated the culture, who wove long, sinewy threads from the past into a garment of affirmation we must wear.

In all the many projects in which you were involved, you were a soulful, take-charge, no-white-gloves-wearing, unapologetically Black woman-scholar adorned in a short natural who sang, "A change is gonna come," and then went about the business of effecting change, and changes.

Small dark woman from Kentucky. Mother of a son named David. Daughter of a weak woman who didn't know how to love you. Granddaughter of a strong sister who did. Womanperson in a country that did not and still does not love too-dark, too-short, too-round Africanic sisters. Roseann Pope Bell. A wild woman running naked in the night.

I never told you that I envied your nakedness, your love affair with the night, your daring freedom to be free, but you knew. You understood it was envy rather than judgment that asked you to cover your nakedness, and that is why you claimed your wildness with even greater passion, telling me that moonbeams are Nature's raiment for a woman whom Spirit loves.

For myself. For Rhoda Hendrikson. For C. T. and Rick Powell. For Yvonne Robinson Jones. For Miriam Willis. For Vickie Crawford. For Toni Cade Bambara, Bettye Parker-Smith, and Beverly Guy-Sheftall. For all the sisters who love you and who miss you. For all of us, I want to testify that you were connected to the Spirit. Our memory is a witness for the nights you gathered many of us into your parlor for bonding, for healing, for visitations of Spirit. Your candles flickered even during daylight, so sure you were of our need to challenge darkness and of the power of our spiritual bonding to give us light. Say no to it, you told us. The darkness, you meant.

Some sisters only write about sisterhood and the Spirit. You lived a life devoted to both. Networking was as natural to you as breathing. Ideas belonged to all of us, and power belonged to none of us. And being at the center was an impossibility, you said, for women gathered in a circle of sisterhood. You shared selflessly, unconditionally. You wrote when we needed to read the poetry of genuine sisterhood. You called when we needed to hear the rich laughter of love. You complimented when doubt, that ailment which afflicts Black women, put hurdles in the path of our clarity. You were our sister-comforter. "Girl, how are you feeling today?" you would ask. "I said, how are you feeling. Don't give me any intellectual stuff. I want to know how you are *feeling*." And you always ended by saying, "You know I love you." We knew. We know.

You gave away your strength, and in the end you were too weak to fight the demon that claimed your life. Stole you from us when you were writing inspired essays about Black women writers (especially Morrison, whose *Beloved* was "sacred text"); defending brothers while holding them accountable for being brothers; loving sisters while holding them to their promise to be sisters; designing projects that brought the academy and the community into a revolutionary relationship; clarifying what Black nationalism means and does not/should not/cannot mean; collecting tales from sistren who trusted you; laying on your hands and singing our songs . . . Stole you from us when you were in recovery and yet too alone and too weak to recover. We began missing you.

Though we owe you so much we have not invoked your spirit at rituals, have not called your name at CLA and MLA, have not cited you in Black women's scholarship that—when the whole truth be known—you envisioned and, by dogged example of troubling the waters, made possible. We must put an end to this affliction of amnesia and, like you, challenge the naming rules that prevent us from preparing our own roll calls. Accepting validation from the outside is a conspiracy against our own souls.

In writing this tribute, I/we understand why the flowers and mourners in the small Memphis church were few and why the aisles were not alive with choir members enrobed in purple, swaying from side to side the way you said they did in the old church: the Spirit wanted us to remember you, not in a church service that observes procedure, but in a book that celebrates Spirit. We hear you, Roseann. We hear you singing with us and, therefore, are our octaves higher, our notes more sustained, and the paths for our healing and renewal more certain to be revealed unto us.

Contributors

Riua Akinshegun has gained national recognition for her work in art and healing. Drawing upon a shooting incident in 1971 which left her paralyzed, she uses sculpture, ceramic masks, traditional batik, and African wrap dolls to teach people how to manage both spiritual and physical pain. "Home-grown Juju Dolls," an exhibit of African wrap dolls, has toured throughout West Africa and the continental United States. Her most recent project is "The Most Mutinous Leapt Overboard," an interactive installation for African-Americans that seeks to heal the pain of the Middle Passage. *The Seed of My Soul*, an autobiography, will be released soon.

Maya Angelou has authored several autobiographical works, among them the best-selling *I Know Why the Caged Bird Sings*, five volumes of poetry, and most recently a collection of inspirational writings, *I Wouldn't Take Nothing for My Journey Now*. She is the first African-American to be honored with an invitation to write the inaugural poem for a U.S. president, a poem which she read at the 1992 inauguration of President Bill Clinton. Ms. Angelou is Z. Smith Reynolds Professor at Wake Forest University in North Carolina.

Toni Cade Bambara is credited with ushering in the Black women's movement of the seventies with *The Black Woman*, a collection of essays by Black women concerning their own reality, which, two decades later, remains one of the most frequently consulted books in the field. Scholar and activist, Bambara is celebrated as one of the most versatile and gifted twentieth-century Black women writers, having produced major books in several genres. In addition to many essays, her works include *Gorilla My Love*, *The Sea Gulls Are Still Alive*, and *The Salt Eaters*.

Lisa Pertillar Brevard is a performer and scholar of African-American sacred music. She has been associated with the Smithsonian Institution since

1987, working primarily on *"Wade in the Water" African-American Sacred Music Traditions*. She coedited with Bernice Reagon and Tonya Bolden *Wade in the Water Educator's Guide* and prepared an extensive bibliography to date on African-American gospel music for *"We'll Understand It Better By and By": Pioneering African-American Gospel Music Composers*. Brevard is currently a doctoral candidate at Emory University.

Valerie J. Bridgeman Davis is a poet and an ordained minister. She is currently completing a doctorate in biblical studies at Baylor University in Waco, Texas.

Dilla Buckner earned her doctorate at Rutgers University and has been actively involved as planner and participant in conferences, programs, and projects that advance excellence in English at historically Black colleges. Currently chair of the humanities division at Tougaloo College, she is conducting research on representations of the South in Black autobiography.

Imani Constance Johnson Burnett is founder and director of Sisters in Divine Order, a self-help collective, and their Word-of-Mouth Band (WOMB), a performance artwork in progress. Her publications include a collection of short stories and poems entitled *Soul Kiss*.

Katie Geneva Cannon is nationally recognized as one of the pioneers of womanist scholarship. Her works are published in leading journals and in collections of essays that are on the cutting edge of this new scholarship, most recent among them *A Troubling in My Soul: Womanist Perspectives on Evil and Suffering*. She is a tenured Professor at Temple University.

Lucille Clifton is Poet Laureate of the State of Maryland and is the author of four volumes of poetry and one prose memoir. Her many distinctions and awards include the University of Massachusetts Press Juniper Prize, a nomination for the Pulitzer Prize in poetry, and an Emmy Award from the American Academy of Television Arts and Sciences.

Johnnetta B. Cole is an anthropologist and editor of *All American Women: Lines That Divide, Ties That Bind* and *Anthropology for the Nineties*. President of Spelman College, she recently authored a memoir, *Straight Talk From America's Sister President*.

352

Marsye Conde is the author of *Tree of Life*, *Segu*, and *I, Tituba*, a novel which won France's prestigious Grand Prix Literaire de la Femme.

Thulani Davis is the author of the novel *1959* (1992) and of *Malcolm X, The Photographs* (1993). She has also authored two volumes of poetry, *Playing the Changes* and *All the Renegade Ghosts Ride*. Her second novel, *Primitive*, is scheduled for publication in 1995. She was ordained a Jodo Shinshu Buddhist priest in 1990 and works with the Brooklyn Buddhist Association in New York.

Carolyn C. Denard is associate professor of English at Georgia State University and the author of numerous scholarly articles on Black women's literature. Founder of the Toni Morrison Society, she is completing a book on Morrison's fiction which will be released in 1995.

Toi Derricotte has published three collections of poetry, the most recent of which is *Captivity of Natural Birth*. She has been the recipient of many honors and awards, among them the Lucille Medwick Memorial Award, the Folger Shakespeare Library Poetry Book Award, and a Pushcart Prize. She is associate professor of English at the University of Pittsburgh.

Rita Dove has published the poetry collections *The Yellow House on the Corner* (1980), *Museum* (1983), *Thomas and Beulah* (1986), *Grace Notes* (1989), *Selected Poems* (1993), and *Mother Love* (1995), the short story collection *Fifth Sunday* (1985), the novel *Through the Ivory Gate* (1992), the verse drama *The Darker Face of the Earth* (1994), and essays under the title *The Poet's World* (1995). In 1987 she received the Pulitzer Prize in poetry, and from 1993 to 1995 she served as Poet Laureate of the United States and Consultant in Poetry at the Library of Congress.

Mari Evans, writer, educator, musician, and activist, is the author of the highly acclaimed *I Am a Black Woman*. Other publications include *Where Is All the Music*, *Nightstar*, *A Dark and Splendid Mass*, and *Black Women Writers: A Critical Evaluation* which has been recognized as a major contribution to Black women's studies. She is the recipient of many awards, among them a John Hay Whitney Fellowship and the Hazel Joan Bryant Award from the Midwest Afrikan American Theatre Alliance.

Ellen Finch, the mother of seven children, is an independent scholar of Kemetic culture with an emphasis on women's rituals and symbols. With a bachelor's degree in premed from Mount Holyoke, she is currently studying to be a midwife.

Ginger Floyd, physician and poet, serves as Director of the Maternal and Child Health Branch for the Georgia Department of Human Resources. Selected as one of fifty W. K. Kellogg Foundation National Leadership Fellows in 1991, she has traveled extensively throughout West Africa, the Caribbean, and South America obtaining hands-on experiences within and understanding of indigenous, traditional cultures. She has published numerous scientific articles and received numerous awards from state and national organizations.

Nikki Giovanni has been one of the most popular and acclaimed Black woman writers since the late 1960s. In demand as a speaker in the States and around the world, she has authored, among other works, nine volumes of poetry and *Gemini*, an autobiography. She is tenured professor of English at Virginia Polytechnic Institute.

Catharine Goboldte, an ordained minister, is a doctoral candidate in religion and theology at Temple University.

Marita Golden first gained attention as a writer in the 1970s with the publication of *Migrations of the Heart*, considered one of the most compelling of Black women's autobiographies. Since then, she has edited a collection of essays on love and sex and published three novels, most recent among them *Do Remember Me*.

Sandra Yvonne Govan teaches African-American and American literature and courses in popular culture at the University of North Carolina in Charlotte. Her poems and essays have appeared in a number of journals, magazines, and books.

Jacquelyn Grant, a womanist theologian, is author of the acclaimed book *White Man's Jesus, Black Woman's God* and many essays on African-American women's religion and spirituality. An ordained minister, she is on the faculty of the Interdenominational Theological Seminary in Atlanta, Georgia.

354

Rachel Harding, who earned an M.F.A. in Creative Writing from Brown University, has published poems and short fiction in several literary journals including *Feminist Studies* and *The Langston Hughes Review*. She is currently completing a Ph.D. in Latin American history at the University of Colorado at Boulder.

Rosemarie and Vincent Harding have been participants in movements for justice, peace, and communities of hope for more than three decades. A native of Chicago, Rosemarie is a counselor and teacher who offers workshops on various forms of personal and societal healing. She is an adjunct faculty member at the Iliff School of Theology in Denver. Vincent Harding, a native New Yorker, is professor of religion and social transformation at Iliff. He is the author of *There Is a River: Hope and History* and the forthcoming, *From "Freedom Now!" to "Black Power!"*

Carla J. Harris began writing as a form of therapy three years ago as a recovering addict. She writes poetry in order to "express the thoughts that live and travel through my mind. I write poetry because I must stay sane!"

Akasha (Gloria) Hull is a well-known feminist scholar and poet whose books include *Give Us This Day: The Diary of Alice Dunbar-Nelson* and *Sex, Color, and Poetry: Three Black Women Writers of the Harlem Renaissance*. Her most recent book is *Healing Heart: Poems 1973–1988*. She is professor of women's studies and literature at the University of California, Santa Cruz, and is currently writing a study of spirituality in African-American women's literature.

Fleda Mask Jackson, who earned a doctorate at the University of Illinois, Champaign-Urbana, uses her training in psychology and anthropology in various social service and research projects that focus on retrieving, using, and retaining African-American cultural strengths. She is currently completing a book on the empowering influence of the Black church for children and their families. She is an administrator in community service at Spelman College.

Deborah James is associate professor of literature and language at the University of North Carolina at Asheville, where she co-directs the Writing Center and works with the African-American Colloquium.

Olaive Burrowes Jones, after more than twenty years as a professional pianist and composer, began practicing transpersonal psychotherapy. Her practice is located in Washington, D.C., where she lives with her husband and their two daughters.

Dolores Kendrick is the author of three books, *Through the Ceiling*, *Now Is the Thing to Praise*, and *The Women of Plums*, which received the Anisfield-Wolf Award. She is the recipient of fellowships and awards from the National Endowment of the Arts, the Yaddo Writers' Colony, and the Fulbright program. She lives in Washington, D.C., and is currently completing the libretto for an opera.

Audre Lorde, one of the most anthologized and quoted of contemporary Black women writers, authored thirteen books, among them *The Black Unicorn*, *Cancer Journals*, and *Zami: A New Spelling of My Name*. Founding member of Kitchen Table Women of Color Press and active participant in various movements for justice, she has been recognized as a pioneer in Black feminist lesbian thought.

Anna-Marie McCurdy, mother and poet, passed away suddenly in July of 1994. The poem included here, "sisters," was her first publication, but not her only poem. A prolific writer, she left behind folders full of poems and the beginning of a series on middle life. Her daughter is preparing the work for publication.

Toni Morrison, novelist and essayist, was awarded the 1993 Nobel Prize for Literature.

Imani-Sheila Newsome-McLaughlin, spiritual director and preacher, writes litanies and meditations for African-American women. She is presently working with her husband on the spiritual resources of black historical figures.

Margo V. Perkins, who earned a B.A. from Spelman College and an M.A. from Cornell University, is currently a doctoral candidate in English Language and Literature at Cornell. She is the recipient of several prestigious awards for academic excellence and the author of four published essays.

Bernice Johnson Reagon is known nationally and internationally as founder of Sweet Honey in the Rock. She is a scholar of African-American music and the author of many essays and books.

Carolyn M. Rodgers has published widely in major journals and anthologies, among them *Jump Bad Anthology*, *Natural Process*, and *Breakthrough*.

Belvie Rooks is a writer whose works have appeared in a number of magazines and in two Black women's anthologies, *Double-Stitch* and *Life Notes*. As coeditor of *Paris Connections: African American Artists in Paris*, she received a 1993 American Book Award.

Sharifa Saa-Atma Ma'at, a lecturer on metaphysics, African Science of Mind, and African literature and history, teaches at DeKalb College, of the University of Georgia. She is founder and director of Light Unlimited Foundation, which is dedicated to reclaiming the original spiritual energies of Ancient KMT (Egypt), and also hosts a popular radio program in Atlanta, Georgia, "The African Experience—Worldwide."

Sabrina Sojourner, a witch, studies the Yoruban tradition of the Goddess. She earned an M.A. in theatre arts and has taught women's studies at San Francisco State University.

Monya A. Stubbs, an ordained minister, graduated from Spelman College in 1993. She is currently a graduate student at Vanderbilt University Divinity School.

Daa'iyah Muhammad Taha is a married Muslim, a mother, a teacher, and a cancer survivor. She holds a degree in printing and designing children's books from Mills College. Taha is an author, illustrator, and publisher of Islamic educational material for children, as well as a magazine editor and freelance writer. She is founder of the American Islamic Life Institute, which provides classes, seminars, and workshops on all aspects of Al-Islam for American Muslim converts.

Susan L. Taylor is the editor-in-chief of *Essence* magazine and author of *In the Spirit: The Inspirational Writings of Susan L. Taylor*. "Your Inner Voice" is adapted from an editorial which first appeared in *Essence* (May 1988).

357

Luisah Teish, a priestess of Oshun in the Yoruba Lucumi tradition, is the author of *Jambalaya: The Natural Woman's Book of Personal Charms and Practical Rituals*. She teaches classes on goddesses, shamanism, and the Tambala tradition.

Rosalyn Terborg-Penn is the author of several books and articles on African-American and African Diaspora women's history. She is professor of history at Morgan State University and founder of the Association of Black Women Historians.

Dorothy Perry Thompson has published poetry in various journals and anthologies, including *The African-American Review*, *Caesura*, and *Catalyst*. She teaches African-American Studies and poetry writing at Winthrop University.

Nancy Thompson has created and facilitated personal growth conferences and workshops for over ten years. She was the founder and former Executive Director of Inner Power, a California non-profit organization formed to help individuals develop their inner potential. Nancy earned a J.D. degree from Hastings College of the Law, and is currently writing a book on the use of ritual for personal empowerment.

Iyanla Vanzant is nationally known for her written and spoken testimony on recovery from incest and suicide and for her workshops on spiritual development. She is author of *Tapping the Power Within: A Path to Self-Empowerment for Black Women*, which provides self-help techniques for spiritual health.

Anthony Walton is a poet and essayist whose works have appeared in *Callaloo* and *The New York Times*, among other publications. He authored *Mississippi* and, with Michael Harper, coedited *The Little Brown Book of Contemporary Afro-American Poetry*.

Alice Walker is a nationally and internationally recognized Black woman writer. She has authored four volumes of poetry, three collections of essays, two collections of short stories, and four novels, one of which, *The Color Purple*, was awarded the Pulitzer Prize in 1983.

Margaret Walker, poet, essayist, and novelist, began her writing career with distinction: her first book of poetry, *For My People*, received the Yale

Younger Poets Award in 1942. Other publications include *Prophets for a New Day*, *October Journey*, *This Is My Country*, and *Richard Wright: Daemonic Genius*. Her historical novel, *Jubilee*, based on the life of her great-grandmother, has been a national and international best-seller since its publication in 1966. She is currently completing *Minna and Jim*, a sequel to *Jubilee*, and another novel, *Mother Broyer*.

Mary Helen Washington pioneered as a scholar of Black women's literature with the publication of *Black-Eyed Susan* in 1975. Since then her name has been synonymous with the discipline. Other publications include *Midnight Birds* and the acclaimed *Invented Lives: Narratives of Black Women, 1860–1960*. She is chair of the department of English at the University of Maryland, College Park.

Leona Nicholas Welch, poet and playwright, has published in a number of journals, among them *Journal of Black Poetry*, *Encore*, and *Callaloo*. She is the author of a volume of poetry, *Black Gibraltar*.

Delores S. Williams, associate professor of theology and culture at Union Theological Seminary, has published widely in books, scholarly journals, and magazines. Her recent book, *Sisters in the Wilderness: The Challenge of Womanist God-Talk*, a seminal work, positions her in the cutting edge of womanist scholarship.

Paula L. Woods, a native of Los Angeles, is a graduate of the University of Southern California and the University of California, Los Angeles. In addition to owning a consulting firm, she is co-author of *I, Too, Sing America: The African-American Book of Days* and co-editor of *I Hear a Symphony: African Americans Celebrate Love*.

Amina Wadud-Muhsin is an Islamic scholar who has published widely on women and social justice in Islam, focusing on women's spiritual empowerment. *Qur'an and Woman*, recognized internationally as a groundbreaking work on egalitarianism in the Islamic holy book, challenges the patriarchy which has characterized Islamic theology for over fourteen centuries. Wadud-Muhsin, the mother of five children, is assistant professor of philosophy and religion at Virginia Commonwealth University.

Credits

Index

363